MW00611723

A VAST SEA OF MISERY

A History and Guide to the Union and Confederate Field Hospitals at Gettysburg July 1–November 20, 1863

by
Gregory A. Coco

Foreword by Kathleen Georg Harrison
Maps by Daniel E. Fuhrman

Design and layout by Dean S. Thomas

Copyright © 1988 Gregory A. Coco

Printed and bound in the United States of America

Published by THOMAS PUBLICATIONS, Gettysburg, Pa. 17325

All rights reserved. No part of this book may be used or reproduced without written permission of the author and the publisher, except in the case of brief quotations embodied in critical
essays and reviews.

Library of Congress Catalog Card Number: 88-050263

ISBN-0-939631-88-1

PHOTO CREDITS

Front cover and title page—The Union
Second Corps hospital near Rock Creek,
July, 1863. (William Frassanito Collection)

Back cover—Unidentified Union officer (left)
and unidentified Confederate soldier (right).
(Author's Collection)

Page 208—Greg Coco and Kathy Harrison
on the Gettysburg Battlefield, July 1988.
(Robert H. Prosperi)

This book is affectionately dedicated to
Cindy L. Small and Marvin Lee Aday

Additions and Corrections to the Second Printing, 1992

Captions describing buildings as they "appeared in 1863" does not mean they were photographed then. Photos of buildings in Gettysburg were rarely made before the 1880s.

Many of the photographs credited to G.N.M.P. and A.C.H.S. were copied from the *Gettysburg Bicentennial Album*, and are reproduced courtesy of William A. Frassanito.

P. 3, col. 2, line 4 should read: About this time it began to "be" warm work.

P. 23, col. 1, line 20 should read: "Washington House Hotel." John Wills' correct last name is "Will," the son of the owner.

P. 25. Lt. William H. Myers, 76th NY, was in charge of the Sheads and Buehler warehouse hospital.

P. 31, col. 1, line 14 should read: "It was the College Hospital"; delete "brigade."

P. 32. The President's House was built in 1860. Baugher and other pastors at his church were all volunteers. In 1832 he became a faculty member of the college and in 1850, became president.

P. 37. "Ziegler" is spelled wrong in the lower caption.

P. 39. Mrs. Horner was probably the former Kate Arnold. Mary may have been the daughter of Dr. Horner. One of the wounded cared for in Horner's house was Lt. Col. James M. Thomson, 107th PA.

P. 43, last paragraph, delete "and across the alley."

P. 52, col. 2. Professor Jacobs was a teacher in mathematics and natural science.

P. 59, col. 1. The Rogers house in the photograph was built after the Civil War. Col. 2: George and Dorothy Rose were from Germantown, PA. His brother, John, managed the farm during the battle. Both house and barn were used by the wounded.

P. 62, col. 1. In the caption, the word "farmhouse" should read "barn."

P. 67, col. 1. Site 77 should be changed to the "John Musser Farm." Musser purchased this place just prior to the battle. The Swisher farm was located east of Musser's house.

P. 79. John Howard Wert's mother was Catherine Wert. Col. 1, line 1: "Eva Schwartz" should read "Verna A. Schwartz."

P. 80. Two other sources place the amputation of General Sickles' leg at the J. Bushman farm, southeast of Hoke's tollhouse and at the H. Beitler farm, along the Baltimore turnpike.

P. 83, col. 2, line 21, "Mrs. Spencer" mentioned here was "Elmina Keeler Spencer" born in 1819, and mustered in as a hospital matron of the 147th NY.

P. 86. Henry Beitler may have been the Andrew H. Beitler, who claimed a hospital was present on his 33-acre farm for three weeks. And, Site 97, line 6, should read: "Sergeant" Isaac N. Durboraw.

P. 89, col. 1, "Worley" in the caption is misspelled. Site 100A is possibly the John Bair farm. Bair owned a farm along the Baltimore pike as early as 1829, somewhere near Daniel Sheaffer's house.

P. 90. The A.J. Schwartz farm is very possibly the David Little farm mentioned on page 98.

P. 91. Jacob Schwartz died about 1860 of smallpox.

P. 93, col. 2, line 7, "hospital" is misspelled.

P. 96, top photo credit should read: "G.N.M.P."

P. 101, col. 2, Site 106, line 1 should read: About four-tenths of a mile "west" of....

P. 102, captions should read: "John" Trostle.

P. 109. The man who operated the store in Hunterstown was Jacob King, the son of Hugh King.

P. 115, col. 1. A new source indicates several Confederate wounded were in Culp's barn. Also, Colonel Avery is supposedly buried in Hagerstown, MD. Col. 2: Another source lists a small one-and-a-half story log structure on the Benner farm that was used as an aid station during the battle.

P. 116. Henry Monfort's house was built in 1860, and he died in 1877. According to some records his family never did move to California. Today the house and barn have been repaired and are in good condition.

P. 124, col. 1, last line, the word "whose" should not be italicized.

P. 126. The location of this site is totally incorrect. Recently it has been determined that Jacob Kime's farm was located on the west side of the Harrisburg Road, just north of the Josiah Benner farm. The first paragraph in column 1 and the last paragraph in column 2 should be totally ignored.

P. 126-128. Footnotes 14, 15, and 17 are not in the correct order in the text.

P. 132. On the map Site 139 at Cashtown is really Site 137.

P. 134, col. 1. The Michael Crist house was built in 1806-7 by J.T. Hartzell; the barn was built in 1800 and burned by rebels in 1863. John Crist's farmhouse, which stood just northwest, was destroyed in 1979. The barn had burned in 1924. The word "Christ" in the first line is incorrectly spelled.

P. 134, col. 2: Herr's Tavern was purchased in 1860 by Joseph Weible. In 1941, an article in *The Gettysburg Times* stated that the tavern was used as a Confederate hospital.

P. 135. Lohr's original barn burned in 1947. The stone foundation was still visible when this book was written. By 1992, the house was completely demolished.

P. 151, col. 2, Mrs. J. Paxton Bigham's name in 1863 was Mary Cunningham.

P. 166. The Theological Seminary, used as a hospital, was in Mercersburg, PA.

P. 168, col. 1, the barracks were dismantled in 1862, by early May.

P. 171, col. 1, line 4, should read: *"The Adams Sentinel."*

P. 179. Dunn was in the 111th PA.

P. 184. Tate's middle initial should be "T."

P. 186. Holt was in the 2nd Miss. and Parramore was in the 50th GA. J.M. Hays' first name was "John." F.W. Patterson's first name was "Frank."

P. 187. Pearce was in the 8th SC.

P. 196, Part III, #2, the correct author is: "O'Neal, John W.C."

Additional Field Hospitals or Aid Stations

Henry G. Carr Grocery Store-northwest corner of Baltimore and High Streets
John Houck House-adjacent to the Adams County Prison
Nicholas Codori Farm-Emmitsburg Road
John Wentz Farm-Emmitsburg Road
Joseph Sherfy Farm-Emmitsburg Road
Christian Shefferer Farm-north of the Millerstown Road
George Weikert Farm-north of the Millerstown Road
Elizabeth F. Schultz Farm-Fairfield Road
John Horting Farm (owned by George Arnold)-south of the Fairfield Road on Willoughby's Run
John Butt Farm-Fairfield Road
Belmont School-Herr's Ridge on the Chambersburg Turnpike
John Weible Farm-Hunterstown Road
Christopher B. Young Farm-Baltimore Turnpike near Two Taverns
Dr. Raymond S. Seiss House-Littlestown, PA

CONTENTS

FOREWORD

"I turned away and cried."

The words of Sarah Broadhead reflect the first reaction of many volunteer nurses who first gazed upon the hospitals of Gettysburg. Public buildings, private homes, orchards and groves, barns, outbuildings, and lush meadows had lost their pastoral and tranquil purposes. They had been transformed into "a vast sea of misery," sheltering and housing the tens of thousands of Union and Confederate soldiers who had been cut and maimed and crushed by the days of battle surrounding the small Pennsylvania town. On these farms and in these buildings the Battle of Gettysburg would continue for four more long months.

No shots were fired in that new battle, but the pain and misery, the struggle between life and death, and the individual cases of heroism and pathos continued unabated on these far flung battlefields. These were the hospitals, where surgeons and civilians worked incessantly to alleviate the sufferings of that "mass of ragged, naked, torn and mangled mortality" who were the living casualties of this July 1863 battle.

The surgical record of those days of grim convalescence and slow dying are sparse and curt. The lists of wounded in the hospitals give us only the antiseptic description of wounds and fate:

| INJURY | | | | |
Seat of.	Nature of.	TREATMENT	RESULT AND DATE OF	REMARKS
Right side	Penetrating wound	Simple Dressings	Died July 11th	By Bullet
Right side	Penetrating lung	Simple Dressings	Died July 5th	By Bullet
Right arm	Comp. Fracture	Amputation		By Shell
Inferior maxillary & calf	Comp. Fracture	Simple Dressings		By Shell

The words of those who suffered, those who visited them, and those who tended to their needs are more descriptive but still must fall short of fully painting that scene which the armies and their attendants beheld. A visitor to the battlefield shortly after its close could only write, "And then, these scenes themselves, who can adequately describe them?"

The vast corps and division hospitals cared for hundreds of men at one time, each man's wound bleeding like that of his suffering neighbor, and each demanding the attention of the overwrought surgeons. Often smugly maligned from our twentieth-century armchairs, the doctors who remained to care for the armies' wounded were heroes of these hospital battlefields.

An observer from the U.S. Sanitary Commission could report after the battle:

The labor, the anxiety, the responsibility imposed upon the surgeons after the battle of Gettysburg were from the position of affairs, greater than after any other battle of the war. The devotion, the solicitude, the unceasing efforts to remedy the defects of the situation, the untiring attentions to the wounded upon their part, were so marked as to be apparent to all who visited the hospitals. It must be remembered that these same officers had endured the privations and fatigues of the long forced marches with the rest of the army; that they had shared its dangers. . . . The battle ceasing, their labors continue. While other officers are sleeping, renewing their strength for further efforts, the medical are still toiling. They have to improvise hospitals from the rudest materials, are obliged to make 'bricks without straw,' to surmount seeming impossibilities. The work is unending, both by day and night, the anxiety is constant, the strain upon both the physical and mental faculties, unceasing. Thus, after the battle, operators had to be held up while performing the operations, and fainted from exhaustion, the operation finished. One completed his labors to be seized with partial paralysis, the penalty of his over-exertion.

But, the story of the hospitals at Gettysburg is more than a story of medical and surgical prowess and endurance, although there was plenty of that. It is also a story of the untold thousands of officers and men who underwent physical punishment and privations quite foreign to most of our own experience. The battle wounds of these soldiers effectively stripped away the uniforms of blue or butternut and gray that each wore. To the doctors, to the ministers, to the nurses, to the mothers and fathers and sisters and brothers, these were no longer Confederate or Federal. It was hard to look at such a scene of mutual suffering and endurance and not feel compassion for all alike.

> . . . [In] every direction lay men of all classes, the rich man and the poor man, the commander and the private. At one place, near a fence, lay privates, corporals, lieutenants, majors and colonels, from New York, North Carolina, Indiana, Mississippi, Connecticut, Georgia, New Hampshire, Alabama, Maine and Delaware side by side, on the bare ground, or on a little wet straw; no distinction.

The story of the hospitals is symbolic. It is the end of battle, and the end of war. It is not a Confederate story or a Union story. There is no North or South hidden in the meaning of the hospitals. It is a story of Americans coping against almost insurmountable odds for the common good. It is the story of hundreds and thousands of acts of individual kindness, of bravery and courage, of charity and love, faithfulness and patriotism. It contrasts markedly with the story of the battle. The victims of that brutality and madness are transmuted from the helpless fallen who can no longer affect the outcome of battle to the central characters of these hospital scenes. Numbers on casualty sheets become names on lovingly carved headboards; medical case studies become the fathers and sons and friends of those receiving blood-stained letters from Gettysburg; and images of piles of amputated limbs by blood-soaked tables yield to memories of the empty sleeves and the crude crutches that led parades and brought these old veterans back to that battlefield to remember and honor.

Through countless hours of research and field work, Greg Coco has finally documented those hospital sites and the human drama that unfolded around the tents and within the walls. In this book, he reminds us of the significance of each of those sites. The battlefield of Gettysburg was the benefactor of a national pride that preserved it and memorialized it, and each year our attention is drawn again to that place as periodicals, television, books, and works of art analyze and recount that moment in our history. Yet, it has been many years since anyone has spoken for the hospital sites that were such a vital part of Gettysburg's legacy. The heroes, the wounded, the families, the owners are all gone now. But many of the hospital sites still exist as the only monuments and memorials to those days of suffering.

Almost all of these sites are unprotected by law or statute and many have already fallen casualty themselves to development and change which is the result of apathy, ignorance, or disdain. We can only hope that this book will educate and convince us that the preservation of these sites is a duty of our generation to that generation which found the necessity to use them. Let us remember the significance of places like Camp Letterman (the General Hospital east of Gettysburg), Black Horse Tavern, the Lohr Farm, and act to save them for the next generation. There was a sense of urgency about the work of the surgeons, the Sanitary Commission, the Christian Commission, and the nursing volunteers in 1863. A community and national emergency demanded immediate and effective attention then, and the soldiers benefitted from those urgent efforts. Today, there is another sense of urgency—to prevent the alarming, growing, and imminent development which is eliminating these sites as historic resources forever. To see farms that were vast hospitals and cemeteries subdivided for suburban housing and developed for shopping centers, to see an abandoned hospital site fall to repeated arson and vandalism, is to see a people who have forgotten its history.

Sarah Broadhead was affected and moved to tears by what she saw in 1863. Today, we have a different reason for grief. When I looked at the Camp Letterman site. When I looked at Major Lohr's Farm. When I looked at the White Church site. When I looked at the Currens Farm site. When I looked at the Johns Tenant House site. When I looked at the Poorhouse site.

"I turned away and cried."

Kathleen Georg Harrison
Hanover, Pa.
July 1988

PREFACE

What's that sound
What's that dreadful rumble
Won't somebody tell me what I hear
Is it only a storm approaching—
All that thunder
And the blinding light . . . *

Human beings are naturally affected by what happens to them personally or of occurrences near to them. Every person is impressed differently by each particular or singular event. And of all humankind's experiences, war is very likely the most fearful, the most traumatic. What certainly is a devastating experience to a civilian caught up in or in close proximity to war's scourge, can be a crushing and disillusioning blow to a soldier who is made to endure hour after hour or day after day in combat's dehumanizing influence. Even further degraded are the wounded as they lie shattered and helpless on or near a festering battlefield, immobilized in pools of hardening blood and vermin-filled bodily excrements. The sudden and terrifying realization of just how vulnerable and fragile one truly is, often creates a swift and profound psychological change in the persona.

Fortunately, when all is said and done and the terror of the moment has long passed into the subconscious, the participant is often only capable of recalling or writing a refined version of what has actually transpired. Such was the case of a soldier who, years after his fearful experience, wrote:

> When felt at all, bullets through the flesh usually produce a burning sensation more or less acute. When bones are broken, stinging accompanies the burning. When bones are hit but not broken, there is a numbing sensation in the whole region involved in the shock, followed very soon by severe and sometimes intense pain. When muscles and tendons are involved, there is a tugging sensation, sometimes very slight, and shell-wounds produce feelings similar to those by bullets, more or less exaggerated, according to the size of the missile and the degree of velocity. Bayonet-wounds I never saw except upon corpses—for I was not a hospital attendant—and as for cannon-balls, they do not, as a rule, leave anything behind to exhibit feelings.

In effect, "the horror of the event is lost in its significance."

As Americans, with our relatively short and secure collective history, we sometimes look at war as a kind of nice and neat spectator sport. Martially-oriented books are read and analyzed from comfortable armchairs, and old battlegrounds are visited in a kind of surrealistic fog, the viewer sometimes little knowing or even caring about what actually transpired in these picture-book portrayals of warfare. The visitor to a manicured battlefield park, or the casual reader of military history, moreover, is generally satisfied with this depiction. He or she is often content to romanticize and trivialize these tragic moments of mankind's misery into a travesty of flag-waving patriotism. Or as William James said: "From time immemorial wars have been, especially for noncombatants, the supremely thrilling excitements."

This book, then, shall attempt to take you into a different realm than you may be accustomed. Throughout these pages, many people of the 1860s will show you the dark side of glory, the not-so-thrilling aspect of battle, another view, another facet, of the relentless pursuit of power and victory at all costs. And what Ernest Hemingway believed all through his life may hopefully make us pause:

"Never think that war, no matter how necessary, nor how justified, is not a crime. Ask the infantry and ask the dead."

*From "Soldiers" by ABBA, copyright 1981

INTRODUCTION

"It was a field of Blood on which the Demon of Destruction revelled."

Jonathan Letterman
writing about the wounded of Gettysburg

"On the field of Gettysburg,
When the battle fierce was o'er,
A soldier of the Union
Lay weltering in his gore;
Around him, there, on every side,
His brother soldiers lay,
Groaning and moaning in their pain,
Waiting the coming day. . . ."

Ena Walton

In this 125th anniversary year of the battle, there are probably in excess of three thousand books, articles, and other publications available which chronicle the Gettysburg Campaign. The unpublished letters, diaries, and memoirs which are hidden away in so many private homes and public repositories, go uncounted. Very few, if any, of these printed sources deal entirely with the medical aspects of the famous battle; a fact which is truly astonishing when one considers the magnitude of the drama.

To write a history of all of the approximately twenty-six thousand wounded of this battle and the generally noble work accomplished in their behalf, including the stories of hundreds upon hundreds of surgeons, nurses, and other civilians would require many volumes of the size of this one. With this thought in mind, I have selected to present a general guide and composition of the nearly 160 hospital sites themselves, with emphasis on allowing the participants to tell the stories in their own words. In this form, I shall attempt to cover several subjects at one time. Hopefully, this study may serve as a small but acceptable tribute to the all-but-forgotten men who were struck down in combat at Gettysburg, many never to rise again. This sentiment was clearly acknowledged by Arabella Willson in 1870:

> Perhaps those of us who were not called upon for a sacrifice in our country's cause, are in danger of forgetting our debt to her brave defenders. Their scars and maims and other disfigurements of war, . . . in our eyes, honorable and even glorious, are after all, sad companions for a lifetime. A hand, a foot or an eye, is, next to a life, the most precious sacrifice which can be laid on any altar. To lose in life's morning one of these inestimable possessions, to go through life deprived of the cunning of the right hand or the exceeding service of the foot or the eye, is, no doubt a great calamity.

I may even be presumptuous enough to believe that the existence of this book might excite sufficient interest in the subject to lead the citizens of Adams County, Pennsylvania to preserve and protect these historically and architecturally valuable sites for future generations.

This two-fold task has been extremely perplexing and even difficult at times. For instance, the common eyewitness of that day had a vague manner of mentioning where these hospitals were located, such as 'a barn near a road,' or a 'grove near a stream' or some other equally cloudy description which can cause great confusion and frustration to the modern researcher.

And, finally, being primarily interested in and more accomplished at research rather than the writing end of this business, I hesitate somewhat in presenting a book to the public which obviously contains many shortcomings and imperfections. In view of this, but also in the expectation of the possibility of compiling another edition, I would like to request that anyone having additional information on the Gettysburg area field hospitals to please forward the same to me without delay.

It is my anticipation that *A Vast Sea of Misery* will serve as only the forerunner of a more complete and elaborate work by some other writer in a not-too-distant day.

ACKNOWLEDGEMENTS

In the research for and the writing of this book, the author is under obligation to many talented men and women. To all of them who kindly assisted me, I offer my deepest affection and sincere thanks. In the future, I shall endeavor to return, in full, all that was given.

Cindy L. Small, especially and foremost, deserves much more than a mere thank you, and probably more than I am capable of repaying. She is not only my beloved spouse, but also my most cherished companion and friend.

Cindy has spent too many long hours transcribing my almost undecipherable, handwritten manuscript into a word processor, and hours more editing and printing out the final copy. We kidded often that she, indeed, was floundering in her own "vast sea of misery." Had it not been for her, the fact simply remains that this book would still be only an elusive dream. Thank you, Cin, for everything.

Kathleen Georg Harrison, one of my dearest friends, was to be the coauthor of an often-discussed book on the wounded and hospitals of Gettysburg. With her complete cooperation on such a project, it would have been so much better. However, due to other important and pressing commitments, she was not available to join me in the writing portion of this project during the past year. Fortunately, Kathy was always there to direct me, answer questions, and ponder and search for hospital locations not easily established. Her beautiful foreword clearly expresses the love we both feel for these endangered historical sites and the sorrow which compels us to fight on to do what we can to save them from eternal destruction. I truly consider myself fortunate to have even one friend in life like Kathy.

William A. Frassanito, the noted Civil War photographic historian and author, was more than a great help to me on several occasions. Many telephone calls and visits to his home enabled me to become untangled from certain nagging pieces of information that I just could not seem to find a proper place for. Aside from being truly dedicated to saving as much of the remaining Gettysburg battlefield as possible, Bill is also totally unselfish when it comes to sharing information or giving assistance. His infinite store of knowledge on the borough and people of Gettysburg is truly impressive. Thank you, Bill, for the many enjoyable research sessions we spent together during the last year.

Another historian who it is my pleasure to acknowledge is Dr. Charles H. Glatfelter. Although a full-time teaching professor, Dr. Glatfelter still finds an opportunity to volunteer many hours of his rare free moments to the Adams County Historical Society, where his wisdom and amicability has won many friends for that fine institution. His insight into the people and places of Adams County is truly amazing—and his help to me on my many excursions to the Society at the Lutheran Theological Seminary "Old Dorm," was always informative and gratifying.

My thanks and gratitude also go out to:

—Daniel E. Fuhrman for his excellent professional cartography. His maps befit a much finer publication than I could ever produce.
—Lewis Leigh, Jr., of Fairfax, Virginia, whose kindness and devotion to history allowed several hundred documents from the personal collection of Surgeon Henry Janes, of Camp Letterman U.S. General Hospital, to be saved as a group for future reference.
—Robert H. Prosperi of the Gettysburg National Military Park and Edmund J. Raus, Jr., of Manassas National Battlefield Park, who guided me toward much useful medical-related information.
—Dean S. Thomas, Keri E. Coco, Robert B. Moore, Henry Deeks and Clara Lee Gunn, for photographic assistance.
—Michael Musick of the National Archives, Daniel W. Bennett, III, of the Armed Forces Medical Museum, and Michael W. Winey of the U.S. Army Military History Institute, for generous help with the collections at those institutions.
—Jay Gobrecht for the use of his fine courier service.
—Todd E. Meisenhelter for bringing the Justin Dwinell manuscript and photographs to my attention; and Walter L. Powell, Ph.D., for information on several 1860s county farm families.

And, again, a 'thank you' to the many kind folks who allowed me into their houses and onto their farms and who went out of their way to assist me whenever possible; especially, W.E. Jordan, Jacob

(Jake) Stoltzfus, John Lott, Maebelle Sachs, Mrs. William (Ruth) Witherow, Kenneth Sease, Mary Kepner, Mike Redding, Henry R. Schaeffer, John Pannick, Lieutenant General Chieu Xuan Pham, Margaret Neff, Kenneth Andrew, and Julian and Angela Nadeau.

Finally, to Dean S. Thomas of Thomas Publications, who had the faith in me and this book to take on the many burdens and commitments, which has enabled it to reach the public.

Gregory A. Coco
Bendersville, Pa. 17306
July 31, 1988

MAPS

ABBREVIATIONS

A.C.H.S.—Adams County Historical Society
A.F.M.M.—Armed Forces Medical Museum
G.N.M.P.—Gettysburg National Military Park
L.C.—Library of Congress
MOLLUS-MASS—Military Order of the Loyal Legion-Massachusetts Commandery (USAMHI)
N.A.—National Archives
U.S.C.C.—United States Christian Commission
U.S.S.C.—United States Sanitary Commission

Alphabetical Listing of Field Hospital Sites

SUMMARY OF EVENTS

I visited the battleground...when the evidences of the horrid carnage...lay on every hand in fearful sights.

Battered canteens, cartridge-boxes, torn knapsacks, muskets twisted by cannon shot and shell, rusted tin cups, pieces of rent uniforms, caps, belts perforated with shot, and heaps of death's leaden hail, marked the spots where men were stricken down in solid ranks.

...right above my head, at one place, so close that it touched me, hung a sleeve of faded army blue — a dead hand protruding from the worn and blackened cuff — I could not but feel a momentary shudder.

Boots, with a foot and leg putrifying within, lay beside the pathway, and ghastly heads, too — over the exposed skulls of which insects crawled — while great worms bored through the rotting eyeballs. Astride a tree sat a bloody horror, with head and limbs severed by shells, the birds having banquetted on it, while the tattered uniform, stained with gore, fluttered dismally in the summer air.

Whole bodies were flattened against the rocks, smashed into a shapeless mass, as though thrown there by a giant hand, an awful sight in their battered and decaying condition. The freshly turned earth on every hand denoted the pits, from many of which legs were thrust above the scant covering, and arms and hands were lifted up as though pleading to be assigned enough earth to keep them from the glare of the day.

So wrote Sophronia Bucklin, a volunteer nurse on her first visit to the fields around Gettysburg, Pennsylvania in July of 1863. Her endurance among these sights existed simply because she had seen worse. Miss Bucklin had already spent two weeks with the real horror that was Gettysburg — the wounded. And she aptly stated, "I had grown familiar with death in every shape."

Veritably, Gettysburg had become an immense charnel house. Farmers noted to each other that even the songbirds had abandoned the surrounding fields, meadows, and woods. The clatter of ambulances and supply wagons replaced the normal din of small town commerce and business. And the soothing sounds of children playing, or people gossiping in the streets were transposed on all sides by the groans and shrieks of mutilated humanity. The air reeked with the stench of blood, decaying bodies, and burning horseflesh. A pall of death and putrescence hovered over the scene as the armies, gone now, gave way to throngs of gawking visitors. Many came to help; but just as many were attracted by curiosity or morbid fascination; some paid their way by plying the trades associated with death and destruction, while the most sorrowful of the multitudes came to look for dead, wounded or missing relatives.

Seldom had anything resembling this nightmare ever visited an American community; and never in such an overwhelming manner. Only Fredericksburg, Virginia would experience something worse. But Gettysburg would be remembered longer.

* * *

The armies that descended upon the little village of 2,000 inhabitants with their hundreds of wagons; cannons; limbers; caissons; ambulances; and tens of thousands of horses and mules, numbered nearly 165,000 men at arms. In less than five days the bulk of these forces disappeared, leaving in their wake the wreckage of the most terrible single event in our history. Dead men lay thick, totalling over 7,000; more than 5,000 animals had been killed; and nearly 26,000 soldiers were wounded, 21,000 of which remained in and around Gettysburg. The Rebels managed to transport several thousand of their wounded comrades back to Virginia in a 17-mile-long wagon train of suffering and anguish that even today lacks a comprehensible description.

The respective Medical Departments for both sides during the Civil War were rarely prepared for the tremendous problems that followed a large military engagement. There were never enough doctors, nurses, ambulances, tents, food or medical supplies. However, by 1863 the U.S. Army realized that one surgeon accompanying each regiment was not the best method for the application of medical science. These regimental surgeons, who were more like our modern day military "medics" or corpsmen, generally administered only first-aid techniques at "dressing stations" near the firing line, prior to sending the patient to the rear and out of danger. Thereafter, and in time for the Gettysburg campaign, each division in the army was assigned an operating staff of only the most skilled physicians, who after setting up field hospitals in safe areas (1-3 miles from the action) took over more serious medical pursuits such as applying anesthetics, performing amputations, probing and extracting bullets and shell fragments, tying of ligatures, and fighting fevers and infection.

* * *

During the actual hostilities at the Battle of Gettysburg, regimental medical staffs attempted to establish field depots or dressing stations as near the engaged regiment as possible, taking care to use natural or man-made shelters to their advantage. In a typical wartime reduced regiment of 300-500 men, three to five stretcher teams were set up — four bearers to each stretcher. The surgeon, with his attendants, secured a few basic instruments, many bandages, some opium pills, sought out the location of the division hospitals and ambulance parks, then began to stabilize the wounded as they walked or were carried to his aid station. If the combat was sustained, the surgeon generally kept up with the flow of stricken men. But as the fighting escalated or the lines surged back and forth, he usually requested or formed additional stretcher teams, or moved his dressing station accordingly.

Meanwhile, wounded men slowly filled every available public place and even private dwellings. Many of these troops were unsure of the whereabouts of rear area field hospitals, so they appropriated shelter wherever possible. Later on July 2 and 3 when Union and Confederate lines became permanently lodged, soldiers more easily found their way back, following hospital marker flags, or by appealing to teamsters and ambulance drivers passing by. (It should be appreciated that literally thousands of wounded men, some very seriously hurt, walked to hospital sites as far away as five miles or even further.)

On July 1, when the fighting was concentrated west and north of the town, many temporary field hospitals quickly took root in local churches, the buildings of Pennsylvania College and the Theological Seminary, the High Street School, the Courthouse and a few private homes. By nightfall of that tragic day, those medical facilities had fallen into Confederate hands and the Federal positions were now concentrated south of Gettysburg. Correspondingly, much of the medical portion of the Army of the Potomac withdrew to secured regions behind Union battle lines. A scattering of hospitals remained in the captured town, while the majority of the Rebel medical staffs assumed positions a few miles away in homes, barns, and schools along the Fairfield, Mummasburg, Newville, Chambersburg, Harrisburg, and Hunterstown Roads. These field hospitals were not as well-organized as in the Yankee counterparts and dotted the landscape in a somewhat haphazard fashion. Nonetheless, the resounding fact remained that both sides' facilities were extremely primitive — especially in the beginning. Every available barn, shed, stable, schoolhouse, and many homes within the areas encompassed by the field hospitals were impressed into service. Within the Union rear, corps and division hospitals sprang up in this order: the First Corps along the Baltimore Pike, south of and including White Church (2,379 patients); the Second Corps at the Granite Schoolhouse, moved later to west of Rock Creek southeast of the George Bushman farm (3,152 patients); the

Third Corps along the Taneytown Road, moved to the south side of White Run near its junction with Rock Creek (2,500 patients); the Fifth Corps along the Taneytown Road, then transferred to woods along White Run, the Baltimore Pike, and near Two Taverns (1,400 patients); the Sixth Corps near the John Trostle house on Rock Creek (315 patients); the Eleventh Corps at the George Spangler farm, the County Almshouse, and Pennsylvania College (1,400 patients); and the Twelfth Corps at the George Bushman farm and near Rock Creek (1,200 patients).

The newly-formed corps and division hospitals were by no means the answer to a soldier's needs. In particular, the two to four days following the great battle found most wounded soldiers — principally the ones severely hurt — in a kind of medical limbo. These men may have been fortunate enough to make contact with a major field hospital, possibly even one within their own corps, but they were still far from being safe and comfortable.

Disorganization bordering on chaos was the prevailing status. With men in every conceivable state of injury (some with ghastly wounds) scattered over the countryside, organization was virtually impossible at first. Scores of injured troops lay in the open with not even a blanket for covering, much less the security of a tent. Soon after July 4 because of heavy rain, both Rock Creek and White Run overflowed their banks, possibly claiming nearly two dozen helpless victims who were unable to crawl out of harm's way. When the mid-summer's sun did appear, it mercilessly tortured the already dehydrated bodies of many caught without shelter. Soldiers fortuitous enough to be indoors, sometimes lay for days as prisoners trapped in their own filth, blood, and body wastes. Flies by the millions, and their maggoty off-spring treated these helpless men to a long and hellish ordeal. Strong veteran warriors, now weakened by blood loss, adverse weather conditions, and lack of nourishment, as well as the mental anguish aggravated by the cries of the unfortunate souls on every side, called out for mercy from their God, or from absent mothers or wives. Frequently they had to wait several days to be visited by a surgeon, and by that time, these soldiers nearly out of their minds with pain and despair, literally begged to have a precious wounded limb cut off — *anything* to stop the horrendous pain and misery.

The army doctors, so often criticized as "sawbones" for their "cut first, ask later" attitudes, were now heroes immersed in a vast wasteland of human agony. In 1895, one physician, Bushrod W. James, told of his memories of the aftermath of the great battle:

No written nor expressed language could ever picture the field of Gettysburg! Blood! Blood! and tattered flesh! shattered bones and mangled forms almost without the semblance of human beings! faces torn and bruised and lacerated...groans and cries, screams and curses, moans and grinding teeth! And the horrible silence of torture beyond all expression...those weeks of sickening work, when the cut of the knife and the rasp of the saw...grated on my overtaxed nerves.

Another medical officer recalled that he stood at the outdoor operating tables for the better part of four days:

...my legs swollen and painful, my arms and hands immersed in blood and water so long that it became difficult to hold the knife...my muscles cramped, eyes burning from sun, sweat, and dust, and flies over it all, covering the gore that lay everywhere...the pile of severed limbs nearby that grew with each passing hour...

* * *

Although the week following the Battle of Gettysburg was crucial to the survival of many ravaged bodies, assistance flowed by degrees into the surrounding hospital sites as early as the second week in July. So, by the end of the month, the army medical service was receiving tons of supplies daily. Typical items that finally flooded the camps were:
dried fruit — 3,500 pounds
lemons — 116 boxes
preserved fish — 3,600 pounds
catsup — 43 jars
pickles — 400 gallons
canned oysters — 72 cans
fresh eggs — 8,500 dozen
concentrated milk — 12,500 pounds
ice — 20,000 pounds
fresh bread — 10,300 loaves
crates of medicines, such as: aloe, alum, ammonia water, calomel, camphor, cantharides, collodin, copaiba, creosote, digitalis, hyoscyamus, laudanum, quinine and tannic acid
drawers, shirts, clothing — 40,000 pieces
sheets, blankets, mosquito nets — 11,700 pieces
towels and napkins — 10,000
sponges — 2,399
bandages — 110 barrels
soap, castile — 250 pounds
crutches — 1,200 pair
fans — 3,500
bay rum — 100 bottles
candles — 350 pounds
The abovementioned list was only a small percentage of the articles which arrived in only one corps hospital in a 10-day period. This changeover from "famine to feast" primarily came about due to the efforts of several civilian organizations. The most prominent of these was the U.S. Sanitary Commission, a group that was originated in April of 1861 by the combined influences of several womens' relief societies. The Sanitary Commission and its sister

agencies simply did what the U.S. Government could not or would not do. They became a medium whereby the material wealth of the nation, along with willing human resources, assembled their power to help relieve the suffering within its midst. In this way, a mostly grateful country was able to shower some of its war casualties with love and kindness.

Even before the close of the battle, the Commission assumed possession of a schoolhouse on the Baltimore Pike and established a central distribution point for its agents who were already amassing male and female nurses, medicines and other supplies. On July 7 the schoolhouse was abandoned and the Fahnestock and Co. Store and Warehouse on Baltimore Street became, in the words of a Sanitary worker, "the centre of the busiest scene which I have ever witnessed in connection with the Commission." A relief "lodge" was also constructed near the depot to aid the men who were continually being transported to major hospitals in large eastern cities.

Around about the second week in August, the corps and division field hospitals in the countryside were broken up and the remaining casualties were consolidated into a huge 500 tent city on the York Pike, east of Gettysburg, where the railroad ran close by the pike. Camp Letterman, as this General Hospital was named (after the Medical Director of the Army of the Potomac), became a showplace of sorts, with its clean, orderly appearance, wide streets, and first-class facilities and staff. But by no means were the wounded out of danger even here — for hundreds still died, right through to November when the Camp was officially closed.

And that same month as the leaves and the fields turned brown, President Lincoln travelled to Gettysburg to turn a final page of the tragic story, his only reminder now of the battle was a small portion of the Dead...who still remain today.

PART I
The Borough of Gettysburg Area Field Hospital Sites

"...thousands of wounded defenders of the flag tossed in agony on the bare ground or moaned on tailor's tables, on rough boards laid across the pews of churches and on improvised beds of straw in hallways, offices and store-rooms."

J. Howard Wert
the son of an Adams County farmer

Often, when reading about the aftermath of the Battle of Gettysburg, one comes across the expression, "every house was a hospital," or some other similar statement. However, most citizens who commented on the subject simply stated that *"many private houses in town cared for the wounded of the battle."* This section, which deals with the wounded who were "hospitalized" in the small borough of 2,400 inhabitants, falls somewhat short of that first dramatic quote.

In my research, I have found mention of over forty-five private dwellings in the town, out of nearly three hundred, which housed one or more of the wounded from both armies. For instance, a soldier of the 15th Massachusetts Infantry, Caleb H. Arnold, died on August 16, 1863, at the Gettysburg house of Francis C. Gardner, a thirty-eight-year-old carpenter. Since Gardner did not own property during the 1860s, his place of residence is still unknown. Obviously there were more "hospitals" like Gardner's, of which little is known, but until further information becomes available, this small number uncovered will serve as a good illustration of that particular situation, in which private houses became temporary hospitals.

Throughout this book, I have attempted to classify a field hospital (or aid station) as *any* building or other location that housed a wounded soldier, or a hundred, or any number, as long as documented evidence was found to support the fact.

Generally, injured men who were found to be located in a private domicile got there in one of two ways. They either "stumbled in," due to supreme necessity during the Union retreat on July 1, or, they were taken in by the family *after* the battle, with the thought that the personal treatment there would be better than the disjointed care in an outlying military field hospital. Unfortunately for some of these this did not always prove to be the case.

To exemplify the crowded conditions in some areas of Gettysburg, civilian Catherine Foster said that on July 2, "Six public buildings and nearly all the private houses on High Street (are) now well filled with the first day's wounded." This situation did not last long as most of these men were soon transported to regular hospitals in churches, other public buildings, and to the corps and division hospitals which were springing up all around the village. Another local citizen, Sarah Broadhead, wrote in her diary on Tuesday, July 14, 1863, that all patients in private houses were being ordered to the General Hospital, that same day.

Part I also delineates the many public buildings used as temporary shelters for the overwhelming numbers of wounded which inundated Gettysburg. Some of these hospitals remained in operation long after the middle of July, even after a "general hospital" was opened just west of town.

1

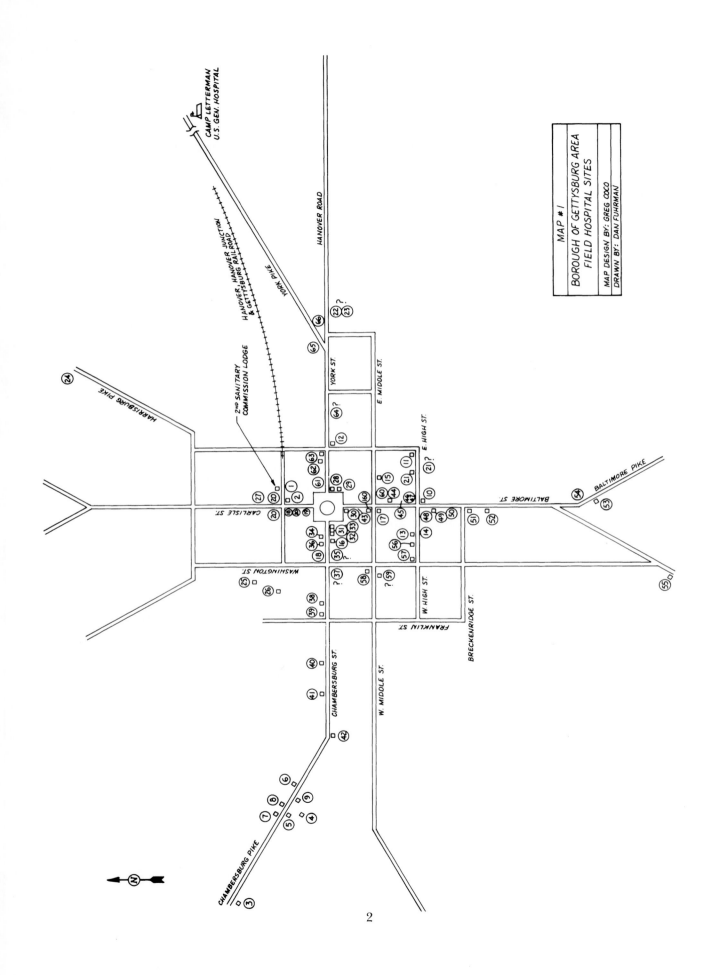

MAP # 1

BOROUGH OF GETTYSBURG AREA
FIELD HOSPITAL SITES

MAP DESIGN BY: GREG COCO
DRAWN BY: DAN FUHRMAN

THE HANOVER, HANOVER JUNCTION, AND GETTYSBURG RAILROAD DEPOT

This depot is easily one of the most notable structures in Gettysburg. Built in 1858, it still stands on Carlisle Street on the railroad, looking (from the outside) much like it did when it was a hospital during the battle, and when Abraham Lincoln stepped off of a train there on November 18, 1863. As Historian Bill Frassanito remarks, "The depot *has* survived the ravages of time," and even more so, the hungry "ravages of progress." We are indeed lucky as citizens of Pennsylvania, to still be able to enjoy this fine building.

More remarkably, the depot may have been the very first hospital established in the Gettysburg area—even as early as June 30. A quote from Robert G. McCreary, a prominent citizen and lawyer, confirmed this in a letter he wrote late in 1863:

> In the afternoon . . . (June 30) Buford's cavalry division entered town. . . . Their medical office requested accommodations for six or eight of the command who were sick. I procured the use of the railroad depot and . . . soon had it cleared out and twenty comfortable beds carried in and arranged.[1]

Then on July 1 the 8th Illinois Cavalry opened the battle and was one of the units, if not the first unit, to come under fire. Its surgeon, Dr. Abner Hard, who wrote the regimental history, remembered:

> The long line of the enemy came in full view (July 1—early morning). . . . About this time it began to warm work. Sergeant Goodspeed, of Company H, *was* wounded and taken to the depot where a temporary hospital had been established. . . ." (Later), ". . . a row of batteries . . . opened a torrent of shot upon us, and we soon found that our hospital, at the depot, was in their range. . . .[2]

Surgeon Jacob Ebersole, 19th Indiana Infantry, remembered clearly:

> About 4 o'clock (July 1) I was ordered to go into Gettysburg to take possession of the railroad depot, and establish our hospital therein. This depot was at the north edge of the town.
>
> In the afternoon, the Eleventh Army Corps . . . were fiercely driven back through the city past my hospital. . . . I saw my horse fastened to the fence across the street (we were on the second floor), with great saddle-bags and blankets . . . strapped upon him. At that moment . . . there leaped into the saddle one of our own boys in blue, in full retreat, and both rider

The rear of Hanover, Hanover Junction and Gettysburg Railroad depot in 1987. The area you see here was used for a Sanitary Commission "lodge," which catered to the wounded as they left by rail to hospitals in major cities along the east coast.

Surgeon Abner Hard.

3

and horse disappeared in an instant. That was just before sunset. Looking from the upper windows of the hospital, I could see our lines repulsed. . . . The enemy were enveloping the town from (every side), sweeping past the hospital, and completely filling the streets.[3]

Surprisingly, Dr. Ebersole found his horse and traps safe and sound at brigade headquarters on July 5.

2 THE ADAMS EXPRESS OFFICE

A map drawn in the 1960s, using research collected from many sources, shows the "railroad freight station," situated on the east side of North Stratton Street, right beside the track. I first thought that this may have been the "Express Office." However, later I discovered an advertisement in an 1861 newspaper listing "C.H. Buehler, agent of the Adams Express office on Carlisle Street near the depot." This may be the solution to the mystery. Buehler operated a warehouse business just across the street from the depot and probably situated the Express Office very near or adjacent to the railroad depot.

Another indication that the depot and Express Office were quite near each other came from Henry Marsh, 19th Indiana Infantry. He stated: "I was acting as hospital steward at the Express building in the town, when Dr. Ebersole said to me: 'Henry, you had better go to the regiment.'" This was during the time when the Eleventh Corps was driven through the streets in retreat.

(If you recall, Dr. Ebersole was just quoted as having been ordered to take possession of *the railroad depot* for a First Corps hospital.)

On July 2, a twelve-year-old girl, Mary E. Montfort, wrote in her diary that while she and her mother cared for the wounded in the railroad depot they found her father who had been struck by a shell.

On July 24, a wounded man, Eli A. Blanchard, 24th Michigan Infantry, said in a letter to his parents:

I am at the express office where our doctor stays. We have a large house full of (wounded) and the most of them are pretty bad cases nearly all of them have some of their limbs off. It is getting to be rather unhealthy here now and we lose a patient about every day. If it was not for the bad smell about here we should not have lost half as many as we do.[4]

Blanchard headed his letter "1st Division Hospital" of the First Corps. He also mentioned they had a

The front view of depot in 1988. The Adams Express Office was probably nearby. (G.N.M.P.)

brass band at this hospital which serenaded the other hospitals in town every evening.

In a letter to a Detroit newspaper on August 7, Chaplain William C. Way, 24th Michigan Infantry, stated that there were thirty men still at the Express Office hospital with two or three who could not survive their wounds. He listed all of the Michigan wounded and said that Drs. Beech and Collar were doing a good job with these men. He also related how it was "saddening to stand near the office of the Express Company and see the coffined remains of scores and even hundreds, being sent to their former homes. . . . Many are dying, and it is almost impossible to get a coffin . . . so great is the demand."

Way had previously written home on July 20, that the Express Office hospital was finally furnished with bedsteads.

A notation in the regimental history of the 6th Wisconsin Infantry said that Dr. John C. Hall, "was on duty in a building used for a hospital near the railroad station in Gettysburg." This was very likely the Express Office.

THE EDWARD McPHERSON FARM

With only the restored barn now remaining, this famous farm sits peacefully and safely within the boundaries of the Gettysburg National Military Park. During the battle, it was rented by John Slentz, while owner Edward McPherson resided in Washington, D.C., where he had been appointed Deputy Commissioner of Internal Revenue by Abraham Lincoln in April of 1863.

This farm became a shelter for some wounded of the Union First Corps, and probably a few Confederates, because it stood directly in the path of heavy fighting on July 1, 1863. It was common for wounded men to crawl, walk, or be helped to a temporary shelter such as this farm, even though its location adjacent to the firing lines was dangerous to men who had already been hurt in battle. In many cases, stretcher bearers could not keep pace with heavy casualties, thus leaving some men to care for themselves. As noted earlier, most regimental aid stations were generally set up several hundred yards or more to the rear. However, during actual hostilities, few ambulance drivers or their attendants ventured too close to the action.

Captain Francis B. Jones, 149th Pennsylvania Infantry, crawled 125 yards to this barn after being wounded twice in the left leg. He was helped into the straw of a horse stall and found Colonel Roy Stone, a brigade commander, lying in the next stall along with many other injured men. On July 2, Jones received some assistance from a Northern surgeon who was a prisoner. He remembered a Rebel surgeon with the Provost Guard who came in to examine the wounded to determine who could be moved off as prisoners. The morning of July 6 brought to the barn a Gettysburg clergyman who helped Jones get safely to David Wills' house in town. Mrs. Jennie Wills, who visited the farm, handed out baked goods to Colonel Stone and the others in the barn. Jones was surprised to find General Winfield S. Hancock in the Wills home.

Two weeks later, Captain Jones left this house for his family in Duncannon, Pennsylvania.[5]

On July 2, Lieutenant R.B. Beath, 88th Pennsylvania Infantry, who acted as a medical attendant to avoid capture, visited the McPherson barn to assist Sergeant Ramsey and other wounded personal friends. He "found it full of bleeding and mangled soldiers in a most distressed and sickening condition, without a surgeon . . . many so shockingly lacerated that they were unable to move, being in some cases, glued to the floor by the blood flowing from their gaping wounds." Beath spent the day caring for them, tearing his underclothes into strips for use as bandages.[6]

A Gettysburg attorney, William McClean, wrote in a memoir that he visited the barn on Saturday, July 4. He brought raspberries, biscuits, and other food with him and found some men who had been without food for four days. "There was so many of these wounded and so closely packed together, that I was obliged to tramp on some of them in distributing my supplies.

The Edward McPherson farm as it appeared at the time of the battle. (G.N.M.P.)

One of them told me, as he was lying on the field, General Lee had given him a drink out of his canteen."

Leonard M. Gardner, a Methodist minister from Clearfield, Pennsylvania, came upon the McPherson place on July 5.

> I found the barn above and below, the wagon shed, the tenant house, the pig sty, and the open barnyard were all crowded with badly wounded soldiers. . . . I happened to be the first to come to their assistance. . . . About noon, part of the hospital corps arrived. In the wagon shed a few boards were laid on some trustles and the work of amputations began. I was asked to assist in holding the limbs. . . . The heat was intense . . . the odor from the wounds was repulsive. One after another was placed on the scaffold, put under chloroform and while the surgeon performed the operation, I would hold the limb until it was separated from the body![7]

A surgeon of the 143rd Pennsylvania Infantry, James Fulton, visited Slentz's tenant house on the McPherson farm on the morning of July 1. "Spread over the floor the men of the battery (possibly Hall's Maine artillery) lay, wounded and bleeding. There was no one to care for them." Fulton attempted to find his orderly who carried the medical supplies, but shortly thereafter, both were ordered into town to establish a hospital there. (That location was the St. Francis Xavier Church on West High Street.)

THE LUTHERAN THEOLOGICAL SEMINARY (MAIN BUILDING)

4

There are several sites in this book which, alone, contain almost enough research material to warrant an individual study. This is one of them. The main building, in later times referred to as the "Old Dorm," was one of the first structures in or near Gettysburg to be used as a field hospital, and along with Camp Letterman, was one of the last to close its doors. In 1863, the Seminary was thirty-seven years old and consisted of the main building, 100 x 40 feet, made of brick and completed in 1832, and two professors' houses, also of brick. This building was rich in history prior to the battle, but the several weeks it served as a Union and Confederate hospital, make it easily one of the most historically valuable buildings today anywhere in Adams County.

At the time of the battle, Emanual Ziegler was steward of the Seminary where he and his six children had quarters on the first floor of the building.

About 1900, one of those children, Lydia, wrote a memoir which told how the family all arrived back home on Monday, July 6, to find "everything we owned was gone—many things destroyed and the rest converted to hospital purposes. It was a ghastly sight to see men lying in pools of blood on the bare floor. . . ."

Lydia's brother, Hugh M. Ziegler, who also lived in the main Seminary building, wrote his memoirs of the battle in 1933. In them, he said:

> We succeeded in getting back to our home but it was in use as a hospital. . . . The doctors in charge, learning it was our home, cleared two of the rooms and we moved in and got busy helping care for the wounded. My mother took charge of the kitchen and did the cooking. . . . There was one of the large rooms of the building used as a clinic, where many arms and legs were amputated and several times I was called on to carry one to the rear of the hospital and deposit with many others that had been placed in a pile. There had been an accumulation of several days before they were taken away and buried: and the pile . . . placed there like a pile of stove wood, would have filled a wagon bed.[8]

Early on July 1, after having been used as an observation point and possible signal station, Surgeon George W. New, 7th Indiana Infantry, recalled:

> I was surgeon in chief of the 1st Division of (Reynold's First Corps) on General Wadsworth's staff, and as such opened the first hospital for the wounded, the Lutheran Theological Seminary. . . . But as our forces were compelled to fall back, leaving a few Medical Officers there, I went back into the town . . . (and) took possession of several large rooms, halls, hotels, etc.[9]

Private Thomas L. Hann, 83rd New York Infantry, mentioned that the structure was already being used as a hospital even as General Reynolds was killed.

Dr. Robert Loughran of the 80th New York Infantry, remembered that after being captured on July 1, he "remained in the village in charge of the wounded, located in the Catholic Church until our recapture . . . and was then placed in charge of the 'Seminary Hospital,' remaining in charge of the same for seven weeks and until near the time it was broken up. . . ."

Many interesting people and incidents filled the building in those weeks, as may be gleaned from the following accounts.

Colonel Robert Powell, 5th Texas Infantry, was transferred to the Seminary after a stay at the Pennsylvania College. He reminisced in 1884:

> . . . there were only a few Confederate officers (here),

President Samuel S. Schmucker's residence on the Seminary grounds also served as a temporary shelter for wounded during the battle.

The Lutheran Theological Seminary main building in 1987. Hospital tents would have occupied the ground next to the structure.

the buildings being almost exclusively appropriated to the use of Federal officers. Here, also, we found the militia . . . guarding Generals Trimble and Kemper and Major Douglas and myself. Douglas has been Stonewall Jackson's aid. I was a Texan and credited with dining on negroes and unhappy unless I had killed a man every morning before breakfast.

Powell reports that the militia guards were kept in a constant state of agitation by the few Rebs located there, especially in trying to keep many and various curious women from visiting the Southern soldiers.[10]

General Trimble, wounded on July 3, noted in his diary that after his leg was amputated he was taken on July 6 to Mr. McCurdy's house in Gettysburg for two weeks. He was then *forced* by military authorities to relocate to the Seminary. On August 3, he wrote:

This day a month ago I was wounded—my leg is healing fast and I suffer no pain. Colonel H.V. Allman comds . . . post Dr. Jones, Dr. Ward, Surgeon 1st Corps, a gentleman. The Lt. of the Guard, Rice—a Penna. blackguard takes every occasion to vex us. . . . May the chances of war put him some day in our power.[11]

A visiting minister, Reverend F.J.F. Schantz, who had once been a student at the Lutheran Theological Seminary, recalled on July 23, that:

In the afternoon I took Hospital stores to the Seminary and visited the many sick and wounded . . . many (who) had lost an arm or leg told me that they still felt sensations in the parts separated from their bodies."

Again on July 26: "Later in the afternoon, I went . . . to hold Service as I had been requested to do by the Surgeon in Chief (Dr. Ward). . . . When I reached the Seminary, he had a party of men in his room drinking

and singing negro melodies. At the appointed time. . . I stood near the stairway in the second hall of the building. As the noise in the Surgeons room had not ended, I sent a messenger. . . . Very soon the surgeon and his party . . . passed me on a rush down the stairway and out of the Building. . . . As (only) the doors were open—I preached to an audience which I did not see. . . .[12]

Between July 5 and 12, Sarah M. Broadhead spent many hours tending to the wounded in the Theological Seminary. She stated in her diary on July 8:

The work of extracting the balls, and of amputating shattered limbs, had begun, and an effort at regular cooking. I aided a lady to dress wounds. . . . I found that I had only seen the lighter case, and worse horrors met my eyes on descending to the basement of the building. Men, wounded in three and four places, not able to help themselves the least bit, lay almost swimming in water. (We) called some nurses to help, and getting some stretchers, the work was begun. There were somewhere near 100 to be removed to the fourth story of the building.[13]

Major Henry K. Douglas, who was a patient and prisoner here for several weeks, remembered, "two young ladies who were great favorites in the Hospital . . . and on occasional nights when Dr. Ward was conveniently absent or not visible, I would stroll with them to make visits to the town . . . we generally landed at *Duncan's* and made an evening of it."[14]

On about August 9, 1863, one hundred to two hundred injured soldiers were sent to the Seminary Hospital from the Courthouse and Christ Lutheran Church hospitals, which were closing at that time. (Colonel G.F. McFarland of the 151st Pennsylvania Infantry said that on July 6, 173 wounded men were present in the Seminary's main building.)

Damage to this fine brick edifice was severe—from shell fire, bullets, and hospital purposes. The place had held over five hundred wounded, and damages exceeded $2,300.

Today, through the attentions of the Adams County Historical Society, the "Old Dorm" still rises majestically over the famous ridge which bears its name, and over the town itself. This wonderful spot is always worth a visit, for its history and for the view.

An invoice of medical stores issued at the Seminary Hospital by Surgeon Ward.

The Lutheran Theological Seminary main building in 1863. (G.N.M.P.)

8

THE HOUSE OCCUPIED BY
CHARLES B. KRAUTH

5

Standing just north of the Lutheran Theological Seminary is another building which became a hospital in conjunction with the previous site. In 1863, it was owned by the Seminary, but was lived in by Reverend Dr. Krauth, an employee, and his wife, Harriet. In applying to the State of Pennsylvania for a war damage claim, they declared that the house, "was used for Hospital purposes . . . (the) first floor filled with wounded; the surgeon and wounded officers upstairs. . . and that the beds were brought down for the wounded." A neighbor, Mrs. Hanna A. Foulk, whose own home was filled with wounded on July 1, later verified Krauth's claim, and said that by July 6 the house was vacant.

Professor Michael Jacobs of Pennsylvania College wrote in June of 1864 that on July 1, 1863, Dr. Krauth's family was forced out of this dwelling by Union soldiers "bringing in their wounded and filling parlor, study, dining room, and hall with them, . . . and then by the rebels when they gained possession of the (ridge) . . . and (the family) returned after the battle to see their floors and carpets saturated with blood and their comfortable home made a scene of ruin."

In 1908, Elizabeth M. McClean, a Gettysburg civilian, wrote that in Reverend Dr. Krauth's home was a surgeon of the First Corps, Richard M. Bache of Philadelphia, a member of Reynold's staff, who had cared for the wounded there.

An interesting note is the fact that for several weeks after the battle, hospital tents were set up between the Krauth home and the Seminary's main building. A Lancaster, Pennsylvania nurse, Mrs. C.A. Elher wrote in 1864 that she could see, "the white tents beneath the spreading branches of beautiful trees in which (their) wounded lay. . . ."[15]

Fannie J. Buehler, another woman living in Gettysburg, commented in 1896: "I was able to go out every day to the hospital tents between Dr. Krauth's house and the Seminary. . . . The tents were filled with wounded men who craved good, nourishing food. So . . . a cooking stove was taken to the woods behind the Seminary, and there we spent every day for weeks cooking. . . ."[16]

The Seminary today remains a mostly picturesque and peaceful landscape much like it was just prior to the hostilities of '63.

The C.P. Krauth house in 1987. Hospital tents stood
on the ground pictured here.

9

THE ELIAS SHEADS HOUSE

6

This house, located on the old Chambersburg Pike northwest of Gettysburg, sits on the north side of what is now Buford Avenue. The two-story brick building was a fairly new house at the time of the battle and housed a girls' school known as the "Oak Ridge Seminary."

Caroline Sheads was the principal of this academy, and early on July 1, she was able to give shelter and comfort to wounded men who passed by the house. An article written about Ms. Sheads in the 1880s stated that she nursed seventy-two wounded soldiers during the battle. A Confederate officer allowed her to keep five Union prisoners as attendants to help care for them. Several of her students returned, and "all devoted themselves to the great number of wounded with whom their halls and large rooms were crowded." The article continued by saying that "for many days after the fighting ceased . . . these poor fellows remained there, and were most kindly cared for, till all whose injuries were serious had been removed to the general hospitals. . . ."[17]

Elias Sheads, in his damage claim filed after the battle, attested: "My premises were inside the rebel lines from . . . July 1 until after the battle. . . . My house was filled with wounded Union soldiers . . . (from) the first day's engagement."

The Elias Sheads house in 1987.

THE MARY THOMPSON HOUSE

7

This small, one-story stone house is currently a museum just across from the orchard site which served as Robert E. Lee's headquarters during much of the Battle of Gettysburg. Although severely damaged by fire in 1896, it has been nicely restored by its present owner. It is located on the north side of the Chambersburg Pike, opposite the Lutheran Theological Seminary.

Catherine Foster, a Gettysburg citizen, wrote in 1904:

Old Lady Thompson . . . walked back and forth from her house to her daughter's near town taking bread to the wounded in her house and yard until her clothes were perforated with bullets and yet she would not be dissuaded. . . . All her clothes and bedding except those on her person were used in dressing the wounded and her carpets in wrapping the dead for burial. An empty stone house and fenceless yard were all that was left the widow of seventy years.[18]

The house was probably used only temporarily for the wounded on July 1 and 2. Mrs. Thompson was the widow of Joshua Thompson. Her maiden name was Todd.

The Elias Sheads house around 1900. (MOLLUS-MASS)

The Mary Thompson house in 1988.

The Mary Thompson house at the time of the battle. (G.N.M.P.)

8

THE HENRY DUSTMAN FARM

A widower and carpenter in 1863, Mr. Dustman was sometimes referred to as "John Henry." He lived on a small three-acre farm next to, and on the east side of, Mrs. Thompson. At the time, Dustman had at least one daughter, Emma, living with him. She was thirty-seven years old.

John Burns, who was wounded three times on July 1, and lay on the field all night, recalled in 1865, how he got help:

"About sun-up, next morning, I crawled to a neighbor's house, and found it full of wounded Rebels." The neighbor (Dustman) took Burns to his own house, which was also a hospital by this time. A Confederate surgeon dressed his wounds. Burns said he received decent treatment at the hands of the enemy, they not knowing, of course, that he had been shooting at them the day before.

9

THE SAMUEL K. FOULK HOUSE

In a damage claim filed after the battle, fifty-six-

An 1863 photo looking west on the Chambersburg Pike. The Dustman farm is in the distance before the ridge. The Foulk place would be to the left, just out of sight. Note the railroad "cut." (G.N.M.P.)

year-old Mr. Foulk described his farm as "on the west side of town, near Elias Sheads and C.H. Dustman." He noted in the claim that he lost several acres of grass and corn which were trampled down, board and rail fencing was destroyed and his house was filled with wounded men on the first of July.

The site today is on the west side of Buford Avenue, about two hundred yards northeast of the "Old Dorm" of the Lutheran Theological Seminary, and across the street from the Sheads house. At least *prior* to the Civil War, a blacksmith shop was located just east of Foulk's residence.

In 1863 Mr. Foulk lived with his wife, Hanna A.

11

THE PRESBYTERIAN CHURCH

The Presbyterians had a congregation in the Gettysburg area as early as 1740, and were worshipping in a log meeting house in 1747.

In about 1839 or 1840, a lot was purchased at the corner of High and South Baltimore Streets, and a building was completed there in 1842. Reverend H.G. Finney was pastor from 1861 to 1864, which included the time during the battle. This church was said to have been one of the first actual field hospitals used during the fighting. The U.S. Hospital Tablet on this site states that as early as June 30, it became the hospital of the First Division Cavalry Corps and remained so until captured by the Confederates on July 1.

However, Surgeon Abner Hard, 8th Illinois Cavalry, who was medical director of the First Cavalry Division, said that his first hospital was set up at the railroad depot. Soon the Southern artillery got the range and he noted, "some of the shots (began) striking the buildings and tearing them to pieces. We removed our wounded to the Presbyterian Church near the center of town, and were engaged in amputating the arm of a rebel soldier, when a messenger announced . . . we must fall back." Surgeons Beck, Rulison, and Vosburg were left in the church to attend the wounded.

A brief mention of wounded in the church was made by Reverend Schantz who remembered "the wounded Cavalry man in (the) Presbyterian Church who sang so beautifully. . . ." He mentioned that on two trips to Gettysburg (July 7 to 9 and July 22 to 27) he visited the wounded in this church.

Young Albertus McCreary, who lived near this church, stated,

> There were a number of hospitals within a block of us. The Presbyterian Church just across the street. . . . We cooked for the patients in (our) house, (and) sent quantities of food to those in the church. . . . The pews in the church were covered with boards, and then straw and blankets were spread on them to make beds for the wounded. There were many cases of severe wounds and many deaths in that church. One day I was watching them bury the dead in this trench, when men with a stretcher brought out a body covered only with a sheet. They drew back the sheet and disclosed the form of a young man perfect in every way, with only a small black hole in his breast.[19]

In November of 1863 when Abraham Lincoln came to Gettysburg to be a part of the new Soldiers' National Cemetery dedication, he attended this church on the evening of November 19. Today, unfortunately, this fine old and illustrious church is gone, replaced, as usual, with an unappealing modern structure which has little historical value.

The Presbyterian Church on Baltimore Street in 1914. (G.N.M.P.)

One of the nine U.S. Government hospital markers which are located in the Gettysburg area.

The new Presbyterian Church in 1987.

THE TRINITY GERMAN REFORMED CHURCH

11

In the claims file of 1907, this church was described as being built in 1851 as a two-story brick building with a basement and audience room, and a gallery across one end. The measurements were 70 x 46 feet, with white plaster walls, and white-painted pews, pulpit and woodwork.

Several witnesses reported that Union wounded were in the church as early as eleven o'clock a.m. on July 1. A Mr. Carver also stated that it was occupied by both Union and Confederate soldiers.

Eva Danner, who was sixteen years old at the time of the battle, lived on the Square in Gettysburg. She remembered: "The wounded were carried into the lecture room of the church and there was so much amputating done there that the seats were covered with blood and they had to bore holes in the floor to let the blood run away. . . ."

Another woman saw "men lying on boards on the tops of the pews," while others mentioned the walls were splattered with blood, and pews so badly soaked in it that, later, they had to be replaced.

Dr. Abraham Stout, assistant surgeon of the 153rd Pennsylvania Infantry, gave an excellent account of how the Trinity Church was opened as a hospital.

(On July 1) I was captured between the Poor House and the town. Colonel D.B. Penn (7th Louisiana In-

fantry) saw me and dismounted. He walked by my side . . . told me I was his prisoner, (and) taking me to the German Reformed Church, said to me: 'You ought to take this church for a Hospital.' I said, 'Yes, if it is not locked.' But we found the doors unlocked and took possession. In less than half an hour, it was filled with wounded, mostly Union men. I was in attendance there three days. . . . After that, we removed the wounded to the public school building. . . .[20]

One other soldier of the 153rd, Reuben Ruch of Company F, ended up in this same church with a slight leg wound.

I found the (church) full. . . . I should call it a slaughter house. There must have been ten or twelve amputation tables in (one) room . . . they were all busy. . . . The doctors had their sleeves rolled up to their shoulders and were covered with blood. I saw all I wanted to of this part, and I climbed the stairs to the floor above. I found an empty pew. . . .[21]

Ruch mentioned several men he knew in the church, and how he struck up a conversation with

The Trinity German Reformed Church in 1863. (front) (G.N.M.P.)

13

a Rebel guard, a North Carolina soldier. From a window he could view some parts of the battle and he later witnessed the attack on Cemetery Hill on the evening of July 2. On July 3, he saw a Confederate sharpshooter killed near the hospital. The next day, he made his way to the Eleventh Corps hospital on the George Spangler farm.

Private Justus Silliman, 17th Connecticut Infantry, was another soldier who was wounded and captured. He was first taken to a Rebel hospital and then on July 2 was taken to the Reformed Church. He noted that most of the wounded there were from the Eleventh Corps and said in a letter to his folks, ". . . nurses were not abundant and I have done what I could to relieve the suffering. Several of our own surgeons are in attendance but to their shame are more neglectful to our wounded than were the Rebel doctors. They will remain for hours at the windows watching the progress of the battle while our wounded were in agony for want of proper attention."[22]

One last note: A Lutheran minister who came to help the wounded after the battle visited several hospitals in the area. Among them was the German Reformed Church which he called the "Seceders Church," which was another name in use for this particular denomination at that time.

The Trinity German Reformed Church as it appears in 1988.

Stratton Street looking south to the Trinity German Reformed Church in 1863. (A.C.H.S.)

The Trinity German Reformed Church as it appeared in 1863. (rear) (A.C.H.S.)

ST. JAMES LUTHERAN CHURCH

This church, located on the south side of York Street, at the corner of Stratton Street, became a hospital on July 1, like almost every other such public building in Gettysburg. The building located there today is a modern replacement; the original having been demolished in 1911. The old structure, built in 1848, was of brick, two stories high, with a gallery at one end that measured 48 × 70 feet. From the description given in the claims file, it must have been a beautiful building—there were thirty-three windows and four exterior doors. It was topped with a steeple/cupola which a witness said was used as an observation post during the battle.

Reverend Abraham Essick, who was pastor at the time of the battle, wrote in 1864, that the church was used as a hospital for five weeks and damages totalled $2025, of which they finally received a $120 check from the government in 1915. The claim further stated that the wounded occupied the entire church, upstairs and downstairs, and everything in the church that could be used was appropriated for hospital purposes.

Mary Stallsmith, who was one supporter of the claim, wrote:

> . . . they sent (word) up to our house, (which was near the church) reporting that a man was dying in the vestibule of that church, and I went there and saw him . . . (he) was a Union soldier, a young drummer boy, . . . I saw into the room of the lower floor, . . . the basement floor, that they had soldiers lying on boards on top of the seats all over. I did not go to the upper floor.

Martha Martin, who lived near the church, remembered one young man there who had a gaping hip wound. She found that his wound was alive with maggots, and went to Christ Lutheran Church to find a doctor to help this soldier. The surgeon was very busy but finally came later that day, showing how scarce medical personnel were at that time. The pews, floors, windowsills and walls were covered with the blood of both Union and Confederate soldiers. Even the hymn books and record books showed evidence of soldiers' scribbling—messages, old familiar names, etc. The word "mother" was written in one book almost twenty times in succession.

The St. James Lutheran Church as it appeared in 1863. (G.N.M.P.)

The St. James Lutheran Church in 1987.

ST. FRANCIS XAVIER ROMAN CATHOLIC CHURCH

13

At the time of the Battle of Gettysburg, this church was only about eleven years old. It was brick, 98 × 48 feet, 28 feet high to the eaves, and had three windows made of plain, clear glass arched at the top, on each side of the church. There were sixty-four white pine pews, with doors, at the aisles. Father A.M. McGinness was pastor in 1863.

Adam Errter, a local man, recalled that there were Federal and Confederate wounded and doctors at St. Francis. He related that the dead were carried to the basement, which was 44 × 21 feet, where he assisted, "a man who was preparing bodies of the dead for burial or for shipment away." Errter also hauled wounded soldiers and dead bodies in his wagon for a while. He remembered blood all over the church, with boards on the pews for the men to lie on, as the pews were too narrow for this purpose.

George E. Stock, who was a member of the Catholic Church and lived four blocks away, said that every other pew was removed to make it easier to get to the wounded.

Another church member, Joseph H. Carver, stated in the claim application that,

> They amputated in the basement. I think I saw one amputation performed in that basement. The attendants stayed around in two little rooms at the side of the altar. . . . The surgeons and nurses passed back and forth from (St. Francis) to (the) church across the street, which was also a hospital.

Lieutenant Colonel Henry S. Huidekoper, 150th Pennsylvania Infantry, gave one of the best accounts left by a wounded soldier who was quartered in the Catholic Church. He was shot in the elbow near the McPherson farm on July 1.

> On arrival at the Church (about 5:30 p.m.) I found an operating table placed in the entry, with the double doors open for light during operations. . . . I went into an empty pew on the left hand side of the church, i.e., on the side towards the west and the third or fourth pew from the street . . . asked some men to tear the pew door off its hinges and place it crosswise on the back and front of the pew. On this, I placed my swollen arm. . . . About six o'clock . . . I went to the (operating) table and got onto it with my head towards the west. I took some chloroform but not enough, for I distinctly remember having said, 'Oh, don't saw the bone until I have had more chloroform.' What I next remember was my saying, 'You took my arm off, did you, Doctor?' He was Dr. Quinan,

Surgeon of my Regiment. . . . I then swung off the table feet first and was told to seek a place in the pulpit to lie down . . . stepping carefully among the hundreds of soldiers who were lying in the aisles. . . . Spying the gallery at the other end of the church, I worked my way back to the operating table and ascended the stairs to the gallery, which, as I had thought was empty. . . .

> The night was a horrible one. All night long I heard from downstairs moans, groans, shrieks, and yells from the wounded and suffering soldiers.[23]

Huidekoper also recalled how on July 2 General Ewell and some of his staff came up to the gallery for observation from the church cupola. Having only one leg, Ewell had to stay down in the gallery. The Colonel remained in the church until July 9. He mentioned that the Sisters of Charity from Emmitsburg were very active and helpful to the injured men.

Colonel Henry S. Huidekoper. (MOLLUS-MASS)

Huidekoper even hired a town doctor to assist the wounded for four or five days. The Colonel paid him $20.00.

Colonel Huidekoper was visited by John B. Linn on July 7. The colonel was then in a house (Peter Myers') about five doors "below the Catholic Church," recuperating from having had his right arm amputated above the elbow. Sharing the same bed with Huidekoper was Major Thomas Chamberlain, who

16

was wounded in the chest.

Incidentally, in a house just "two doors below the church" were several members of the 142nd Pennsylvania, including W.H. Specht who was wounded "in the privates."

Later, Reverend Mr. McCullough, a Christian Commission delegate, and two other men, made bunks for all of the patients in the Catholic Church, raising them from the floor; the wet, musty straw then was cleaned out and fresh bedding was obtained. It was said that the windows were fixed so that they could be lowered from the top to supply more fresh air.

A young Gettysburg schoolteacher, Elizabeth Myers, recalled her first sight as she entered this hospital: "I knelt by the first wounded man inside of the door (Sergeant Alexander Stewart of the 149th Pennsylvania Infantry) and asked, 'What can I do for you?' He looked up with mournful, tearless eyes and answered: 'Nothing, I am going to die!' That was too much for me, and I went hastily out and sat down on the church steps and cried."[24]

Later that day she was able to control her emotions and give service to many of the wounded there and in her home on West High Street.

On July 5, two Sisters of Charity were assigned to the church. They found it packed with men, "the air vitiated by the odor of gangrenous wounds. . . . (and) A considerable number of them were dying from lockjaw. . . ." The Sisters were very popular, and due to the lack of surgeons, were in constant demand as both nurses and makeshift doctors.

Surgeon James Fulton, 143rd Pennsylvania Infantry, was in charge of the hospital in St. Francis Xavier Church on July 1. He ordered that cooking for the patients was to be done in a nearby house belonging to Mr. Peter Myers. Fulton recollected that food got so scarce that he finally went to Confederate General Ewell to request flour to make bread. It was promised, but never delivered.

William H. Locke, a chaplain in the 11th Pennsylvania Infantry, told how Confederate stragglers were constantly coming into the church to help themselves to the private belongings of wounded soldiers. They took items such as shoes, caps, haversacks, and in one case, he saw two Rebels fighting over a Yankee captain's sword. There are several other sources which verify Locke's complaint as being a common occurrence.

A private, Joseph R. Balsley, 142nd Pennsylvania Infantry, stated he was moved to the Catholic Church on July 5 after having been wounded and made a prisoner. He was placed in the gallery with fourteen others and remained there until July 14 when he was removed to the "Cotton Factory" hospital in Harrisburg.

A visitor to this church, on July 7, said:

> The Dr. in attendance seemed to me to be a brute, he stepped about smoking and swearing, and paying no attention . . . to the frequent appeals made to him, and for the sake of appearing to do something commenced sweeping out the house which anyone else could have done better.

On July 7, William F. Norris, M.D., working at Lincoln General Hospital in Washington, D.C., was ordered to Gettysburg. Arriving in town on July 10,

The St. Francis Catholic Church as it appeared in 1863. (G.N.M.P.)

West High Street looking toward St. Francis Catholic Church in 1987.

17

he wrote on July 11 to his father of his experiences:

> (I) was immediately assigned to the Hospital of the 3rd division, 1st Army Corps which occupies at present a Catholic Church and that of some Protestant organization. . . . The Hospital contains 200 patients and is in a state of utter confusion. Men with serious wounds lying about . . . with very little attention. There are no intelligent assistants or surgeons. . . . Even the food is insufficient.
>
> I . . . slept last night on the floor of the private room of the priest adjoining the confessional which I . . . use as a storeroom much to the disgust of the Sisters who are in attendance.

On July 13 he noted:

> I draw and superintend the distribution of rations to the men. (I also tend to) the cooking, the cleanliness of the wards, the outside police, . . . burial of the dead, supplying . . . medicines, sheets, etc. My greatest difficulty is (getting dirty) shirts, blankets, sheets, etc. washed.
>
> The Hospital is now getting into fair condition. We have arranged beds on top of the alternate pews . . .

On July 18 he recorded:

> Each bed consists usually of a bed tick filled with hay or straw and one or two blankets. A few base sheets.
>
> . . . there is no one at all (here) capable except Dr. Quinan (surgeon in charge) . . . I think . . . that in about 10 days this Hospital will be broken up. . . . The sooner this can be done the better. We have been entirely without oiled cloth, gutta-percha cloth, splints, and . . . ordinary medical supplies. . . .[25]

On or about July 22, Norris was placed in charge of the two churches of this division's hospitals, when Dr. Philip A. Quinan was sent to Philadelphia. He wrote home on July 26 that the hospital had been closed a few days earlier and everyone was moved to Camp Letterman.

This hospital finally closed five or six weeks after the battle, but it wasn't until 1864 that the church was able to raise nearly $1,000 to continue the work of cleaning up the war damage. In the words of Father Joseph A. Boll: "On the 4th of January (1864) I arrived here and took charge of my commission. Having found the church much out of repairs by reason of the battle . . . I took immediate action toward cleansing and renovating. . . ."

THE UNITED PRESBYTERIAN AND ASSOCIATED REFORM CHURCH

In 1753, this church was organized and they used for worship services a log house near Rock Creek. About 1805, a church building was erected on West High Street, where it stood during the battle.

Elizabeth "Sallie" Myers, who lived near this church and the Roman Catholic Church on High Street, wrote that the United Presbyterian Church, like the Catholic Church, was used as a hospital. Dr. James Fulton, 143rd Pennsylvania Infantry, was in charge of both locations during, and some time after the battle.

The United Presbyterian Church stood some distance from the street and had a picket fence enclosing the grounds. At the time of the battle, it was considered an old church, even a "relic" by 1863 standards. Two trenches were dug on these grounds near the church, and the dead from the hospital were laid to rest there, wrapped only in blankets. Later, before the trenches were completely filled, heavy boards had to be placed over the bodies to keep them from floating during the heavy rains which followed the battle.

Although there are no good sources from wounded soldiers who used this particular church, we are fortunate to have a short but informative account left by the young Gettysburg civilian, Albertus McCreary. He wrote:

> The surgeons were at work in the hospital that adjoined our back yard (United Presbyterian). I spent hours on the fence watching them operating on the wounded. On a table out of doors operations of all kinds were performed. I must say I got pretty well hardened to such sights![26]

The United Presbyterian and Associated Reform Church site as it appears in 1988.

The United Presbyterian and Associated Reform Church as it appeared in 1863. (G.N.M.P.)

15

THE METHODIST EPISCOPAL CHURCH

This structure served as a hospital, but is harder to document due to the lack of corroborating sources. The church was founded around 1815, and the first permanent building was erected on East Middle Street in 1822, at the cost of about $2,000. When a new structure was completed in 1872, this old brick church became the property of Post No. 9, of the Grand Army of the Republic. It is now owned by an organization called the Sons of Union Veterans.

On August 30, 1863, the United States government paid a bill submitted by the Gettysburg Gas Company. Listed on this bill were several hospitals and the amount of gas used there during the month of August. The quote for gas furnished reads: "At Hospitals in the Methodist, Christ and German Ref'd Churches—$12.80."[27]

Another source for describing the use of this church as a hospital comes from Mother Ann Simeon Norris, a Catholic Sister of Charity, who reported that there were Sisters, "on duty in the Methodist Church Hospital."

Unfortunately, this is all of the information I have been able to find which names this church as a hos-

pital site. Sadly, as you read on, there is sometimes little more than this for documentation of many of the succeeding sites.

The Methodist Episcopal Church in 1988.

19

THE CHRIST LUTHERAN CHURCH

One of the most aesthetically pleasing and stately public buildings anywhere in the Gettysburg area, is this church, located on the south side of Chambersburg Street. It may be the only church in the town which outwardly appears as it did in July of 1863. Adams County is fortunate to have it standing mostly unchanged. The first-hand accounts of this "hospital-church" are quite numerous and generally interesting.

The lot for this "second" Lutheran church was selected in 1835 and the present structure was completed some time later. It was referred to as the "college church" for many years, because its ministers were mainly supplied by professors of that institution (Pennsylvania College) and the students regularly worshipped there. Reverend Henry L. Baugher, president of the College in 1863, was pastor here at that time.

This was probably one of the first public buildings in the town of Gettysburg to be commandeered as a hospital by Union soldiers. Mrs. Nancy Weikert, widow of Peter Weikert, lived nearby on Chambersburg Street. From the frightened sexton, she secured the key to the church to open the doors so that wounded soldiers might have a place of refuge. Mrs. Weikert and Mary McAllister were probably the first citizens to assist these early wounded.

During the Federal retreat through town on July 1, Reverend Horatio Howell, chaplain of the 90th Pennsylvania Infantry, was killed, and several others were wounded on the steps of this church—whether by accident or otherwise, is still debated.

An interesting incident was recorded by a youngster, Albertus McCreary. He knew a black woman, their "washerwoman," "Old Liz," who was being taken south into slavery by Confederates on July 1. When near this church, she slipped away and climbed up into the belfry or attic, staying there for two days without food or water.

Another young man who lived in town, Charles M. McCurdy, recalled:

Two doors below our house, the College Lutheran Church was filled with wounded. The auditorium of this church was on the second floor and the wounded had to be carried up a long flight of stairs from the street. Surgeons were at work under very rude conditions. . . . The Church yard was strewn with arms and legs that had been amputated and thrown out of the windows. . . .[28]

Melvin Walker, 13th Massachusetts Infantry, pinpointed where these operations were performed:

I was taken to a large church on (Chambersburg) Street where our division hospital had been established on the ground floor. The large vestry was fast filling. . . .

An operating table was placed in an anteroom opening off the Main hall and here our Surgeon worked with knife and saw without rest or sleep, almost without food, for 36 hours before the first round had been made. . . . A Confederate guard was placed over the hospital, but otherwise we were left to ourselves.

After the surgeons work was done we had no care save such as the few less seriously wounded comrads could give. . . . The first night 23 dead were carried from our room. . . .[29]

Jennie S. Croll, a Gettysburg resident, remembered that,

The first public building that was opened for hospital purposes was the Lutheran Church. . . . Forty men were laid in the lecture room, and 100 in the church proper, beds being improvised by laying boards on top of the pews. . . . On the Sunday following the battle there was a religious service conducted by Dr. Baugher . . . though it lasted but a short time, five men died.[30]

Thomas L. Hanna, 83rd New York Infantry, stated in a memoir in 1900 that his regimental surgeon, "then First Corps Medical Director, Dr. (C.J.) Nordquist," became a prisoner and he, with other surgeons, served the wounded there, both blue and gray.

Mrs. C.A. Elher, a nurse with the Patriotic Daughters of Lancaster, wrote in 1864 that the church was occupied by the Second Division of the Union First Corps. She worked in the church many days, cooking, cleaning and assisting the 150 plus men there. The menu was "tea and toast in the morning with soft-boiled eggs; dinner, chicken or mutton soup, always two vegetables and sometimes a simple pudding; for supper, tea, with stewed fruit, and buns. It was very simple . . . (but) you may form some idea of the amount of labor performed over a blazing wood fire in the middle of July."[31]

Later, she added that, "Military bands played for us, and the Gettysburg 'Glee Club' came in and sang patriotic songs. . . ."

After four weeks, there were seventy-eight soldiers left in the church. Mrs. Elher remembered that after a while there were no Rebels remaining in the hospital, and that it was closed after about six weeks. The remaining wounded were moved to Camp Letterman.

Mary McAllister, mentioned earlier, lived with the John Scott family on Chambersburg Street. She recalled an experience in this church:

> Every pew was full; some sitting, some lying, some leaning on others. They cut off arms and legs and threw them out of the windows. . . . There was a boy with seven of his fingers near off. . . . The surgeon came along (and) just took his knife and cut off the fingers and they dropped down.[32]

She also mentioned that an artillery shell struck the roof at one point on that day, on July 1.

This last unusual incident, which shows the frustrations brought on by some military regulations, should be recorded. Private Enos B. Vail, 80th New York Infantry, was wounded on July 1. He was "refused admittance" to the Christ Lutheran Church because he said he was told it was an Eleventh Corps Hospital and he was a member of the First Corps. He attempted to make it to the Catholic Church Hospital but could not, so he was brought back to the Christ Church Hospital. He stated that, "The surgeons were working from the front to the rear of the church taking each pew in turn. When the Surgeon reached me, he saw the Corps badge on my cap, passed on and took the next patient. After a short argument . . . he consented to treat my case." Writing in 1915, Vail may have his churches confused; however, it is very possible that during the turmoil of July 1, an Eleventh Corps surgeon working at Christ Church may have refused to treat Vail. This same type of incident happened to a Third Corps man on July 3 when he attempted to enter a Sixth Corps Hospital.[33]

The Parish House, located next door on the west side, was the home of Dr. John L. Hill from 1851 to 1857. It was used as a "supply depot" for this church hospital for several weeks after the battle. A small plaque gives this information on the east wall of the building.

The Christ Lutheran Church a few years after the Civil War. (G.N.M.P.)

The Christ Lutheran Church in 1987.

The Christ Lutheran Church in 1988. The Dr. L. Hill house to the right of the church was used as a supply depot for the hospital. The Eagle Hotel stood on the site where you see the gas pumps today.

THE ADAMS COUNTY COURT-HOUSE

17

The courthouse was built in 1858–1859 at the cost of between $17,000 and $20,000. As a public and prominent structure near the center of town, it quickly became a large and significant hospital.

As early as July 1, the courthouse was seized for a hospital as noted by Gates D. Fahnestock who lived diagonally from it. He recalled that he and his family brought food to the men there and stayed to render aid to the surgeons during amputations from the afternoon of July 1, onward.[34]

On July 4, a soldier, Franklin F. Pratt, 76th New York Infantry, who served as a temporary nurse here, wrote home that there were at least 250 men in that hospital.

Shortly after the battle, a Rhode Island man in the U.S. Sanitary Commission remembered:

> In the courthouse, in the very heart of Gettysburgh, we found our own soldiers lying on the bare floor, covered with blood, and dirt, and vermin, *entirely naked* having perhaps only a newspaper to protect their festering wounds from the flies! . . . Oh! it is impossible to describe these mangled and marred fragments of humanity. One we saw with a great cavern in his side, from which the lungs protruded several inches. Another . . . whose eyes had been shot out . . . was struck in the body five times! Of the number above named, 83 were shot in the body; 77 were cases of amputation, the rest were wounded mostly in the lower limbs.[35]

A woman who lived opposite the courthouse recalled:

> The sights and the sounds at the courthouse for a week after the battle are too horrible to describe. Limbs were amputated amid the cries and groans of suffering humanity and often have I stopped my ears that I might not hear. . . . Loads of arms and legs of these poor soldiers, that were amputated . . . were carted outside of the town, and were either burned or buried. The Regimental Bands . . . came every afternoon and played . . . in front of the hospital. . . .[36]

Another Gettysburg citizen, Elizabeth M.McClean, said at one point, "I started one day with others to go into the Court House, but the sight of the men lying on the floor on straw in the clothing they had worn during battle, and the dreadful odor turned me sick and I had to leave in haste."[37]

A visitor to Gettysburg on or about July 6 recalled: "In the Court House sickening sights met our gaze. Every available place in the rooms, halls, vestibule and stairway was crowded with suffering heroes. Many had lost an arm or leg. Groans of agony were heard on every side."

A wounded Confederate, W.H. Swallow, "found himself in the court-house from which all the seats had been thrown out the windows. It was lined with wounded. In the center was a row of tables, upon which miserable victims were lying, writhing under the surgeons' knives." Oddly, Swallow said that in a few weeks he was removed from this place to a grove of trees near the stonewall that Longstreet had assaulted on July 3.[38]

An account I have in my files tells of a seriously wounded 6th Wisconsin soldier named Levi Steadman who was a patient in this hospital. He lay in the main hall for several days until he died.

Another wounded man, Frederick Neff, 24th Michigan Infantry, was assisted to the courthouse on July 1. He found all of the rooms crowded except the judge's locked chamber off the main courtroom. He broke a window from the outside and he and a few comrades took shelter there for several days. He recalled that the building was struck several times by bullets, and on July 2, a shell burst in the cupola. Hiding out in the still-locked judge's chambers, Neff escaped the notice of the many Rebels who occupied the village.[39]

After several weeks the courthouse ceased to be used as a medical establishment. The wounded were transferred to the Seminary and to Camp Letterman.

The Adams County Courthouse in 1988.

THE GETTYSBURG HOTELS

This section includes information on one or *possibly* two hotels in Gettysburg which were used as hospitals. An account written by John C. Wills, the owner and proprietor of the Globe Hotel or Inn in 1863, said: "During and after the Battle the churches the Public Buildings of the town, the warehouses and one Hotel were filled with sick and wounded soldiers. . . ."[40]

The fact that he mentioned *one* hotel is interesting, because I have found very little to indicate that more than one hotel was used as a hospital. It would seem *likely* that all of the hotels, taverns and inns would have been taken, but such does not appear to be the case. The following information is all that I have found regarding hotels being used for hospital purposes.

The "one" hotel Wills spoke of was not the Globe Inn because no mention of a hospital in their inn was made in accounts left by Wills or his son.

Two different sources do mention the "old" hotel or "The Washington House" hotel as a hospital and "embalming house." It was located on Carlisle Street at the railroad on the southwest corner of Railroad Street, and was built in 1860 and razed about 1930. The Washington House is also noted on a U.S. government voucher to the Gettysburg Gas Company dated September 7, 1863. The paper authorized payment of $10.40 to The Washington Hotel, a U.S. hospital, for 2,600 cubic feet of gas used from July 7 and for a period of two months. On July 2, John Wills noted that, "(Mr. Israel) Yount and Family moved out and

The Eagle Hotel in 1888. (A.C.H.S.)

the Hotel was used as a hospital."[41] Yount was proprietor of The Washington House. He was forty-eight years old; his wife Mary was fifty.

A newspaper article in the *New York Herald* on July 24, 1863, reported:

. . . Surgeon Jas. L. Farley, of the Brooklyn Fourteenth, who had some fifty or sixty of his boys, badly wounded, in the Washington Hotel.

This house was almost in line of the shelling . . . and two shells struck it, pieces of it taking off the thumb and thigh of one of Dr. Farley's attendants. . . . Dr. Farley and his efficient steward, John H. Fisher, of the Fourteenth, stayed with the boys during the (rebel) occupation. . . .

Dr. George W. New, 7th Indiana Infantry, was Surgeon-in-Chief of the First Division, First Corps on July 1 when he recalled:

(I) . . . opened the first hospital for the wounded, the Lutheran Theological Seminary. (Later) I went back into town with other Medical Officers who took possession of several large rooms, halls, hotels, etc., being first also to open hospitals in the town for the wounded of that battle.[42]

Leander Warren, who lived along Railroad Street, noted that, "Every warehouse, hall, and the old hotel along the railroad were converted into hospitals." Warren was another who seemed certain about only one hotel in use.

A journal kept by Dr. Theodore Dimon, a former military surgeon from New York, was the best ref-

The Eagle Hotel as it appeared in 1863. (G.N.M.P.)

The site of the old Washington House hotel in 1987.

erence to a hotel being used as a hospital. Arriving in Gettysburg on July 12, he was told by the Medical Inspector, Dr. Cuyler, that he would be sent to the Second Army Corps Hospital to assist Confederate wounded. However, on July 13, he was ordered to,

> (a) . . . hospital in the town, known as the United States Hotel* (the Eagle Hotel or the Washington House), where it was reported things were not in satisfactory condition and that the wounded consisted of New York troops. I proceeded there . . in charge and a full corps of nurses, ward masters and a steward. There were beds in most of the rooms and the regular cooking arrangements of a hotel with a supply of hydrant water. But every part and parcel of the premises were disorderly and filthy inside and outside. . . . A considerable part of the time of the surgeon was spent in concocting iced drinks for himself and visiting friends. . . . At ten o'clock, the surgeon commenced dressing the wounds on the first floor. I . . . commenced in the attic or third floor. . . . These were wounded of the 1st Corps, . . . they had fallen into the hands of the Confederates and their their wounds were neglected till the 5th. They were placed then in this building and a detail of our surgeons furnished them. . . .
>
> July 14, 1863. I dressed personally every wound in the house, extracted a ball . . . and tried to get an amputation for another. . . .
>
> July 15, 1863. From representations made of the condition of things at this hospital the patients—all but 3 or 4 cases—were moved to three other hospitals.

Later, Dr. Dimon assisted the New York State Relief Agent in various corps hospitals, primarily in recording deaths and the burial sites of New York soldiers. He left Gettysburg on July 30.[43]

*"The United States Hotel" was located in Harrisburg. Dimon may have mistaken the two places.

One last note of interest—Dr. Dimon gave thought to establishing a central cemetery for deceased soldiers in the Gettysburg area. He took the outline for the project to the Relief Agency and David Wills, and the end result was the Soldiers' National Cemetery, which was dedicated by Abraham Lincoln in November of that year.

THE PUBLIC OR TOWN HALLS OF GETTYSBURG

19

Similar to the warehouses and hotels, at least one and possibly several, public or town "halls" in Gettysburg were taken over early on July 1 to serve as temporary field hospitals. And like the warehouse and hotel sites, these halls are somewhat hard to document. The best known hall was McConaughy's, once located where *The Gettysburg Times* building now stands. The Gettysburg Gas Company was paid by the U.S. government for McConaughy's Hall's use as a hospital as late as September of 1863. Several local citizens mentioned "halls" as being converted to hospital use. Likewise, a number of surgeons made this distinction also, such as George W. New of the 7th Indiana, who related: "I went back into the town (July 1) with other Medical Officers who took possession of several large rooms, halls, hotels, etc. . . ."

I have noticed that on occasion several of these sources list "halls and warehouses" interchangeably.

The site of McConaughy's Hall in 1988.

McConaughy's Hall as it appeared in 1863. (G.N.M.P.)

 THE GETTYSBURG WARE-HOUSES

20

The fact is not generally known, but several warehouses were extensively used as hospitals during and after the Battle of Gettysburg. Documentation is scarce; however it stands to reason that warehouses were "perfect" for that use, since they were large, airy, close to town and water, and usually near the railroad. The information on several warehouses in use is combined in this section.

One of the first to observe a warehouse for hospital use was Robert G. McCreary who lived on the first block of York Street. He wrote in an 1864 letter that in the early afternoon of July 1, ". . . I hastened to the nearest hospital, which I found in a warehouse about two hundred yards from my residence. I went to work." He later left the hospital to check on his family when the shelling got worse; one shell, in fact, passed through a corner of the warehouse. On July 2, he resumed his aid to the wounded, as he carried soup to several hospitals, and even secured a pound of chloroform which was needed for operations.[44]

Matilda "Tillie" Pierce, a fifteen-year-old girl, also noted the use of these buildings as hospital sites when she wrote: "Sometime after the battle had commenced, my father went down the street, he having heard that the wounded were brought to the warehouse located in the Northern part of town."

In another account published in 1906, Sarah King, a woman who lived at the southeast corner of York and Liberty Streets, described her experience on July 1: "Soon we heard the firing (uptown) and saw wounded men brought in and placed in (a) warehouse."[45]

Writing a diary entry for July 9, Sarah Broadhead stated: "Nearly every house is a hospital, besides the churches and warehouses, and there are many field hospitals scattered over the country. . . ."[46]

Leander H. Warren, another resident, wrote many years after the battle that, "Every warehouse, hall, and the old hotel along the railroad were converted into hospitals."

Leander H. Warren, years after the war.

Later, Warren's family prepared to leave the town to seek shelter elsewhere. Some other people were leaving, "and started up by the warehouse now owned by G.R. Thompson. When they got there, the soldiers who were caring for the wounded came out and told us not to go, because our homes would be robbed while we were away."[47]

Robert McCurdy and Jeremiah Diehl owned and operated a grain and produce business warehouse on Carlisle Street in Gettysburg. In a state claim filed for damages they reported that the warehouse was used as a hospital and the Confederates had complete possession. Robert Sheads and Charles H. Buehler also owned a warehouse, constructed in 1858, for their coal, stove, and lumber business. Many wounded occupied this building since, like the McCurdy-Diehl building, it was also near the depot.

An article in a Gettysburg newspaper of November, 1885, related how Alexander Ivey of the 7th Wisconsin, had been wounded on July 1 and was taken to the warehouse of Colonel C.H. Buehler on Carlisle Street. His leg was amputated on the second floor of that building.

One of the best accounts of a warehouse hospital

25

The Sheads and Buehler building as it may have appeared in 1863. (A.C.H.S.)

was the reminiscence of Nellie Aughenbaugh who was a girl of nineteen during the battle. She recalled:

> Over the (grocery) store was a large hall, which was turned into a hospital. (This was the Sheads and Buehler Warehouse or Hall.) When the surgeons amputated, they would throw arms and legs out the windows into the yard to lay there in the sweltering sun of that hot July. Sometimes afterwards they came with horses and carts, shoveled the amputated parts up and hauled them away and buried them in long trenches. We could not open our windows for weeks because of the terrible stench.[48]

The "grocery store" she mentions, may have held its own burdens. George Duffield a cleryman from Detroit said on July 9: "We were shocked at the sight of Peter Bird . . . (24th Michigan Infantry) lying in a food store shot through the thigh. . . . Alas, the doctors say he is doomed to die."

In a letter to his father dated July 9, 1863, William Harvey, a wounded Michigan soldier, wrote: "The ball passed through the chord below the knee. . . . I feel well and in good spirits. . . . Fish and I are now in Spangler's warehouse hospital." The site of Spangler's old warehouse was very likely at the northwest corner of Carlisle and Railroad Streets, diagonally across from the railroad depot.[49]

An interesting inscription found on the inside cover of a bible picked up after the Battle of Gettysburg reads: "Taken from the knapsack of a dead rebel at Warehouse Hospital, Gettysburg, July, 1863." The bible supposedly belonged to a William M. Nichols,

Carlisle Street in 1988, taken from the site of the Sheads and Buehler store and warehouse.

21st Georgia Infantry, who is *not* listed as being killed in the battle.

Charles Wills also mentioned that "during and after the Battle the Public Buildings of the town, the warehouses and one Hotel were filled with sick and wounded soldiers. . . ."

21

THE PUBLIC SCHOOLS

Completed in 1858, the two-story public school on East High Street was quickly taken over as a hospital during the first two days of the battle. Its importance as a hospital cannot be overlooked. In fact, as late as October 18, 1863, Surgeon Henry Janes, who had been in command of more than fifty hospitals in the Gettysburg area, wrote:

"There is but one building *well* adapted for hospital purposes in Gettysburgh—that is the school house which the people will be unwilling to spare for that purpose, it will accommodate about 60 patients."[50]

Actually, on about August 20, the public school hospital *had* been broken up due to pressure from the citizens of the borough who saw the need for it in late August for its original or intended purpose.

Dr. Abraham Stout, 153rd Pennsylvania Infantry, gave an excellent account of this school and its role as a hospital. After doing duty in the Reformed Church for three days, he remembered:

After the battle we removed the wounded to the public school building back of the church. The Union men occupied the first floor and the Confederates the second floor. Dr. (Theodore H.) Tate of Gettysburg had charge of the upper floor. I remained there for about three weeks, then had orders to remove all patients to Harrisburg, where they were put in an improvised hospital in a cotton factory.[51]

In a July 9 letter to the family of a wounded soldier, the chaplain of the 24th Michigan said: "I found Alfred (Ryder) of the 1st Cavalry, who was also wounded, I believe on the 2d and is now lying in a dangerous condition in a hospital, at the Union school House. I conversed with him for a long time. He does not expect to live."

In another letter on August 7, the chaplain wrote: "There are about forty Union and thirty reb soldiers still at the 'School House Hospital.' Besides these (and 230 he had previously mentioned) all have been removed from town, with the exception of a few at private dwellings."[52]

Mrs. Agnes S. Barr said that the school building was filled with Confederate wounded who were cared for by "Ladies of the Confederate Aristocracy of Baltimore."

Another letter written by Justus Silliman, 17th Connecticut Infantry, is headed, "Hospital 11th Corps, Public School, Gettysburg Pa, Friday July 3rd, 1863." In it, Private Silliman recorded that he was wounded on July 1, then taken to a Rebel hospital at a farm, then to the German Reformed Church, and next to the school. At the time of this letter, he said,

. . . the firing has now become general . . . and bullets and fragments or shell are rattling against our hospital, making a great racket. One shell from our (batteries) entered a house adjoining but did not explode.[53]

In 1868, a Christian Commission delegate recalled another occurrence here:

In the school-house Prof. Stoever found together two interesting and intelligent young men, who had just had amputations performed. They were Confederates, and both from Lutheran colleges—one from Roanoke College, Va., the other from Newberry College, SC. Their teachers had been students in the college at Gettysburg, and were well known to the Professor.

The delegate then went on to relate the messages the two boys sent home, both dealing with their faith in Christ, etc.[54]

In another incident, a Union soldier actually hid in the belfry of the schoolhouse from July 1 to July 4. He had survived on a few drops of water in his canteen and a couple of pieces of hardtack. The modern

The public school on East High Street as it appeared in 1863. (A.C.H.S.)

The public school in 1987.

photograph shows that the belfry is no longer a part of that structure.

Several accounts were found which mentioned that "two public schools" were used as hospitals in Gettysburg. However, the other school was not then and has not yet been positively identified. It is possible that the "other" school may have been one of two small schoolhouses which stood along the alley directly behind the old jail, which is presently across from the old "Union" school. One of these structures was known as the P. Weikert School in 1850.

Margaretta Kendlehart, a sixteen-year-old in 1863, wrote in 1923:

On the south side of (High) street between Baltimore and Stratton there were two small houses, a brick school building and the jail. On the north side were two houses, between which was a brick building used for school purposes. This building had high stone steps leading up to the entrance. The present High street school building was comparatively a new one at the time. The Reformed Church was on the corner . . .[55]

The school she mentioned as being on the "south side" of High Street was very likely the "second school" mentioned in several sources as a cavalry hospital.

The "second" school on East High Street after the Civil War. (A.C.H.S.)

BLACKSMITH SHOP(S)

A few contemporary references have mentioned a blacksmith's shop or shops which were used as temporary hospital sites.

Lieutenant Henry E. Shepherd, 43rd North Carolina Infantry, a Confederate of Daniel's brigade, Ewell's Corps, was wounded on the morning of July 3. He was soon carried to a blacksmith's shop which "was an improvised hospital, some distance in rear of our line of battle." He was later carried to a principal hospital "out of the range of Federal artillery."[56] It is impossible to determine which shop this was since there were four or more in the town in 1863 and several more in the outlying countryside.

Ephraim Whisler's blacksmith shop, near Jacob Lott's farm on the Chambersburg Pike, contained five identified Confederate burials on the property, possibly indicating a small hospital or aid station.

CARPENTER'S SHOP

An excellent account of a Confederate hospital in a carpenter's shop was written by Liberty Hollinger, who lived, in 1863, at the junction of the York and Hanover Roads just east of the Square.

There was an emergency hospital in a carpenter shop not far from our house. The Carpenter's bench was used as an operating table, and (my sister) who had gone there several times said that there was a big pile of legs and arms outside the window.

On Saturday afternoon (July 4) a Confederate surgeon came into our yard . . . Mother . . . invited him to eat with us. But he very politely declined, . . . as he (said) he was too weary and heartsick from amputating limbs all day. We could see on his knee-high boots how he had tried to get rid of the blood stains which had splashed on them while he was at work. . . .[57]

There is no doubt that he had been operating in this shop mentioned by Ms. Hollinger. The carpenter shop nearest to the Hollinger house was that of Jeremiah Culp, who operated the business at what today is 141 York Street, about three houses west of the southwest corner of the intersection of Liberty and York Streets.

The Jeremiah Culp house in 1988. (second from left)

THE ADAMS COUNTY ALMSHOUSE AND FARM

This once handsome and historic set of buildings is long gone by way of "progress." The site is now marked by only a few ragged trees which follow the course of the old road which led into the heart of these large brick structures. The Alms "House" or "poor farm" could not help but become a temporary hospital; it stood directly in the path of the U.S. Eleventh Corps' retreat route and was overrun by a part of Ewell's Confederate Corps.

Private Justus Silliman, 17th Connecticut Infantry, wrote in a letter to his parents on July 7 how he went out searching for his friend Sam Comstock. ". . . I finaly (sic) found him lying out in the storm in a puddle of water . . . he (had) lay on the field of battle all night (July 1) and part of the next day, when he was taken to the poor house where he remained until the fourth. . . ."[58]

Another soldier, this one from the 153rd Pennsyl-

vania Infantry, wounded on July 1 near what is now named Barlow's Knoll, recalled:

> Lying . . . until the afternoon of July 2nd (and) then removed to the Poor House. No room being available there—the place was filled with Rebel wounded—(I) was put down in the yard near the driveway.
>
> Shortly before noon of the third, a Rebel signal corpsman got up upon the roof of the Poor House, and started to signal the Confederate Army.
>
> Then began a terrific cannonade from the Union forces in their efforts to dislodge this fellow . . . shells passed over our heads and landed in the garden nearby . . . the suffering of the wounded in the Poor House must have been terrible. . . .[59]

A Confederate officer soon rode up and ordered the signalman to cease his actions thus ending the fire on the Almshouse.

In another account of the first day's fighting at Gettysburg, one soldier mentioned several times in his narrative of "a big red barn at the Alms house." No doubt, the barn, too, was used by wounded men. It can just barely be seen in the photograph.

John Rush, 153rd Pennsylvania Infantry, said he

The Adams County Almshouse farm as it appeared in 1863. (G.N.M.P.)

The site of the Almshouse farm in 1987.

by the Eleventh Corps during the battle, and eight identified burials took place on the grounds of that institution.

25

THE COLLEGE EDIFICE

Now situated on the campus of Gettysburg College, this important site was the main building of what was Pennsylvania College in 1863. Completed in 1838 on land purchased from Thaddeus Stevens, the "College Edifice," as it was called then, has changed significantly on the outside and totally inside since the days of the battle when it was a large hospital which remained in operation for at least two months afterwards. This large edifice was 150 feet in length, four stories high, surmounted by an octagonal cupola which was 17 feet in diameter and 24 feet high.

This was one of the hospital sites where Southern sympathizers, mostly women from Baltimore, came to assist the wounded Confederates. In some cases, these women were able to furnish soldiers with civilian clothes and new identities, to help them escape back to the South.

The cupola of this building was used as a signal station as early as June 30, and by both armies during the battle.

Late on July 1, some of the Eleventh Corps retreated across the campus, leaving in its wake, scores of Federal and Confederate wounded. Many of them ended up in this field hospital, the President's House, and another building on campus, referred to as Linnaean Hall (which no longer exists). Later, some of the wounded men from this corps, a large number being of German descent, found themselves in the library room of the main college building. Ironically, their heads were supported by old volumes written by German theologians, and the pages of some of the books became sealed together by their blood.

Michael Colver, a student returning to the College to see about his personal possessions, found, "All rooms, halls, and hallways, were occupied with the poor deluded sons of the South. The moans, prayers and shrieks of the wounded and dying were heard everywhere."[62]

Another visitor to the college was John Linn who said that "every room was filled with them, some rebel surgeons were amputating a man's leg on the portico. It is said that 900 rebel wounded were left here with only two medical cadets."

Andrew Cross, a Christian Commission delegate,

was taken to "a large brick house, I think it was the almshouse, but the place was full of wounded and the late comer had to wait till some poor fellows died before he could get a bed." Rush was there until the fourth of July when he was finally taken to a Baltimore hospital where his wounds were *first* dressed.[60]

Reverend F.J.F. Schantz, assisting the injured at the Eleventh Army Corps Hospital where he said he met Colonel William H. Jacobs, 26th Wisconsin Infantry, who told Schantz that he had "been four days among the idiots in the County Poor House. . . ."[61]

At the time of the battle, Jacob Culp and presumably his family, lived at and attended to the Almshouse farm. In his state damages claim filed after the war, he stated that he personally lost a "wagon when a Rebel officer took (it) to transport his wounded father to Virginia."

The physician for the Almshouse was Dr. John O'Neal who, on July 2 and 3, said he attended the "sick" there during the fight. Whether he meant "wounded" is unknown, but undoubtedly he must have been of some assistance to them.

One other wounded man who was carried to the Almshouse was Lieutenant Bayard Wilkeson, 4th U.S. Artillery, who was mortally wounded in the fighting around Barlow's Knoll. At the time, a story was circulated that Wilkeson completed the amputation of his shattered leg with a pocket knife, then crawled into the Almshouse barn where he later died. Young Wilkeson's father* wrote on July 4: ". . . (my) oldest born son, crushed by a shell in a position where a battery should never have been sent, and abandoned to death in a building where surgeons dared not to stay."

An official U.S. War Department hospital marker lists the Almshouse as one of the first hospitals used

---

* Samuel Wilkeson was a reporter for the *New York Times*.

entered the College Hospital on July 6 and found it, ". . . almost entirely filled with Rebel wounded, (where) a young, pleasant-faced lad asked us rather anxiously for food. He had not had a meal from Tuesday before, six days . . . we said we had a few dried apples. There happened to be just one apiece for them, (there were sixteen, lying on the floor) and never did we see men enjoy a little thing more." (Official Confederate sources listed The College Edifice as a hospital for General Heth's division.)

A wounded officer of the 47th North Carolina Infantry wrote in his diary:

> July 7. Today I was carried to the hospital. It was the College Hospital brigade . . . we were furnished with one blanket a piece. . . . In this hospital, there were six hundred of our wounded men, and about 5 of our surgeons remained with them.[63]

One other Confederate officer who was confined at the College Hospital, Colonel Robert M. Powell, 5th Texas Infantry, said that a Doctor (James K.) Shivers was the Surgeon-in-Charge. (On July 26, Dr. Lennox Hodge was reported in charge.) He reported that the building attracted many visitors, even that of

Decimus et Ultimus Barziza in the 1880s. From a photograph in his published memoirs, edited by R.H. Shuffler.

The College Edifice, a few years ago.

a Northern schoolteacher, who attempted to "teach" the ignorant Rebels their ABC's.

Captain Decimus et Ultimus Barziza, 4th Texas Infantry, recalled visitors during his stay at the college building, saying:

> The rooms and passages were densely crowded, and wounds of every shape and description afforded subjects for the attention of the humanitarians. There was a handsome yard adjoining the building, interspersed with shade trees. Thousands of citizens from all parts of the North flocked to Gettysburg to see a battlefield and get a view of the terrible rebels.[64]

Barziza went on to condemn many of these sightseers, especially hypocritical New England preachers, and fanatical, condescending men and women who were astounded that the many Rebels actually believed in their cause, and could even read and write. He remembered it was easy to get rid of these types—all the Rebs had to do was ask for money or something to eat.

Four Sisters of Charity were assigned to the six hundred or more Confederates at the College. The Sisters, ". . . could only take time to dress (the soldiers') wounds, for surgeons were too scarce everyplace. Every morning when they returned to the College, eight or ten bodies lay at the entrance waiting for interment."[65]

26

THE PRESIDENT'S HOUSE

In 1852, Reverend Professor Henry L. Baugher resigned as full-time pastor of the Christ Lutheran Church in Gettysburg, to begin his duties as president of Pennsylvania College. During the battle, Dr. Baugher lived with his wife and daughter in this house, which was then, and is now, known as "The President's House." It, along with The College Edifice, became a temporary hospital. A very good account of this site reads:

> Some eighteen of the wounded of the 1st Corps were carried to the splendid mansion of the Professor. Day and night the family were unremitting in their attention to the wants of the sufferers, and although the rebels held possession of the town . . . and the home was searched repeatedly (a wounded officer of the 90th Pennsylvania Infantry who was on the staff of General Reynolds) was so effectually concealed that he escaped being taken prisoner. This noble family . . . refused compensation . . . (for their losses).[66]

George Kimball, a twenty-year-old corporal in the 12th Massachusetts Infantry, was wounded in the left groin and carried in a blanket off the field by the Rebels to Dr. Baugher's house. Kimball wrote of that experience:

> My wound being pronounced mortal by a rebel surgeon who came in—Dr. Frazer of Galveston, Texas—it seemed like a waste of time and effort to endeavor to thwart the busy Reaper: so I came to the conclusion that there was nothing left for me to do but to die. . .

Kimball did not die, however, but was nursed to better health by Baugher's daughter, who he said was unceasing in her efforts toward the wounded. Kimball continued:

> . . . there were twenty or more of us lying in the hallway and lower rooms—and though shells were frequently bursting about the grounds . . . she paused not in her noblework. . . . Once, during a heavy cannonade on the second day, she (and her father) brought in a supply of straw for us to lie upon (from a neighboring farm). During the afternoon of July 2, General Lee paid us a visit. The look she gave him left no doubt in my mind as to her sympathy with the loyal army and her contempt for rebels.[67]

It may be interesting to some readers to know that Mrs. Baugher's son had been killed in an earlier Civil War battle in 1862 at Pittsburgh Landing, Tennessee. One wonders if young Baugher, a Union solder, might have received comparable aid and comfort from a Southern mother.

The President's House, a few years ago.

THE JACOB SHEADS HOUSE

27

In 1863, the Sheads family lived in a house on the east side of Carlisle Street, four buildings north of the railroad depot. Jacob Sheads, one of eleven children, married Agnes Flora Gehr in 1854. He was a tailor by trade, but in 1866, became a dealer in lumber, coal and firewood. In the year of the battle, Sheads was forty-two years of age and Agnes was thirty.

A letter written to Sheads after the battle indicated that his family cared for at least one wounded soldier. In the letter, which is now in the collection of the Gettysburg National Military Park, the father of a New York City soldier, wrote to ask for the rifle of his son, who died on July 15 of wounds received in the battle. He also thanked Sheads for taking care of his son until his death. There were many wounded men in this area, and it is likely that this house became a shelter and temporary hospital for this New Yorker and perhaps others.

THE DAVID WILLS HOUSE

28

Constructed in about 1818, this brick three-story house has become famous for being the place where Abraham Lincoln stayed overnight on November 18, 1863. It was the home of attorney David Wills and his family during and after the battle. Mrs. Wills was the former Jennie Smyser of Norristown, Pennsylvania. David Wills was the son of James Jack Wills of Bendersville, Pennsylvania, and had graduated from Pennsylvania College in 1851.

Captain Francis B. Jones, 149th Pennsylvania Infantry, who was wounded in the leg on July 1, spent over four days in the McPherson barn before being "rescued" by Mrs. Wills, who brought food to the barn on July 6. She then sent an ambulance for Captain Jones.

At six o'clock that day, he explained:

> An ambulance with attendant came and took me into (town), where Judge and Mrs. Wills received me into their home most cordially, and I slept in a clean comfortable bed, after the hospital attendant had given me a refreshing bath. Mrs. Wills told me she already had Major General Winfield S. Hancock from Norristown

The Jacob Sheads house in 1988.

David Wills in 1886.

The David Wills house after the Civil War. The house of Robert G. Harper may be seen to the right. (G.N.M.P.)

33

in another room. . . . The Wills family looked up any others they knew and could find who were from Norristown. In fact, their house was full of wounded.[68]

The Captain said he was there over two weeks, and when he left, Hancock* was still at the house.

Another officer who found aid here was Captain William H. Rexford, 24th Michigan Infantry, who had been shot through the hip. He said in a letter on July 9, that, "(the) ball had been extracted, (I) had a good nights' rest (and) got a clean shirt and felt better." His wife also had arrived that day from Michigan.[69]

Colonel Henry Morrow, commander of the 24th, who was wounded in the head, was in the Wills' house for awhile on July 1 before he was captured and marched to the rear. After the Confederate retreat, Morrow returned to thank the Wills family for their kindness.

*This is unlikely, as several people saw Hancock in Westminster, Maryland, on the afternoon of July 4.

THE ROBERT G. HARPER HOUSE

29

Robert Harper was editor and proprietor of the *Adams Sentinel* in 1863. He lived at the southeast corner of the Square in the same two-story brick building as the *Sentinel* publishing office.

An article in the July 14 *Sentinel* mentioned that a hospital was in operation at the Harper's residence. Also, a letter published in a Detroit newspaper on July 9 stated that Lieutenant Colonel Mark Flanigan, 24th Michigan Infantry, was a patient at Mr. Harper's house, with his wife serving as a nurse. His leg had been amputated, but he was, "cheerful and happy, and did not grudge his leg to his country. . . . Capt. (R.J.) Dillon, and several of our regiment and others of our brigade, have been cared for at (this) residence. . . ."

THE JOHN L. SCHICK STORE

30

The building, operated as a store by John Schick during the Battle of Gettysburg, still stands at the southwest corner of the public square in Gettysburg. Schick, however, did not live here at that time. His personal residence was located on Carlisle Street, north of the Square. Therefore, the following account is not clear as to whether Major Lee was cared for in the store or the house. Also, it is entirely possible that Rowland Howard, quoted below, assumed that Schick lived in the store.

In any event, while visiting the battlefield in 1887, General Oliver O. Howard's brother, Rowland, recalled that he returned to, ". . . the house of Mr. Schick where I took my dangerously wounded cousin Maj. S.P. Lee (3rd Maine Infantry) and was hospitably received."[70]

General Howard also mentioned the cousin, this time in his autobiography. "Lee's arm was shattered and had to be amputated at the shoulder. Lee had first served acceptably in the naval force, but concluded to change into the army, entering my old regiment as lieutenant . . ."[71]

Mr. Schick was born in Lancaster in 1822. He was married to Sarah J. Welty in 1863, his wife Mary Hereter had died in 1851. In 1870, he purchased the store building that he had only rented during those memorable times. After the battle, and until his death, Schick became very active in the Gettysburg Battlefield Memorial Association, attempting to preserve for posterity as much of the historic ground as possible.

The John L. Schick store as it appeared in 1863. (A.C.H.S.)

34

The John L. Schick store in 1988. The M.L. Stoever house may be seen to the left. Stoever lived on the upper floors.

31

THE SMITH S. McCREARY HOUSE

McCreary's hat workshop and residence were located on the south side of Chambersburg Street, between the Square and Washington Street. It was three buildings east of the Lutheran Church.

Mr. McCreary, a widower living with his three daughters, opened his house to both wounded men and "boarders." Surgeon William F. Osborn, 11th Pennsylvania Infantry, and the chaplain and another surgeon of that regiment, stayed in a room on the third story of the building. At the same time, several wounded men occupied the house. Among them was General Gabriel Paul, a brigade commander in the First Corps.

Jennie McCreary, seventeen years old and the youngest of McCreary's daughters, wrote an interesting letter to her sister on July 22, 1863. In it, she told what she found when she returned home on July 1 from a neighbor's house where she had been rolling bandages:

I found two wounded at our house. Col. (Samuel H.) Leonard shot in the arm and Dr. Parker slightly in the head, (both from the 13th Massachusetts Infantry). They are both from Massachusetts. Dr. Parker was wounded whilst coming down the (Lutheran) church steps.[72]

General Paul, seriously wounded and blinded by Rebel fire on July 1, was expected to die. His son, Captain Paul, arrived in Gettysburg on July 9, with a

coffin and other preparations for the burial. However, as J. Howard Wert explained in an article he wrote in 1907, the funeral did not come off.

"(The surgeon of the 11th Pennsylvania Infantry) had the General carried to the residence of S.S. McCreary, on Chambersburg Street, near the public square."

The surgeon, Osborn, continued,

It were gross injustice and worse ingratitude not to acknowledge my obligations to Mr. McCreary and his courteous daughters, who generously shared with us what they had upon their tables. . . . When I sought more comfortable quarters for General Paul, Mr. McCreary cheerfully gave up his own room and bed.[73]

A month after the battle, General Paul was able to travel to Washington, D.C., where he took up permanent residence.

The Smith S. McCreary house site in 1988. (large, three-story)

Gen. Gabriel R. Paul (MOLLUS-MASS).

32

THE ROBERT McCURDY HOUSE

Robert McCurdy, president of the local railroad in Gettysburg and co-owner of a warehouse, lived with his wife, Mary (Marshall), and family in a three-story brick house on Chambersburg Street. On July 6, they received a most interesting guest.

General Isaac R. Trimble, commanding a division in Lee's army on July 3, had been wounded in what is now called "Pickett's Charge." He kept a diary in those days and wrote:

> July {3}—I was shot through the left leg on horseback near the close of the fight and my fine mare after taking me off the field died of the same shot. . . .

After the amputation of his leg in a Confederate hospital, he could not be removed to the South, so—

> I decided to fall a prisoner—was taken to Mr. Mc-Cardy's (sic) house in Gettysburg and well treated with the most tender kindness for two weeks when I was removed by *orders* to the Seminary Hos. 1/2 mile west of town.[74]

Charles McCurdy, Robert's son, remembered the general:

> Father offered to care for the prisoner during the night (July 6), and he was carried on his cot into the parlor. . . . The men (who were carrying him) promised to return the next morning and send him on his way. The day passed and as they did not return he was taken upstairs to a properly furnished bedroom. The prisoner proved to be Major General Trimble. . . . The room adjoining . . . (his) was occupied by a young officer of our own army whose arm had been badly shattered. The poor fellow would not permit the surgeon to amputate and afterwards died. . . . General Trimble proved to be a delightful and appreciative guest. . . .He was attended by this aide . . . and by his orderly. . . . (who) had been a sailor. . . . Trimble was very angry about being moved to the Seminary. It seems that several Gettysburg citizens had complained that he, a Rebel, was getting such good treatment.[75]

In 1871 Judge McCurdy supervised the removal of the Confederate dead from the battlefield.

The Robert McCurdy house in 1988. (second building from trees)

General Isaac R. Trimble.

THE MARGARET ZIEGLER HOUSE

33

A simple reference is made of this Chambersburg Street site by Thomas L. Hanna, 83rd New York Infantry, who was wounded on July 1 and was carried by ambulance to the Christ Lutheran Church. That hospital became very crowded and Hanna remembered:

> That evening (July 3) Mrs. Ziegler, who lived in the small brick house adjoining the Sunday school entrance to the church, gave two or three (wounded) comrades and myself the use of the front room on

The Margaret Zeigler house in 1988.

the ground floor. . . . Twenty-five years later, after attending services in the church with Chaplain Roe, Mrs. Hanna and (my) daughter, I had a pleasant reunion with the dear old lady.[76]

The tax records for 1863 are no help in locating Mrs. Ziegler's residence. Evidently, at the time of the battle, she did not own property on Chambersburg Street, and must have, therefore, been a tenant in some other building very near the Lutheran Church.

THE JOHN SCOTT HOUSE

34

John and Martha Scott lived on Chambersburg Street, in a brick building which was both their residence and a general merchandise store. Martha's forty-two-year-old sister, Mary McAllister, lived with them and worked in the store. The location was on the north side, across from the Lutheran Church, just east of Washington Street and the Eagle Hotel.

Mary McAllister, while writing in 1907, remembered the first wounded man she saw on July 1.

> . . . soon the wounded ones came in so fast, and they took them in different houses and into the church. The first wounded soldier I saw was with John McLean (a civilian). The soldier was on a white horse and John was holding him by the leg. The blood was running down out of the wound over the horse. Our John (Scott) had been sick and was just able to be about and he fainted. . . . They brought him into our house and Martha and I put him on the lounge, and I didn't know what in the world to do.

Just about this time she and a Mrs. Weikert went to the Christ Lutheran Church to help the wounded there. However, Mary was too upset to do anything, so she returned home.

> When I came to the door it was standing open and the step was covered with blood. . . . I could hardly get through for the dining room was full of soldiers, some lying, some standing. . . blood on his face. . . . There was a young Irishman in there, too. His name was (Lieutenant) Dennis Burke Dailey, 2nd Wisconsin. (Dailey had Confederate General Archer's sword, a souvenir, and asked Mary to hide it.)
> Later, the Rebels came in and took many of the Union soldiers in the house prisoners, except the seriously injured ones.
> The next thing then was to get these wounded fixed. . . . We went upstairs to get some of the wounded ones in bed and to get pillows to make the

others as comfortable as we could. Five surgeons came in (and suggested the family raise a red flag). Well, Martha thought of a red shawl she had. She got it and I got the broom and we hoisted the front window (and let the flag fly).[77]

Two of the other officers present in Scott's house were Lieutenant Colonel James M. Thomson and Captain Jacob V. Gish, 107th Pennsylvania Infantry. Both stayed upstairs. One wounded man downstairs had a bad wound and Mary could not get a surgeon to come over to look at it. She had to find Dr. Robert Horner, a civilian, to do the operation. This was on July 2.

On July 4, most of the wounded in the Scott house were taken over to the church, and Colonel Henry Morrow, who had been a prisoner in the College hospital and later at David Wills' house, returned for a visit. Mary also wrote that not only were there wounded in their house, but *five Rebel surgeons* had their quarters in the Scott house, and demanded that Martha Scott cook for them.

Col. Henry A. Morrow
(MOLLUS-MASS).

The John Scott store and house at the time of the battle. Mary McAllister stands in the doorway.

The John Scott house in 1988. The third floor was added after the war.

35

THE NANCY WEIKERT HOUSE

In 1863, Mrs. Weikert lived somewhere on Chambersburg Street, probably on the south side, a few houses west of the Christ Lutheran Church. Nancy Weikert was the widow of Peter Weikert, Sr. A 1928 newspaper article said that her house was, "where the 'Gift Shop' stands now."

Mrs. Amanda E. Reinecker lived with Mrs. Weikert, her aunt, in 1863. Nancy Weikert was the woman who first opened the Lutheran Church, enabling the surgeons to establish a hospital there.

The 1928 article stated that, "(Miss Reinecker) a woman of 22 years helped to wash and bind up the wounds of the injured, and on the night of the first day's battle she made gallons of coffee for the wounded in the church and at the home of her aunt."[78]

From this sentence, it is obvious that the Weikert house was an aid station and/or field hospital, and therefore should be included, if only briefly, in this study.

Nancy Weikert possibly lived in the third building from the left.

36

THE DR. ROBERT HORNER HOUSE

Thaddeus Stevens had once lived in a house which stood on the north side of Chambersburg Street, diagonally across from the Lutheran Church. In 1858, Dr. Robert Horner set up his residence and office in the same building, along with his wife, Mary A. Horner. During the battle, Dr. Horner was kept busy caring for wounded in many parts of the town. In 1887, Mrs. Horner remembered the struggle through the words of writer Jennie Croll:

> (On July 1) Before we fully realized there was a battle wounded men were brought into our houses and laid side by side in our halls and first-story rooms until every available place was taken up. . . . In many cases carpets were so saturated with blood as to be unfit for further use, walls were blood-stained, as well as books that were used for pillows.[79]

Mary McAllister recalled:

> (July 4) By morning they (the Rebels) were all cleared out, and when we came down there was nobody about, only what were wounded. I went out and Mrs. Horner came out and began scraping off her pavement the mud and blood.

Of interest is the fact that Mrs. Cornelia Hancock, one of the best known nurses working in Gettysburg after the battle, stayed in the Horner residence from July 6 through September.

The Dr. Robert Horner house site in 1988.

The Dr. Robert Horner house in 1863.

THE LAZARUS SHORB HOUSE

37

THE DR. CHARLES F. SCHAEF-FER HOUSE

38

This Chambersburg Street site, like many others, is very hard to document. An 1861 advertisement in a local paper listed Lazarus Shorb as a coachmaker with a shop on Washington Street. According to the 1860 census, Lazarus Shorb lived at or near the corner of Chambersburg and Washington Streets. So, possibly in 1863, Mr. and Mrs. Shorb were still living somewhere near this location.

I was unable to find much additional information, except that in July of 1863, Alexander Cobean lived in a brick house on this spot and the Shorbs lived "in another house" nearby. The site is the southwest corner of Chambersburg and Washington Streets.

In any event, a letter written from Gettysburg on July 15, 1863, by Chaplain William C. Way, 24th Michigan Infantry, reads in part:

Sergt. Asa Joy, Co. C, at Mrs. Shorbs, on Chambersburg Street. Augustus Pomeroy, Co. C, slightly wounded, is in attendance as nurse. Mrs. S. is one of the many of those who have manifested the greatest kindness for our wounded. For sometime Capt. (Charles A.) Hoyt shared her motherly kindness, assisted as she was by two daughters. It is enough for us to say in her praise that she has six sons in the Union Army. While the rebels occupied the town Mrs. S. found protection in the cellar of her house from rebel bullets.[80]

Dr. Schaeffer was a professor of german both at Pennsylvania College and at the Seminary. His home was located on the north side of Chambersburg Street, three houses east of Franklin Street. Reverend F.J.F. Schantz, a visitor to the battlefield on July 8, reported:

I could have slept in a bed in the house of my dear friend, Rev. Dr. C.F. Schaeffer. . . . But the doctor could not accommodate five men. He had Col. Lucian Fairchild (2nd Wisconsin Infantry) who had lost an arm in the first day of the Battle, in his house. Another room was occupied by a student of the College who . . . was favored with a bullet from the rifle of a sharp shooter, which lodged in one of his limbs. . . . Our party slept on the floor of the parlour in the house of Mr. Mickley adjoining the residence of Dr. Schaeffer.[81]

Gen. Lucius Fairchild
(MOLLUS-MASS).

The possible area of the Lazarus Shorb house in 1988.

The Charles F. Schaeffer house or site in 1988.

THE DAVID McMILLAN HOUSE

39

THE JACOB W. GILBERT HOUSE

40

David McMillan lived at the northeast corner of Chambersburg and Franklin Streets in 1863. He was an older man, a veteran of the War of 1812, who lived alone. Richard Laracy, formerly of the 95th New York Infantry, recalled visiting this house on July 1 in a letter he wrote after the war.

> I was wounded with (a) fragment of shell that took off the third and fourth toe of my right foot—(I) went to the rear and hobbled along on my heel to the town. There I saw a small cottage with a pump in the yard and some soldiers getting water for the wounded. One of the men cut my shoe off on the uppers and released my foot and washed off the blood and told me to go in the house. In the house were 14 or 15 more wounded men. The house belonged to a man named McMillan. . . . An old lady kept house for him. She tore up all her sheets and pillow covers, to make bandages and attended to the men the best way she could.
>
> That night . . . three other ladies came in to help. One was Mrs. Schaeffer . . . with her daughter . . . Virginia. . . . (Also) Mrs. Neinstead . . . (and) a daughter, Catherine. . . . Then Mrs. Eichelberger came in.[82]

This house was located in what was known as the "Warren Block" on the north side of Chambersburg Street, one-half block west of Franklin Street. During the battle, it was occupied by Mr. Gilbert, his wife Elizabeth (Small), his mother, and two daughters. On July 1, the family went to Mr. Stahle's home on Baltimore Street. They returned that evening and found Confederates all around, on the streets and in houses. Elizabeth Gilbert recounted in 1905:

> Early on the fourth a Confederate soldier, wounded in the leg, came to the Gilbert home and asked to be cared for, offering Mr. Gilbert his horse. The man was taken in, saddle removed and (the) horse placed in Sterner's barn. The horse was never seen again, it was carried off by a soldier. When Union soldiers searched the houses for rebel prisoners they found the wounded rebel . . . and made him go along with them.[83]

It may be of interest to note here that Mr. Gilbert was one of the few civilians to actually be wounded as a result of the battle. On July 4, on Middle Street, he was struck in the left arm by a bullet fired by a sharpshooter.

The site of the David McMillan house in 1988. (on corner with flag)

The Jacob W. Gilbert house in 1988. (second from right with flag)

THE JOSEPH BROADHEAD HOUSE

41

Joseph and Sarah Broadhead lived on the north side of Chambersburg Street, about one-half block south of Franklin Street. This house was also part of the "Warren Block".

Sarah faithfully kept a daily journal and on July 1 wrote how she and others on the street sat at the doorsteps bathing the wounds of soldiers. Later, she walked each day to the Seminary to assist at that hospital. On July 9, her diary reads:

A man called to-day, and requested me to take into our house three wounded men from one of the field hospitals. I agreed to take them, for I can attend to them and not be compelled to leave my family so long every day as I have done.

July 10: At 5 o'clock our men were brought to our home, and I prepared them as nice a supper as I could, and they appeared quite cheerful, not withstanding their dirty persons, having been lying in a field hospital three miles from town, without a change of clothing since before the battle, and with very imperfect attendance.

July 11: This day has been spent in caring for OUR men. We procured clean clothes from the Sanitary Commission, and having fixed them up, they both (one of the three died July 9 or 10) look and feel better,

though their wounds are very painful.

July 12: To-day the lady I sent for came to see her husband. I never pitied anyone as I did her when I told her he was dead. . . . There has been some difficulty in securing proper medical attendance, the surgeons not liking to quit their hospitals and run from house to house, and our own physicians are overwhelmed with business.

July 13: . . . the nurse has just informed me that our sickest man will die soon. It is sad; and even we, who have known him so short a time, will miss him.

July 14: . . . the surgeon having general care over all (the hospitals), ordered the patients from private houses to the General Hospital.[84]

THE JOHN L. BURNS HOUSE

42

Old John Burns, the "hero of Gettysburg," lived in a wood frame house at the corner of Chambersburg and West Streets. On July 1, after being wounded and left on the field, Burns said,

About sun-up, next morning, (July 2) I crawled to a neighbor's house, and found it full of wounded Rebels." John Trowbridge who knew Burns continued: "The neighbors afterwards took him to his own house, which had also been turned into a Rebel hospital. A Rebel surgeon dressed his wounds; and he says he received decent treatment at the hands of the enemy, until a Copperhead woman living opposite 'told on him.'[85]

The "neighbor's house" that was used as a hospital

The Joseph Broadhead house in 1988. (left)

John Burns.

was the Henry Dustman house.

After the Confederates left the area, Burns was visited by Chaplain William Way and Surgeon Alexander Collar, 24th Michigan Infantry. Both men thanked John for his services and dressed his wounds before leaving. Michael Zellinger claimed in 1933 to have been the person (along with Zellinger's father) who transported Burns from Dustman's to his own residence.

The John Burns house in 1863. (G.N.M.P.)

The site of John Burns' house in 1988.

43

THE DR. MARTIN L. STOEVER HOUSE

Professor Stoever, a Doctor of Divinity, described as intelligent and patriotic, was another of the kind Gettysburg civilians who opened his home to injured Union soldiers during the battle. Living on the southwest corner of the Square, Stoever, his wife, and son were happy to assist in any way they could. The following story was written about them:

> As many as twelve wounded Union soldiers at once lay upon his dining room floor, receiving from himself and Mrs. Stoever constant care. His spacious yard was for days a free ordinary where our men ate their fill, without money . . . but with that hearty and cheerful welcome which so re-animates the weary. In his cellar he concealed three Union officers for three days—while the town was in possession of the rebels—anxiously determined to save them from arrest and the Libby prison. His wife fed them steathily during the time.[86]

Stoever's wife, Sue Elizabeth, wrote in 1903 of their experiences, and mentioned that there were *twenty* soldiers in the house. She remembered two Union doctors who assisted these wounded; Surgeons A.J. Ward, 2nd Wisconsin Infantry, and Abraham Stout, 153rd Pennsylvania Infantry, plus a Rebel surgeon named Major Watson from Alabama. Curiously, Dr. Stout had been a student of Stoever's before the war. Sue Elizabeth wrote:

> Dr. (Stoever's) recitation-room became the amputation room and could 'sing of arms' gastly and innumerable. . . .
>
> Among the soldiers who sought safety from the enemy . . . was Captain M.R. Baldwin, 2nd Wisconsin Infantry. . . . The captain chose the cellar, and thus was concealed. . . .[87]

Later, she related how her son hid that officer's sword in a woodpile—saving it for him until years later when it was returned.

On July 3, the Rebels broke into the house and rounded up Union prisoners and on July 4, the house, one of the tallest in town, was taken over for a time by Federal sharpshooters. On the days following the battle, two nurses, Mrs. Brown and Mrs. Glover, (from Philadelphia and Connecticut), stayed with the family while they worked in one of the hospitals.

A final note: Just two houses south and across the alley from Stoever, stood the Moses McClean house. Elizabeth M. McClean, a daughter, recalled that, "in a house across the street" was a wounded captain and a Union soldier left there to nurse him. At the present time, that is the only information available on this unidentified site.[88]

THE DAVID A. BUEHLER HOUSE

44

David Buehler, postmaster, lawyer, and editor of a local "Republican" newspaper, lived with his wife, Frances J. Guyon (Fannie), and six children on the east side of Baltimore Street, just south of Middle Street. Their house was built in 1816 and was one of the first in town with three floors. Mrs. Buehler was left alone with her children during the battle, as her husband, like many other Gettysburg men, headed out for safer localities. In her reminiscences written in 1896, she recalled:

> The battle had commenced. The wounded were being brought in. Here was womens' work and they did it nobly. Public buildings and private houses were quickly turned into hospitals, while the slaughter went on. In less time than I can write it some of the slightly wounded found their way into our house. They had been sent to the Court House, (across the street), but in some way or other the key had been lost or mislaid and during the delay in opening it the poor men hobbled in wherever they saw an open door or alleyway. We had both, so we soon had a number to be cared for.

She also related how several neighbors came in to help bandage wounds, and how the soldiers were taken to the cellar for safety. When the danger created by the Union retreat passed, they were carried upstairs and laid on the dining room floor. She said that most of the wounds were not serious. There were also wounded on the porch, and some men who were merely exhausted.

A German named Frey, and an Irishman, offered to assist Mrs. Buehler in this hospital work. The porch was turned into an open dining room where, for the entire "month of July, on (this) porch, (we were) always ready for any one, citizen or soldier, friend or foe, men of high and men of low estate, Governors, Senators, Congressmen, Officers of the Christian and Sanitary Commissions. All were made welcome, and all ate from this table. . . ."

Another wounded man in the house was Frey's captain named Myers. Mrs. Buehler said she took in three more captains on or after July 4. And, as you shall read in Site #46, Colonel John C. Callis

was moved to this house from Dr. O'Neal's in the latter part of July. Mrs. Buehler placed him on the third story, in the front room along with both his nurse and his wife. He remained in this home until September 1.[89]

The David Buehler house in 1988. (fourth from the corner)

THE HENRY J. STAHLE HOUSE

45

In 1863, Henry Stahle's residence was located on the east side of Baltimore Street, just north of High Street. Stahle was editor and proprietor of a Gettysburg newspaper, the *Compiler*, which he had purchased in 1859 and was situated in the neighboring building. This is one of the many sites which was obviously not a "true" *hospital*, but since wounded were cared for in the house, it is listed here. The house was torn down in 1894.

On July 1, Mr. and Mrs. Jacob Gilbert and several other people gathered here to prepare lint and bandages which were then taken to the Courthouse hospital. Much later in the day, Lieutenant Colonel William W. Dudley, 19th Indiana Infantry, was brought through the alley beside the building and then into the yard of Stahle's lot. Wounded in the leg, Dudley was carried into the dining room of the house and was placed on a couch in that room. Mrs. Gilbert took charge of the colonel and bathed his wound, while Mr. Stahle went to the Courthouse to secure the services of a Confederate surgeon, then in charge at that location. Interestingly enough, soon after the battle, Mr. Stahle was taken under arrest to

Ft. McHenry for allegedly giving aid and comfort to the enemy. These "lack of loyalty" charges were never pressed and he was returned home.[90]

Confederate soldiers later visited the house looking for hidden Union troops, but left Dudley in peace. Then, on the evening of July 4, he was moved to the "White Church," a First Corps hospital on the Baltimore Pike.

In a letter written from the "White Church Hospital" on July 26, 1863, Hospital Steward H.C. Marsh, 19th Indiana Infantry reported: "Lieutenant Colonel Dudley has had his leg amputated a second time and is now improving."[91]

The Henry J. Stahle house and newspaper office as it appeared in 1863. (The house is on the right.)

Henry J. Stahle in 1886.

46 - 47 THE DRS. JOHN W.C. O'NEAL, WILLIAM TAYLOR, AND JAMES CRESS OFFICE AND HOUSE

This building was a two-story brick with a two-story frame attached which sat at the southeast corner of Baltimore and High Streets in 1863. Three local doctors had their offices and homes here. One of them was Dr. O'Neal, from Fairfax County in Virginia. O'Neal, forty-two years old, had attended Gettysburg College, then practiced in Baltimore, Maryland for a time. In early 1863, he had moved to Gettysburg, Pennsylvania, to set up a new office.

Although not an actual "hospital," we know of at least one wounded officer who was cared for here. He was Lieutenant Colonel John B. Callis, 7th Wisconsin Infantry, who was wounded on July 1, in the left breast and lung. Supposedly, Callis had laid on the field, overlooked by both armies, for over forty hours. After a few weeks at O'Neal's he was moved to the Buehler house on Baltimore Street. On the first of September, Callis, accompanied by his wife and in a very weak state, left for his home. The bullet was never removed.

On September 28, 1863, Colonel Callis wrote to Dr. and Mrs. Ellen (Wirt) O'Neal thanking them for their kind attention while, "under your roof."[92]

Dr. O'Neal's house years after the war. (A.C.H.S.)

Drs. O'Neal, Cress, and Taylor office and house site in 1988.

Dr. J.W.C. O'Neal, years after the Civil War.

THE DAVID McCREARY HOUSE

48

Mr. McCreary (1804–1879) was a prominent citizen of Gettysburg, who lived at the southwest corner of Baltimore and High Streets in 1863. His harness shop stood just south of and adjacent to his brick home. In 1887, these buildings were purchased and destroyed by the Episcopal Church, and today, unfortunately, a church occupies the site.

Years later, one of McCreary's sons, Albertus, wrote

of the family's experiences. He recalled that a surgeon was in the house for a while and performed an operation on the front steps. Also this:

Two men were carrying another on a stretcher and stopped to rest at our door . . . his hip was broken (and he was suffering great pain). Father had them bring him into the house, as we still had a bed to spare. He was a captain, and had been in the Mexican War. He refused to have his leg amputated—said he would die first. We sent for his wife, who came on with their little daughter. They were with us six weeks. All the doctors could do did not save him. He died from lockjaw, and his shrieks of pain could be heard half a block away.

We were saved much annoyance (from the rebels) by having a red flag put up at our Door, to show that the house was a hospital. All our beds were occupied. . . . We not only cooked for the patients in the house, but sent quantities of food to those in the church (Presbyterian) across the street.[93]

The David McCreary house as it appeared in 1863. (A.C.H.S.)

The David McCreary house site in 1988. (at church)

THE SAMUEL WITHEROW HOUSE

49

The following Gettysburg newspaper article from 1909 is a source that portrays one of the few "romantic" aspects of the Battle of Gettysburg.

Dr. (James J.) Purman was a First Lieutenant in the 140th Pennsylvania Regiment part of General Zook's brigade and was in the fight at the Wheatfield and was shot in both legs, one of them being afterwards amputated. He was a native of Waynesburg, Green

Co., Pa. and when wounded was carried to the home of Samuel Witherow on Baltimore St., where he was nursed and cared for. Upon his recovery he married Miss Mary Witherow, daughter of Samuel and Eliza Witherow.[94]

Samuel's wife, Eliza Jane, had died some time prior to 1860. Mr. Witherow was fifty-four and an "auctioneer" in 1863. This site is located on the east side of Baltimore Street, about one-half block north of Breckenridge Street.

THE HENRY COMFORT HOUSE

50

Marie and Henry Comfort lived on what was known as "Baltimore Hill", on the west side of Baltimore Street just north of Breckenridge Street and across from what is today called Wade Avenue. Mr. Comfort was fifty-seven, and Marie was seven years younger.

Mrs. Emily B.T. Souder, who came to Gettysburg from Philadelphia to nurse the wounded, wrote in a letter home on July 22, 1863:

A Captain in an Ohio* regiment died yesterday directly opposite to the house where we are staying, another wounded man lying on the floor in the same room, and the Captain's wife in spasms all day. It was pitiful to witness the efforts at consolation made by her son, a little fellow in uniform, who had been with his father in the army, although a meer (sic) child.

* This captain was very possibly John Costin, Company F, 82nd Ohio Infantry, who had been wounded on July 1.

The Samuel Witherow house.

The area along Baltimore Street where Henry Comfort's house stood. (possibly the third from the left)

In another letter on the 27th she noted that the house where the Captain died was that of Mr. Comfort. Mrs. Souder was possibly staying at John Adair's residence.[95]

THE JAMES PIERCE HOUSE

51

The Pierce family lived on the west side of Baltimore Street at the corner of Breckenridge Street. Pierce was the proprietor of a slaughterhouse in Gettysburg.

In an account written in 1889 by his daughter, Matilda J. " Tillie", the following was gleaned:

> (My father) was obliged to enter the house by the back cellar door.
>
> After he got in, (he found) no less than five Union soldiers in the house. They were all sick and disabled; two of them were captains, and were very badly wounded.
>
> Mother nursed them and dressed their wounds during . . . the battle.

One of the soldiers was Corporal Michael O'Brien, 143rd Pennsylvania Infantry, who had been wounded on July 1 in the back, the ball passing into his right arm and shattered it at the elbow. Of the two captains, she remembered one being a member of the 6th Wisconsin.

About July 7, she said:

The James Pierce house in 1988.

Several soldiers came to our house and asked mother if she would allow them to bring their wounded Colonel to the place . . . saying they would like to have him kept at a private house. . . .

The wounded officer was carried to the house on a litter, and was suffering greatly. . . . The Colonel was a very tall man and of fine proportions.

He had been severely wounded in the right ankle and shoulder, the latter wound extending to his spine.[96]

The colonel was William Colvill, 1st Minnesota Infantry. He remained at the Pierce home for several months. At one point during his stay, his sister came to aid in his recovery. Two other nurses at the house, were Milton L. Bevans, a musician in Colvill's regiment and Walter S. Reed, a private of Company G.

Colonel William Colvill, Jr. (MOLLUS-MASS)

THE J. HENRY GARLACH HOUSE

52

This house, which ironically is still owned by the Garlach family in 1988, is located on Baltimore Street on the west side, just north of South Street. The south end of the house was the residence of J.H. Garlach, his wife, and his family of four children, while the remainder of the building was used as Garlach's woodworking/cabinetmaking and coffin shop. Not surprisingly, on the night of July 3, several Rebel soldiers came to the house to obtain or build a coffin for a Confederate officer who had been killed. This coffin was never used for its intended purposes and was later appropriated for the burial of Mary Virginia Wade, a civilian killed in the battle.

On July 1, Henry's eighteen-year-old daughter, Anna Garlach, and fourteen others occupied the house. She helped to bandage wounds during the retreat and later, on July 4, went to the Presbyterian Church to assist an injured soldier named Goodspeed, who was possibly a sergeant in the 8th Illinois Cavalry.

On July 2, Adjutant Charles Roberts of the 17th Maine Infantry was wounded near Houck's Ridge and shortly afterwards his leg was amputated. He secured transportation from the division field hospital on July 6, and was carried to the Garlach house where he was tenderly cared for until his father came for him. Lieutenant Roberts recalled his visit:

> The house was an old-fashioned, two-story brick building, close to the sidewalk; and the front hall being very narrow and small I (lying on a stretcher) was admitted through a window and a comfortable bed made for me in the parlour near the windows overlooking the street. . . . I remained at the home . . . between four and five weeks, receiving every care and attention from the several members of the family.[97]

His nurse was a soldier of the 17th Maine named Thomas M. Dennett.

In 1888, Roberts revisited the Garlach home during the dedication of the 17th's monument in the Wheatfield. Mr. Garlach had been dead one year, but Mrs. Catherine Garlach was still there, now sixty-seven years old. Both enjoyed and relished the reunion.

One other note of interest: Mrs. Emily Souder, who also nursed the wounded in Gettysburg, wrote home to her family in Philadelphia after visiting the Garlach house on July 20:

> On the opposite side of the street (from Henry Garlach's) is a young captain of the same regiment, who has lost his arm, Captain (Milton M.) Young. He was wounded, I believe, in the first day's battle, and like many others laid several days in the woods without attention.

To date, I have been unable to positively locate the house in which Captain Young lay. It may have been the Methodist Episcopal parsonage, or the home of John Norbeck.

Unfortunately, I did discover that Captain Young, who was wounded on *July 2*, died on August 13, 1863.[98]

THE JOHN MYERS HOUSE

Myers, born in 1783, was listed in the 1863 tax rolls as "Captain John Myers, gentleman." His residence was located on the west side of the Baltimore Pike, just north of the Evergreen Cemetery gatehouse. In 1866, this building became the National Soldiers' Orphan Homestead, until it closed in 1877. Myers died in 1872. The orphanage housed up to 130 children.

The *Gettysburg Compiler* of July of 1905, told the story of Mrs. Elizabeth Thorn who lived in the gatehouse. On the evening of July 1, she went to the Myers house to get some meat she had stored there. Mrs. Thorn said: "The house was filled with wounded soldiers and none of the family was about. I saw a lot of

The Henry Garlach house in 1988.

The John Myers house in 1988.

men lying in rows and six of them did not move and that scared me and I took a nervous chill and hurried home without any of the meat."[99]

The building still stands today and houses a gaudy museum. It is almost impossible to recognize it as the 1863 residence of Captain Myers.

THE CATHERINE SNYDER HOUSE

54

Conrad and Catherine Snyder (sometimes referred to as Snider) lived for many years in a house located along the east side of Baltimore Street, just south and across from its junction with the Emmitsburg Road. In 1863, their family consisted of Catherine Snyder and eight children. Mr. Snyder, a farmer, had died in 1860.

In 1944, Mrs. Rosa Snyder Gettle, who was a child of four years during the battle, recollected:

> On the first day of the battle . . . Union soldiers began coming back along Baltimore Pike with the Confederate prisoners. . . . The wounded were being taken back to the courthouse and other public buildings which were being used as hospitals.
>
> The children noticed one prisoner had been wounded in the arm with grapeshot. When the wounded man reached the gate . . . he said, he could go no further. (Mrs. Snyder) took pity on him, and ordered that he be brought into their house. She told his bearers to put him on the bed in the spare room, but when he saw the bed he protested because he didn't want to get it dirty. He asked them to put him on the floor. Mrs. Snyder did not allow them to put him there.
>
> The children who were badly frightened at the sight of the ugly wound, were even more frightened when they overheard someone say the arm would be amputated.[100]

Later, Catherine Snyder sent her youngest children to their aunt's house across Rock Creek. Nothing further is written about the soldier. (Their neighbors to the south were J. Lewis and Georgiana McClellan in whose house Mary Virginia Wade was killed on July 3, 1863.)

THE GEORGE GEORGE HOUSE

55

This one-story stone house is still located on the north side of the Emmitsburg Road (Steinwehr Avenue), just west of South Washington Street.

On July 1, General John Reynolds, who had been killed shortly before, was carried to this house in order to give his staff an opportunity to find a coffin for the general so that his body could be taken home to Lancaster.

A document written by Surgeon Murdock McGregor of the 33rd Massachusetts Infantry, gave a good account of the house's use during the battle. From Gettysburg on July 5, he wrote:

The George George house about the time of the battle. (MOLLUS-MASS)

The George George house in 1988.

50

I certify that the house occupied by George George in Gettysburg was taken by our troops for a Hospital on July 1st. It has been used for the wounded and sick ever since. To this house Gen. Reynolds was brought when wounded. The sheets, quilts and pillows and all provisions have been used for our sick men. George George estimates his loss at one hundred dollars.[101]

During the 1840s Mr. George spelled his name in the older, European fashion, without the "e".

THE PETER MYERS HOUSE

56

"Squire" Myers' residence stood on the north side of West High Street, just west of the Catholic and United Presbyterian Churches. Myers was the Justice of the Peace for Gettysburg and lived with his two daughters, Elizabeth and Sue, both of whom kept records of their experiences during the battle. Peter Myers also had a son named J. Jefferson. In 1861, Mr. Myers had enlisted in Company F, 87th Pennsylvania Infantry, and was discharged in 1862. His son also served, but in a Pennsylvania Reserves regiment.

Elizabeth, a teacher in 1863, wrote that one wounded man brought to their house was Sergeant Alexander Stewart, 149th Pennsylvania Infantry. He had been in the Catholic Church part of the day. Stewart died on July 6.

Sgt. Stewart was the first wounded man brought into our house, but others followed, and it was used in connection with and under the same control as the two churches. . . . We had twelve in all, and two deaths. The sight of blood never again affected me and I was among wounded and dying men day and night. (Lieutenant Colonel Henry S.) Huidekoper, who lost an arm, and (Major Thomas) Chamberlain, (both) of the 150th Pa Vols., were with us a while; also (Capt. Bruce) Blair, of the 149th Pa. Vols., who was left-handed and lost his left arm at the shoulder joint; (Capt.) James Ashworth, (121st Pennsylvania Infantry) of Philadelphia, was with us six weeks. He had seven severe and painful flesh wounds. Captain Henry Eaton and his brother, Sgt. Eugene Eaton, of the 16th Vermont Vols., came late one evening. . . . William J. Sheriff of the 142nd Pa. Vols, . . . was with us for a while. . . . (Private Andrew Crooks) of the 149th Pa. Vols., who was wounded while helping to carry Sgt. Stewart from the field, was also with us, and I . . . stood near . . . while the surgeons amputated his leg. . . . Pvt. A.R. Wintamute (143 Pennsylvania Infantry), another of our boys, recovered . . . (but) in the first engagement (after Gettysburg) was instantly killed. (Pvt. Charles Decker, 142nd Pennsylvania Infantry), another, joined his regiment . . . and a few years later was drowned in the Susquehanna River in sight of his home.[102]

Sue Myers remembered that there were only eleven soldiers in their house. She said many had their mothers and servants with them and paid for the care they received.

Today, this house is a plain, unobtrusive little dwelling giving to the casual passerby no indication of the stirring history which occurred within its walls.

THE SOLOMON POWERS HOUSE

57

Solomon Powers, fifty-nine, a granite cutter, lived with his wife Catherine and family in a two-story house in 1863. His granite cutting yard was on the property, which was at the northeast corner of West High and Washington Streets. Mr. Powers, who died twenty years after the battle, opened the first granite quarry in the area in 1838. One of the first projects he undertook was to build one of the granite bridges on the "Tapeworm" Railroad. This railroad was a dream of Thaddeus Stevens and commenced to be built in 1835. It was originally intended to begin at Gettysburg, and bear southwest, where it would intercept the Baltimore and Ohio Railroad. This did not happen, but it saw use as a railway in later years.

The Peter Myers house on West High Street in 1988, is probably the building on the left.

The site of Solomon Powers' house in 1988. (corner)

J. Howard Wert wrote of Mr. Powers in 1908:

A product of the granite hills of Yankee land was Sol Powers and he had a heart in him ten times larger than his massive frame. Blunt of speech, unmerciful in his exoriation of all shams, hypocracies, and false pretences. . . .[103]

Powers' daughter, Jane, and a friend, Lizzie Sweeney, actually went out and "rounded up" any wounded men they could find during and after the battle. One of those kindly ensnared was Private George Engle, 143rd Pennsylvania Infantry, who had been first a patient in a Rebel hospital near the Thompson house on the Chambersburg Pike, and later in the Catholic Church. When he was brought to the Powers home he found, "some fifteen or sixteen wounded men . . . in the house. . . . Their wounds had been dressed as skillfully as the attention could have been given by the most expert nurse; nourishing dishes had been prepared such as would appeal to the appetites of fevered and pain-worn men."[104]

Another daughter, Alice Powers, remembered in 1903:

A wounded Scotchman had been brought in who seemed so old beside the other boys that we immediately called him grandpa. He had such faith . . . in the ultimate triumph of the Union. . . . His 'na fear man' to father heartened us all.

On Saturday morning Dr. James Fulton came into the room where we were attending the wounded, and told us . . . the rebels had gone. Sure enough when we went to the door, the last gray-coat was seen going out at the end of the street.[105]

Surgeon Fulton himself recalled:

I well remember Mrs. Catharine Powers, one of the heroines of Gettysburg, coming and getting an apron full (of hard bread or 'crackers') for her 'poor fellows' as she styled them. Well were they cared for who had the good fortune to get into her house. The whole family gave their undivided attention to the wounded under their care. . . . They had during the time about 30; one dying, the rest recovering.[106]

58

THE MICHAEL JACOBS HOUSE

This two-story brick structure on the northwest corner of West Middle and South Washington Streets was the home of Professor Jacobs, a mathematics and philosophy teacher at Pennsylvania College.

Jacobs' eighteen-year-old son, Henry, witnessed the scene as the first wounded man was carried into their house.

(During the retreat on July 1) . . . a thunderous pounding fell upon our door of fists and boots. I ran upstairs. One of our own Bucktails named Burlingame (H.L.B., Co. G, 150th Pennsylvania Infantry) wounded in the leg, was there, supported by a group of his comrads. . . . We took him in, with two of the others . . . later a detail of Confederates arrived . . . they took with them (the two men) prisoners; but Burlingame they allowed to remain with us because of his wound. But they did not forget him. Two days afterward they returned and carried him off. His wound, while severe, was not so dangerous that he could not be moved safely.[107]

The Michael Jacobs house in 1988.

Jacobs' house is well cared for in this 125th year after the battle. The exterior probably looks much as it did during that bloody summer.

THE SAMUEL WEAVER HOUSE
59

Diagonally, and just across the street from Professor Jacobs' house, stood the home of Samuel Weaver. He lived on the south side of West Middle Street, the second house west of Washington Street.

Seventeen-year-old Jennie McCreary was present in a "Mr. Weaver's" house on July 1. As of this date, I am still uncertain if she meant "Samuel" Weaver, or some other family. In any event, she wrote about it in a letter to her sister on July 22, 1863:

> We had been downstairs but a few minutes later when we saw an officer dash up the street (Chamberburg Street) and order ambulances to carry the wounded from the fields. Next came a soldier wounded in the arm and then an officer on horseback. He wore no hat, his head was tied up and blood streaming down his neck.
> I then went over to Weaver's to help them roll bandages. We had not rolled many before we saw the street filled with wounded men. Men wounded in arms, limbs, head and breast. Oh, it was sickening to see them and hear their groans. Weaver's house was soon filled. I never thought I could do anything about a wounded man but I find I have a little more nerve than I thought I had. I could look at the wounds, bathe them, bind them up without feeling the least bit sick or nervous.
> The tears only came once and that was when the first soldier came in the house. He had walked from the field and was almost exhausted. He threw himself in the chair and said, 'Oh, girls I have as good a home as you. If I were only there!' He fainted directly afterward.

When Jennie wrote of her return to her family home on Chambersburg Street through the streets of Gettysburg, the route she took corresponded closely with landmarks which would have been passed on a trek from Samuel Weaver's house to her own.[108]

THE JOHN CANNON HOUSE
60

In 1863, tax records indicated that John Cannon did not own property in the town of Gettysburg. However, during the battle, he and James Adair operated a marble works which was located on the southeast corner of Baltimore and East Middle Streets. Cannon obviously lived in this building as will be seen from an excerpt from a letter written at the time by a Michigan chaplain.

As in many other sites, very little is known of this temporary hospital. But, in this case, we are fortunate to have the letter written by Chaplain William C. Way to the *Detroit Tribune* on July 15, 1863. In part of this correspondence, he explained:

> Thomas Ballou, Co. C, is at the residence of Mr. John Cannon's opposite the Courthouse. Alfred Willis, Co. C., who was wounded in the hand, is nurse at this house.

If there was a nurse in Cannon's house, it is possible that there were other soldiers here as well.

As a sidelight, both of these men were 24th Michigan privates. Ballou was part of the regiment's colorguard, and was wounded in the groin on the retreat toward Cemetery Hill. Seemingly, Ballou became a sort of local hero as a result of his actions in the battle, as his name often appears in the hometown paper.

There seems to be a possibility that "Martha White" was a tenant in the same building as Cannon.

THE BANK OF GETTYSBURG BUILDING AND HOUSE OCCUPIED BY T. DUNCAN CARSON
61

At the time of the battle, Mr. Carson was employed as a clerk and teller at the Bank of Gettysburg and lived with his wife in the bank residence on the north side of the first block of York Street, between the bank and the Globe Hotel.

Sometime before July 1, he had been sent to York with the bank's funds which were to be shipped to Philadelphia. His wife, Mary, who remained behind, took nineteen women and children into the bank vault. While there, a message arrived saying that Mary Carson's brother, Lieutenant Charles O. Hunt, 5th Maine Battery, was at the door, wounded. He was taken to the cellar at once, and was placed on a piano box, where Dr. Robert Horner extracted a bullet from his leg and cared for the lieutenant until about July 12 when he left for home.

Mr. Carson recalled having two other soldiers in his house, one, wounded in the face, later died. Carson's mother nursed them throughout the battle while T.D. Carson assisted for several days in another hospital.[109]

One other soldier who spent time in this residence was Lieutenant Charles Fuller, 61st New York Infantry, who had received two wounds, one in the leg and a second in the shoulder. On or about July 13, he was transported to the Carson home. He related:

> Two men carried me on a stretcher . . . I was taken to the house of Mr. Carson, . . . At this time every house in town was at the service of any wounded, or their friends. When I was deposited at his house, Mr. Carson was in Philadelphia to get and return the bank's property, but Mrs. Carson was there, and, if I had been a near relative, she could not have done more to make my stay tolerable. . . .
>
> After a few days in the village, consent was obtained for me to start for home.[110]

THE PETER STALLSMITH HOUSE

62

The small two-story house of Ann and Peter Stallsmith stood just in rear of and northwest of the George Swope house on the northwest corner of York and Stratton Streets. In 1863, a lawn stretched from the house to York Street. An article in the *Star and Sentinel* of April 26, 1887, told their story:

Capt. H.C. Parsons of the 1st Vermont Cavalry was severely wounded in Farnsworth's charge. First taken to the Court-house and afterwards to the house of Mrs. Ann Stallsmith on York Street (about ten days) until removed to the General Hospital. Wounded officers had been placed in the care of Mrs. Stallsmith.

Captain Parsons was wounded in an ill-fated charge on the afternoon of July 3. He and Captain Oliver Cushman fell at about the same moment near where Farnsworth was killed. At that time, Parsons commanded the first battalion of the regiment.

THE GEORGE SWOPE HOUSE

63

Situated on the northwest corner of York and Stratton Streets, this large and attractive house was owned by one of Gettysburg's wealthiest citizens in 1863. George Swope, sixty-two years old, and his wife, Margaret, sixty, occupied the house which may have held wounded men. It is listed here because in searching through a file in the Gettysburg National Military Park library, I came across an old (1930s) photograph of this house with a notation that it was used by wounded men during and after the battle. There is probably some truth in the remark, simply because of its size, and location diagonally across the street from the hospital at St. James Lutheran Church. The house may have taken some of its overflow.

In fact, John Linn, a visitor to Gettysburg from

The Peter Stallsmith house. (The 1863 structure of stone is in rear of this more modern facade.)

The George Swope house as it appeared in 1938. It is much the same today. (G.N.M.P.)

July 6–11, said that this house had been "turned into a refreshment room for wounded." Linn was staying in a boarding house just across the street from the Swope Mansion—on the *southwest* corner of York and Stratton Streets. During the battle a wounded officer, "Lieutenant Murphy" of Baton Rouge, was cared for here. The boarding house was being run by Sarah or Marie Walters.

Mr. Linn also noted the presence of another wounded officer in town. This was Lieutenant Joseph S. Milne, 4th U.S. Artillery, who was at a "Mr. Weikels." Unfortunately, this house can not yet be identified. Milne was being nursed by Lieutenant Jacob H. Lamb when he died on July 9 at 2:20 p.m.

THE SARAH E. MONTFORT HOUSE

64

At best, this site is a "calculated guess." In 1863, Sarah was possibly the only Montfort in Gettysburg and may have shared a brick and weatherboard house with a "Mary Thompson" on the south side of York Street, three doors west of Liberty Street.

One account stated: "By the time I returned home I found the little folks had been called in to Mrs. Montfort's to pick lint (for bandages). The fighting was on in earnest and nearer. (This was on July 1.) A soldier on horse back rode along York Street calling to families to go to their cellars. . . ." The writer lived two doors east of the Montfort house, on the corner of York and Liberty Streets.[111]

The diary of twelve-year-old Mary Elizabeth Mont-

fort of Gettysburg, revealed that on July 2,

"We brought two (wounded) soldiers into our house. One was very young. He was from Connecticut. The other was as old as father and was from Bucks County in Pennsylvania."[112]

On July 1, both Mary and her mother had been at the railroad station assisting the wounded. It is not known at this time if Mary was Sarah's daughter; the only connection is the name Montfort, the only family by that name in the area.

THE ELIZABETH CULP HOUSE

65

Elizabeth or "Polly" Culp lived in a two-story frame and brick house on the north side of the York Pike, near its junction with the Hanover Road. At least one soldier, a wounded Michigan soldier named Smith, was cared for in her home. This man was injured on July 3 in a battle with Confederate cavalry west of Gettysburg. First carried to the porch of the "Rhinehart farm," he was later taken to the "Miller farm" and then to "Aunt" Polly Culp's. He was treated by Culp until he was able to return to his home.[113]

The Elizabeth Culp house or site is located near where you see the white house on York Street.

Sarah E. Montfort possibly lived in or on the site of one of these structures photographed in 1988.

THE JACOB S. HOLLINGER HOUSE

66

Jacob Hollinger owned a warehouse on the corner of Stratton Street, adjacent to the railroad, where he was in the grain and produce business. For some reason, this warehouse was not used as a hospital, however, it was ransacked and pillaged by the Confederates.

A sixteen-year-old daughter, Liberty Hollinger, described the location of their house this way:

> We were living on York Street. . . . Our house, a roomy brick one, stood in the center of a large plot of ground between the York Pike . . . and what was known as the Bonneauville or Hanover Road. . . . There were then only a few houses east of ours, also between the two roads, and a few opposite on the other side.

The family must have cared for several wounded men, but Liberty recalled one young soldier in particular:

> This woman came to Gettysburg with the father of a wounded boy who was at our house. The boy's first name was Paul; I do not remember his other name. His right arm had been amputated at the shoulder, and it was my duty to dress the wound every morning and evening. How still he used to hold while I thoroughly cleansed it! His father took him home and we heard later that though the wound had healed he died from the effects of it. While he was at our house he was so painfully nervous from the pain and shock that he had to have an anodyne every evening on retiring so as to get some sleep and rest.[114]

The Hollingers were well remembered by a 6th Wisconsin officer named Captain Loyd G. Harris. He wrote to his colonel of his experience there:

> After I was wounded, Lieut. W.N. Remington, Lieutenant John Beely and myself, were in a temporary hospital in Gettysburg. Acting on the advice of the surgeon, we found pleasant quarters with the family of Mr. Hollenger (sic), and while there were joined by one of our sergeants (William Evans I think) who had (our captured) rebel flag.* This was about noon. Just after our dinner, firing began in the front. I went up stairs and from an upper porch could plainly see the movement of the eleventh corps but not the first corps. They (the eleventh corps) were over-lapped by the enemy and soon in full retreat. I went below and told Remington and Beely to hurry out and get to the rear as fast as they could. Mrs. Hollenger partly fainted, and assisted by her husband I helped to carry

*This was the flag of the 2nd Mississippi Infantry.

her to the cellar. There were two young lady daughters, (Miss Julia was the name of one of these young ladies). I bade them all good bye, and when I went out, had a narrow escape from being shot down or captured, but by going through houses, (and) after I passed two cross streets, found my companions in an ambulance. Once with them, we lead the retreat.[115]

Liberty Hollinger often saw on the streets of Gettysburg, Dr. Mary E. Walker, an army surgeon, whom she described as wearing "a low silk hat, with bloomers, and a man's coat and collar. . . ." Walker was one of the few women physicians in the United States in the 1860s. She was the first female to be commissioned a surgeon in the U.S. Army. Dr. Walker, a New Yorker, died in 1919.

Today, the site of all this excitement, terror, and history is a gas station.

The Jacob Hollinger residence stood here looking west toward the town square.

Dr. Mary Walker. (MOLLUS-MASS)

PART II
The Union Army Controlled Area Field Hospital Sites

"I don't believe that the world ever saw or ever will see again so much of such awful suffering, woe and despair in an equal space of ground."

An artilleryman near Gettysburg
July 4, 1863

This second section will attempt to take you, the reader, into the rear of the Union Army of the Potomac beginning on July 2, 1863, and then later into the vast hospital "complex" created by the terrific onslaught of fighting which occurred during the remainder of the battle. A few of these field hospitals, notably the Union corps sites, lasted well into August, many weeks after the army had returned to its old area of operations near Fredericksburg, Virginia.

I have tried to arrange these aid stations and field hospitals in some semblance of order of their appearance, to make it relatively easy to be guided to the sites today. For instance, the areas covered first are along the Taneytown Road and on the battlefield park, itself. You will then be directed south along the Baltimore Pike into the countryside where the huge Federal corps hospitals were situated.

As you read Part II, it will become obvious that the July 2 and 3 field hospitals, just in rear of the battle lines, quickly became untenable and soon evolved into the vast division hospitals located several miles away from the ever-present, and dangerous artillery fire, and near the large and desperately needed supplies of water, along Rock Creek and White Run.

Rock Creek (just south of White Run) near the Union
Second, Third and Sixth Corps hospitals.

57

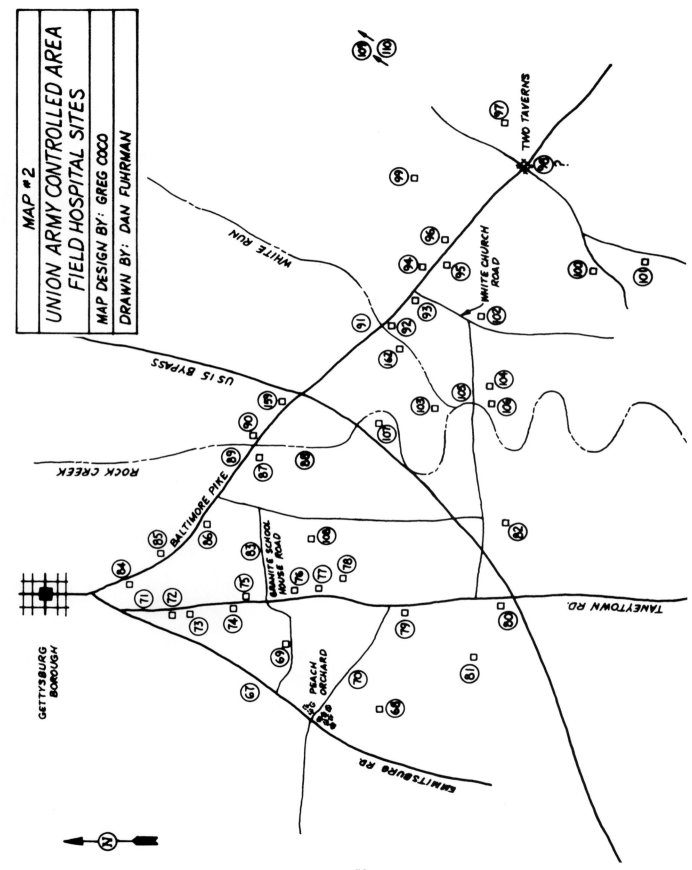

MAP #2

UNION ARMY CONTROLLED AREA
FIELD HOSPITAL SITES

MAP DESIGN BY: GREG COCO

DRAWN BY: DAN FUHRMAN

WHITE RUN

US 15 BYPASS

ROCK CREEK

BALTIMORE PIKE

GRANITE SCHOOL HOUSE ROAD

TANEYTOWN RD.

PEACH ORCHARD

EMMITSBURG RD.

GETTYSBURG BOROUGH

TWO TAVERNS

WHITE CHURCH ROAD

N

67

THE PETER ROGERS FARM

Peter and Susan Rogers lived on a small farm along the Emmitsburg Road. Their small one-story house was located on the west side, just north of what is now the Wheatfield Road. The site is part of the Gettysburg National Military Park, however the farmhouse and outbuildings are no longer standing.

Josephine Miller, who was possibly a niece or granddaughter of Mr. Rogers, lived with the Rogers family. In October of 1863, the twenty-three-year-old Miss Miller married William J. Slyder and moved to Dayton, Ohio.

During the battle of July 2, men of the Third Corps found the house deserted, except for Josephine Miller, who, despite the fighting, continued to assist the wounded, even baking bread and biscuits to give to the men.

An article in a Gettysburg paper on July 6, 1880, reported:

. . . Miss Josephine Rogers (sic) was busy in the house caring for the wounded and doing all in her power to alleviate their suffering. She remained at the house during the entire battle, and after it was over continued to minister to the suffering soldiers.

Another article written in February of 1891 said:

When the battle was over, her house was found to be riddled with shot and shell, and seventeen dead bodies

were taken from the house and cellar, the bodies of wounded men who had crawled to the little dwelling for shelter.

Another source commented that at dark on July 2, two members of Company K, 13th Vermont Infantry, searching for a missing comrade, walked to the Rogers house. They found the buildings at the farm crowded with wounded, some dead and some dying, most being Confederate.

In a claim filed by Susan Rogers (Peter died in 1870), mention was made that the house was definitely used by wounded and that a new carpet was much bloodied and ruined for further use.[1]

68

THE GEORGE ROSE FARM

The famous Rose farm on the battlefield of Gettysburg and now part of the Gettysburg National Military Park is situated along the Emmitsburg Road. It was a temporary Confederate aid station for a short time on July 2 and 3. George Rose had moved to Adams County from Baltimore, Maryland, and farmed about 236 acres in 1863. After the Civil War, when Rose offered his farm for sale, he stated that there were 1,500 Rebels buried on his property. An 1866 list showed about eighty identified graves on the farm, including Lieutenant Colonel Francis Kearse, 50th Georgia Infantry.

The following information concerning this farm comes to us by way of Dr. James B. Clifton, a surgeon of Semmes' brigade which fought through and over the Rose land on July 2. Clifton fortunately kept a diary during the Gettysburg Campaign.

On July 2, about midnight, he wrote:

The Peter Rogers farm years after the Civil War and before it was destroyed. (G.N.M.P.)

The George Rose barn, circa 1880. (G.N.M.P.)

The Moon is shining beautifully, and the ground in front is almost black with Yankees. After riding about for some time I find the Brigade. . . . Near the Brigade, is a large stone Barn at which I find a great many of our wounded who have not been cared for. I immediately go to work to send them off to the rear.

July 3.rd I did not sleep a moment last night, but remained at the old barn trying to get the wounded off. At day-light this morning the artillery commenced firing, and finding myself in a critical place, (the old barn being between the lines) I attempted to make my way to the rear. . . .[2]

It was at the Rose farm as noted earlier that so many Confederates were buried, probably between five hundred and a thousand. The use of this barn, between the opposing battle lines, etc., is a *classic case* of the work of an aid station during the Civil War.

THE ABRAHAM TROSTLE FARM

69

This farm is also a part of the Gettysburg National Military Park and is located just in the rear of the Third Corps' salient position at the "Peach Orchard" and Emmitsburg Road. In 1863, Catherine and Abraham Trostle farmed about 135 acres, and lived in a two-story frame house with a brick summer kitchen. At the time of the battle, Abraham was incarcerated in a "lunatic asylum" due to his tendency to enjoy a periodic fist fight.

The claims file listed the site as a "5th Corps" hospital in use July 2 and 3, rather than use by the Third Corps; it was noted that some Confederate wounded

also ended up here.

During the actual fighting on July 2, the medical personnel of Sickle's old Excelsior Brigade attempted to set up an aid station near the large brick Trostle barn. It soon had to be moved to the rear due to heavy shelling, but some wounded men were left behind in the buildings. One witness in the 5th Massachusetts Battery stated that wounded men were in the house, and one was even discovered behind the chimney. Burial parties too, found it being used as a temporary field hospital.

By July 6, it was definitely not occupied. A Gettysburg civilian, Dan Skelly, visiting the site on that day, said:

The Trostle house was entirely deserted. In the kitchen the dinner table was still set with all the dishes from the meal, and fragments of food remained, indicating that the family had gotten up from their meal and made a hurried getaway.[3]

The Trostle farm in July 1863. (Library of Congress)

The Abraham Trostle farm in 1987.

THE TEMPORARY AID STATION OF THE 32ND MASSACHUSETTS INFANTRY

70

There are two reasons for the use of this particular site in this book: One is to show a typical example of how most regimental surgeons carried out their duties just in rear of their units' battle lines. The second reason is because any hospital marker on a Civil War battlefield is rare, and therefore worthy of mention.

As noted earlier, most regimental surgeons simply

The temporary aid station of the 32nd Massachusetts Infantry. One of many such stations which were in operation July 1–3. (G.N.M.P.)

set up aid stations near to, and just in rear of, the firing line, to quickly patch up many of the wounded and then direct them to ambulances and field hospitals where surgery and more advanced assistance could be rendered. Even though the rarity of this plaque suggests it, this practice as used by Dr. Z.B. Adams behind these rocks, was by no means unusual or heroic.

The plaque reads: "Behind this group of rocks on the afternoon of July 2nd, 1863 Surgeon Z. Boylston Adams placed the field hospital of the 32nde Massachusetts Infantry, 2nd Brigade, 1st Div. 5th Army Corps. Established so near the line of battle many of our wounded men escaped capture or death by it's timely aid."

It may be interesting to note here that Surgeon Adams wrote that while at Gettysburg, owing to someone's neglect, he did not receive his usual orders to report for duty at a field hospital in the rear until *after* the battle. This may account for why he was so close to the area of combat near the Wheatfield on July 2. Adams listed doing four leg and one finger amputations as well as several other operations on July 4. On July 5, he amputated the leg of a Rebel and then rejoined his regiment on July 6. He sadly related how, due to being on duty at the division hospital for two days and three nights without rest or sleep, he suffered an attack of blindness. Adams was honorably discharged on July 7. Later, he returned to the service as an infantry officer with the 56th Massachusetts, where he was wounded and subsequently captured.[4]

Surgeon Z.B. Adams, 32nd Massachusetts Infantry. (G.N.M.P.)

THE CATHERINE GUINN FARM

71

This two-story log house was located along the Taneytown Road, on the east side, a short distance south of the Emmitsburg Road junction. Mrs. Guinn had little choice about what occurred near, or in her home, since the fighting line of the Second Corps, Army of the Potomac, was only a hundred yards west of her front door. It soon became a temporary aid station and hospital of Hay's division of that corps. On the east side of the house, several burials were noted: graves of men of the 8th Ohio, 111th, and 125th New York Infantry regiments. One source also mentioned that Surgeon H. McAbee of the 4th Ohio worked for a time in this hospital.

"Katie" Guinn was apparently a very feisty woman. During the battle, she was said to physically "beat up" any Union soldier she found lurking near her house, including one she found in her cellar who had inadvertantly soiled her clean laundry.

The 1886 history of Adams County states that, "The house immediately south of the National Cemetery was built by William Guinn in 1776, and occupied on July 4th of that year. It was tenanted by Catherine Guinn during the battle . . . , when thirteen shot and shell entered it, one striking the bureau near which the old lady was sitting." She was eighty-five years old in July of 1876.[5]

Unfortunately, her farm and buildings are long gone. Today the site is mostly a parking lot.

The frame house in the center of the photo is where the Catherine Guinn farmhouse probably stood during the Civil War. (G.N.M.P.)

THE LYDIA LEISTER FARM

This small farm on the west side of the Taneytown Road, just south of the Guinn farm, was occupied on July 2 and July 3 by General George Meade, as headquarters of the Army of the Potomac. When Meade and his staff fled this house on July 3 during the afternoon cannonade, it quickly became a temporary hospital and ambulance collecting point. It probably only remained an aid station/hospital for no more than two days. Mrs. Leister, the widow of James Leister who had died in 1859 at age sixty-one, owned this farm which became one of the most historic and important properties on the Gettysburg battlefield. Her neighbor, Mrs. Elizabeth Thorn, stated in 1905 that a "Mrs. McKnight lived at the Leister place. . . ." It is uncertain whether this Mrs. McKnight permanently lived with Lydia Leister or was just staying there for safety during the hostilities.

Later in the afternoon of July 3, General Meade's son, an officer on his father's staff, returned with the

general to the Leister farm only to find:

As the old headquarters house, which had been abandoned . . . in the afternoon, was now being used as a field hospital, General Meade and staff moved down the Taneytown Road, about a quarter of a mile and slept among the rocks in the open.[6]

Private C.W. Belknap, 125th New York Infantry, wrote in his diary on July 3:

After the firing ceased I helped carry Capt. (Ephraim) Wood, (who was shot through the bowels) to Gen. Meade's headquarters where many of the wounded were carried to await the ambulances which carried them to the hospital. A great many of the rebel wounded were also carried there. I stayed and waited on several of the wounded. . . .[7]

Again, on July 3, an eyewitness, Captain Benjamin W. Thompson, 111th New York Infantry, recalled:
"Filling a canteen with water to leave with my clerk, I started back to find my company. I went to General Meade's headquarters, which was now a halting place for the badly wounded, and there found a number of my boys."[8]

Daniel Skelly, a Gettysburg civilian, went to the Leister house on July 6.

In the front room . . . was a bed, the covers of it thrown back; and its condition indicated that a wounded soldier had occupied it. I was told that General Butterfield, Meade's chief of staff, who had been wounded, had been placed upon it before being taken to a hospital.[9]

Butterfield was wounded by a shell fragment during the artillery barrage prior to the great Confederate assault on the afternoon of July 3.

Charles A. Hitchcock wrote to the historian of the

The Lydia Leister farm as it looks in 1988.

battlefield in 1886 and gave additional information concerning the use of the Leister farm as a hospital. He said:

When the heavy artillery-fire opened I was hit in the forearm by a splinter struck from a rail by a shell which bursted nearby. I thought my arm was broken & started to the rear for a surgeon, & reached the [Meade's] head-quarters & went in to the barn. I sat on the floor, my back against a large beam, pouring water on my arm from my canteen. I was in such pain that I thought little of the terrible racket going on all around, when a spent cannon ball crashed through the side of the barn, hitting the beam directly back of my back, & knocked me some distance from where I was sitting, stunned & breathless & conscious, but thinking myself fatally wounded I was lying face downward flat on the floor, & when I got my breath & could stir my arm I carefully put my hand to heel [head?], expecting to find myself all mashed in, & was happily disappointed at finding myself whole. I was helped up & when able went to see where the ball had struck. I found it to be a twelve pound solid shot, it had burried itself half way in the beam & had fallen out.[10]

The site today is nicely preserved as part of the Gettysburg National Military Park.

THE PETER FREY FARM

73

Located within the Gettysburg National Military Park, this farm sits on the west side of the Taneytown Road, approximately one-quarter mile south of Hunt Avenue. On July 2 and 3, Frey's farm was a temporary aid station and field hospital.

An assistant surgeon of the 108th New York Infantry, Dr. Francis Wafer, recalled his service at the stone farmhouse on July 3, during the early afternoon.

When (the) cannonade commenced and for the remainder of the day I was at a small stone farm house on the Taneytown road—about half a mile in rear of the regiment and near the centre or focus of (our lines). . . . This temporary hospital was merely a place where some Surgeons who were on duty on the field, assembled to apply light dressings to the wounds & superintend the removal of the wounded in ambulances to the operating hospital further to the rear. . . . The outbuildings, fences and fruit trees were completely torn to pieces. The roof of the house was torn up and the stone wall broken in one place & the stones thrown upon the floor. It was about the commence-

ment of their cannonade that an orderly came to the house in search of a Surgeon for Genl. Hancock. I did not hear this but my orderly told me afterwards that one surgeon refused to go. . . . It soon became impossible to do much for (the wounded). The few bandages in our medical knapsacks were already exhausted. We found many homespun linen sheets in the house; these were torn into strips & made a good substitute. . . . Our assistants exhausted the only well there giving them water, as that & some *morphia* to those who were in much pain was all we could do for them until (they were) removed to the large field hospital.[11]

This was also possibly the house where Colonel George L. Willard, 125th New York Infantry, who commanded the Third Brigade, Third Division, Second Corps, was first taken after he was mortally wounded late on July 2.

In a letter written by a former soldier, H.H. Bigham, to General Winfield Scott Hancock in 1869, I found another reference to the use of the Frey farm as a hospital. After he was wounded, Bigham recalled:

Hays bound my head up with his handkerchief & told me to go to the Hospital & have the wound dressed. This I did riding back on the Taneytown Road to the stone house just below Meade's old head quarters house, & opposite to the point where we all were when the enemy commenced their artillery firing. The Surgeon dressed my wound. . . .[12]

One unusual burial was noted at this farm among the 122 Union graves nearby—that of a Confederate, Sergeant W.S. Jinkins, of the 7th North Carolina Infantry, whose grave was in the orchard.

General Winfield S. Hancock.

The Peter Frey house in 1938. (G.N.M.P.)

The Peter Frey house in 1988.

The Peter Frey farm in 1988.

74

THE JACOB HUMMELBAUGH FARM

This small farm of frame buildings was and still is located on the west side of the Taneytown Road about 1,100 yards north of the Granite Schoolhouse Road. Today it too is a part of the Gettysburg National Military Park. The Hummelbaugh farm was among the first field hospitals/aid stations set up by medical officers of the Second Corps. An excellent source on this hospital is contained in the regimental history of the 148th Pennsylvania Infantry. The surgeon of the unit, Dr. Alfred Hamilton, reported:

> I established my temporary hospital at the house of Jacob Hummelbaugh. The family had just left a partially eaten meal on the table. A half barrel of flour was in the attic . . . the flour tided us over in the 'slap-jacks' made by Davy McIlhattan and other attendants. The house was soon filled with wounded, chiefly from the Third Corps. . . .
>
> The wounded were carried in during the night of the 3d in such numbers that they filled the barn floor and open space surrounding it. . . .
>
> I was the only medical officer at the left center front during the 2d and 3d of July until night of the latter day. . . . I attended General Barksdale of Mississippi. He was shot through the left breast from behind, and the left leg was broken by two missiles. . . .

Medical operations were definitely conducted here, because a man in the 148th Pennsylvania Volunteers reported hauling straw from the barn to the "amputating table" for Dr. Hamilton.

Major Robert H. Forster of the same regiment recalled the scene:

General William Barksdale. (MOLLUS-MASS)

During the night of the 2d as I approached the little house—now the field hospital—I stepped upon something that felt so peculiar that I stopped and picked it up. It proved to be an arm. Happening to look at the west window I saw an outline of a pyramid of some sort, which on examination I found was a pile of hands, arms, feet and legs which the surgeons had thrown out in their work and which had now reached the window sill. In front of the house lay General Barksdale mortally wounded, his breast torn and one leg shattered. . . . Alternately begging for water, which a drummer boy was giving him with a spoon, and cursing the Yankees, it was a most pathetic scene. . . . He died during the night.

It should be noted that General Alfred Pleasonton, who commanded the Federal cavalry in the Army of the Potomac, had his headquarters at this house July 4 through July 6.

Several men were buried on the farm, (about fifteen were identified), one of which was Captain R.M. Forster of the 148th Pennsylvania Infantry.[13]

The Jacob Hummelbaugh house in 1981.

The Jacob Hummelbaugh farm in 1987.

75

THE WILLIAM PATTERSON FARM

The William Patterson farm was a seventy-five-acre place in 1863, with the house located about eight hundred yards north of the Granite Schoolhouse Road on the east side of the Taneytown Road. The barn, possibly stone, was across this road and just south of the house. This barn, according to a New Jersey artilleryman, was in use as a field hospital. William Patterson, forty, and his wife Lydia, forty-one, lived on the farm during the war. In his damage claim filed in 1874, Patterson stated that, "The 2d Corps hospital was at my house during the first day." He also said that they moved quickly because the house was in full range of Confederate artillery. There were also ten identified Union soldiers buried on his farm. It may be of interest to some readers, that a shell from one of the two Confederate signal guns which started the July 3 cannonade preceding Pickett's Charge, exploded in Patterson's barn. This was about one o'clock in the afternoon. The shell tore off the arm of a fourteen-year-old black boy who was the servant of a New York officer.

For a time after the battle, this farm was the headquarters of the Provost Marshal General of the Army of the Potomac, General M.R. Patrick. His headquarters during the battle was at the Aaron Sheely farm.

The William Patterson barn as it looked in 1863. (G.N.M.P.)

The William Patterson house looking south on the Taneytown Road in 1988.

76

THE MICHAEL FREY FARM

Michael and Sarah Frey's small farm was located along the east side of the Taneytown Road about five hundred feet south of the Granite Schoolhouse Road. Captain Louis Duncan, who wrote a history of the U.S. Medical Service during the Civil War, listed this as a temporary field hospital of the Third Corps, probably only used July 2 through the 4th.[14] Several identified Union burials were noted on Frey's land, none of them were Rebel dead. Although many sources mentioned "barns" or other sites along this road, none that I have found mentioned this particular farm by name.

An excellent source of a Third Corps hospital which could easily have been this site, was from a diary kept by James Houghton, 4th Michigan Infantry. On July 2, late in the afternoon, he carried his captain to,

a 3d Corps Hospital . . . situated in a Barn and Barn yard (about 1/2 mile from Little Round Top) as we came to the gate we (were) informed . . . that they had about 300 wounded in (the) Hospital. . . . The wounded were lying on the ground in rows acrost the yard with Allies between for the waiters and Sergeons to pass through. At the east end of the yard were lying some of the most hopeless cases . . . I took one of the Allies that led to the west end of the yard here the Sergeons were busily at work probing for bullets and amputating Limbs. it requires a man with a steel nerve and a case-hardened heart to be a Army

Sergeon. . . . I took (another) Alley which led in to the Barn. the Barn was filled with the wounded to its utmost capasity and if I ever heard a Barn full of groans it was there—it was more than I could stand.[15]

Thomas Livermore, who was chief of ambulances for the Second Corps, very possibly used this farm for a time as an ambulance collecting point. He said in his memoirs at the turn of the century:

I placed the main portion of my (ambulance) train at a house on the right hand side of the Taneytown road, around a house near which was an orchard. . . . I think it was Mr. Frye's (sic) or Jacob Swisher's or Sarah Patterson's. At any rate, it was a house of considerable dimensions and its vicinity afforded clear ground for the park. As soon as the train was established, I . . . instructed the officers to have all the wounded brought to the house where the park was.[16]

This is a good example of how these initial field hospitals or aid stations were sometimes used by the wounded of several different corps at one time.

Another officer who may have been taken to the barn at this site, was Captain John Bigelow, 9th Massachusetts Battery, who was wounded on July 2.

For a while, this farm was probably the headquarters of General R.O. Tyler, commander of the Artillery Reserve of the Army of the Potomac.

The Michael Frey farm in 1987.

THE JACOB SWISHER FARM

77

THE SARAH PATTERSON FARM

78

By now, it should have become apparent that many of the small farms southward along the Taneytown Road became temporary aid stations or field hospitals between July 1 and 4. The Swisher farm, located just south of the Michael Frey farm, on a curve in the road, and on the same side as Frey's place, was another one of these sites. It was probably used by General Alexander Hays' division of the Second Corps; the evidence being the graves found there after the battle—sixteen identified Union burials, many from his division.

On July 1, at about five o'clock in the evening, a student at the Seminary, Michael Colver, stopped at the Swisher home, seeking shelter from the battle now raging in and around Gettysburg. He recalled:

> Here I expected to find rest and peace. But the 12th Corps was near the house and seemed ready to move—in fact the family supposed an engagement imminent . . . I was told that the body of Gen. Reynolds had been taken past only a short time previous to my arrival.

Colver continued that after he left this house, he came to a cabin, "where a number of wounded soldiers were gathered. I dressed some wounds and won for myself from them the title of 'doctor.' "[17]

This farm on the Taneytown Road is just south of the Granite Schoolhouse Road, on the east side, with the buildings sitting back from the road. Some excellent information has been found concerning the use of this farm as a hospital site. The post-battle damage claims which were filed by the family, are available which pinpoint the Patterson place as a temporary Union aid station and field hospital.

Surgeon Justin Dwinell, who was in charge of the Second Corps hospital also noted this fact. He stated in his report of the campaign:

> The Hospital of the Second Division was located . . . at the stone barn and orchard of Miss Sally Patterson on the Taneytown Road immediately in the rear of the . . . Corps. . . .
> At night the wounded occupied the large barn and the ground under the trees in the Orchard. . . . As near as I can judge we had five hundred wounded men that night (July 2) most of whom belonged to the Second Division. The remainder (were) from the other Divisions . . ., the Third Corps, and Confederates.

Since the farm was directly behind Federal lines, it was a natural selection for this purpose.

It is possible that the barn on this site is original, while the house may be a more modern structure.

The John Musser farm site today.

The Sarah Patterson farm in 1987.

THE LEONARD BRICKER FARM

THE JACOB WEIKERT FARM

The Bricker place still sits along the west side of the Taneytown Road, just south of Blacksmith Shop Road. The stone house and possibly a barn were used as a temporary aid station and hospital for either or both the Third and Fifth Corps. Seven identified Union burials are listed for this farm, including Lieutenant Eugene Dunham, 44th New York Infantry, who was buried in a corner of the garden fence under a peach tree. Captain Larrabee, of the same regiment, was buried alongside the lieutenant. This may give some clue as to which division used this hospital i.e., the Third Brigade, First Division, Fifth Corps.

In 1888, a Vermont historian described Stannard's Vermont Brigade's hospital as being in a barn one-and-one-half miles south of Meade's headquarters on the Taneytown Road. This description places it somewhere near the Bricker place, although it could have been the Sarah Patterson farm. This "brigade" was actually the Third Brigade, Third Division, First Corps. So evidently, there was a First Corps hospital in this area, an unusual situation, for most of that corps medical staff was situated along the Baltimore Pike. In his medical history of the Civil War, Captain Duncan has the Bricker farm listed on a map as being part of the Fifth Corps hospitals in the area east of Little Round Top.

Thankfully, the area has not changed significantly.

The Leonard Bricker farm in 1987.

This 102-acre farm, complete with its stone house and large bank barn is still virtually intact. It is located along the west side of the Taneytown Road, one-quarter mile south of what is now Sach's Road. Weikert's was a fairly important site due to its heavy use by portions of the U.S. Third and Fifth Army Corps. Several good accounts of this hospital exist; one, fortunately, by a regular Army surgeon.

The post-battle claims application listed it as a hospital from July 1 to July 5, by elements of the Second, Third, and Fifth Corps. The family described the farm as having an eight-room house, with the barn and carriage house used by the wounded also. The claim included damages for straw and "bandages" through this use.

Dr. Clinton Wagner was Surgeon-in-Chief of the Second Division, Fifth Corps, known as the "Regular Division." In 1911, he wrote a letter explaining his duties during the battle. He recalled selecting the Weikert farm as a hospital on July 2. Wagner and other surgeons performed operations until July 3 at about nine o'clock in the morning, when he was ordered to send all wounded to a safer location in the rear. One paragraph of the letter was very interesting:

> On the porch of his house (Weikert's), the bodies of three gallant soldiers lay during the night of Thursday, all of whom were killed in the struggle on the summit of "Little Round Top;" they were General S.M. Weed, Col. O'Rourke, 140th N.Y. Vol., and Lieut. Hazlitt.
>
> General Weed was not killed instantly as many accounts of the battle state. I was riding to the front when I met the stretcher bearers carrying him. . . . I dismounted; he begged me not to stop for him, 'he said I could do nothing for him;' I examined and found he was right . . . he was taken to the farm house and survived about an hour or two.[18]

Captain Robert G. Carter, 22nd Massachusetts Infantry, stated that Hazlett, "was temporarily buried at the east end of Weikert's garden."[19]

A wounded lieutenant, Charles A. Fuller, 61st New York Infantry, also recalled the porch of the Weikert house:

> The boys who were toting me came to a stone house with a wide piazza clear around it. I was laid on the floor of it, which made a hard bed. I ached in every bone, but there was nothing to do but, 'grin and bear it.'" Fuller told how another man of the 61st was laid next to him with a bullet hole through his lungs,

The Jacob Weikert house in 1981.

General Stephen H. Weed. (MOLLUS-MASS)

The Jacob Weikert farm in 1987.

". . . and every time they filled a portion of the air went through the wound with a ghastly sound.[20]

Doctor John Billings, a regular army surgeon also with the Fifth Corps, wrote in his official report:

I accompanied my regiment until they were under fire, and was then ordered to repair to a large stone house and barn . . . and there establish a field hospital. . . . On entering the house, I found it unoccupied and bearing evident traces of the hasty desertion of its inmates. A good fire was blowing in the kitchen stove, a large quantity of dough was mixed up, the bake-pans were greased. . . . I immediately set my attendants at work baking bread and heating . . . water. In five minutes, I was joined by the other medical officers . . . (and) fifteen minutes later . . . the wounded began to pour in. I performed a large number of operations . . . received and fed 750 wounded and worked all night without cessation.[21]

Surgeon John Shaw Billings.

Matilda "Tillie" Pierce, a Gettysburg girl who was at the Weikert farm during the battle, recalled the scene:

"On this evening (July 2) the number of wounded brought to the place was indeed appalling. They were laid in different parts of the house. The orchard and space around the buildings were covered with the shattered and dying, and the barn became more and more crowded." She also claimed she saw General Weed in ". . . a little room in the southeast corner of the basement," before he died. Pierce gave him some of the fresh baked bread, but upon returning to the scene the next morning, found him dead. For additional and contradictory information on Weed's place of death, see Site #82, the Lewis Bushman farm. Apparently, Weed and several other officers were first brought to this farm, but due to dangerously close exploding shells from Confederate artillery, these officers were later moved to the Lewis Bushman farmstead.

On July 3, in the evening, Miss Pierce saw,

> The approaches (to the house) were crowded with wounded, dying and dead. The air was filled with moanings, and groanings . . . the house . . . also completely filled with the wounded . . . amputating benches had been placed about the house. . . . Near the basement door . . . stood one of these benches. I saw them lifting the poor men upon it, then the surgeons sawing and cutting off arms and legs, then again probing and picking bullets from the flesh. . . . To the south of the house, and just outside of the yard, I noticed a pile of limbs higher than the fence . . . the whole scene was one of cruel butchery.[22]

Some wounded Confederates were also taken to this farm. A colonel of a Texas regiment remembered being taken to a stone house behind Little Round Top where some "Regulars" were camped. Another source, Lieutenant Graham of the 16th Michigan Infantry, said he saw some wounded Rebels near Weikert's well, and tried to give them water but Mr. Weikert had hidden the pump handle. It was soon located, as the lieutenant remembered:

> I went into the house, found this man, a mean Dutchman, buried in the bosom of his family, and his family buried in the bowels of the cellar . . . I ordered him to give up the well crank. He first refused. . . . I threatened to shoot him . . . this brought it out of its hiding place. . . . Every visit I have since made to Little Round Top, I have seen "old Wikert's" (sic) son—his father is now dead—telling interested hearers of the 'wonderful acts of heroism' his father and he did in taking care of the wounded in their yard that fearful day. . . .[23]

THE JOHN SLYDER FARM

Just to the east-northeast of Big Round Top and about six hundred feet from its base stands the Slyder farm, now called the Granite Farm and today a part of the Gettysburg National Military Park. In 1863, it was a small farm, with a stone house at its center. The historian of the Third Pennsylvania Cavalry wrote:

> During the evening of July 4 . . . (we) . . . posted pickets and established our reserve at the house of J. Slyder on Plum Run. . . . The house was being used as a field hospital and was filled with wounded upon whom the surgeons were engaged in their revolting work. As fast as the men died their bodies were taken out of the house and into the rain and left there temporarily. The scene was so painful and sickening to us that we determined to remain with the picket reserve in the pitiless downpour of rain.[24]

There were five Confederates buried here; one, the body of Colonel John A. Jones, 20th Georgia Infantry, was disinterred on this farm in December of 1865, and returned to his family's home in Columbus, Georgia.

The John Slyder farm in the 1930s. (G.N.M.P.)

THE LEWIS A. BUSHMAN FARM

The Lewis Bushman farm is located southeast of Sachs Road, and south of the U.S. Route 15 bypass. The current brick house is not the Civil War era farmhouse. One hundred to two hundred yards east of the present house was where the old original frame building stood, near a spring which is still in the vicinity today.

Being so near to the Union rear and just east of Little Round Top, it soon became a hospital of the First Division, Fifth Corps. Several sources stated that this farm, not that of Weikert, was the place where O'Rorke and Weed were taken.

Captain Porter Farley, 140th New York Infantry, wrote:

> The general (Weed) was carried at once (after he was wounded on Little Round Top) behind the shelter of a rock, and soon was taken in an ambulance to the

70

farmhouse of Louis A. Bushman, which, as well as his barns and outhouses, had been taken possession of and was being used as our division hospital. Weed suffered intensely. . . . He soon became delirious and died at about nine o'clock that evening.

During the fight our surgeons, Drs. Dean and Lord, had been . . . in rear of the regiment. . . . Here they gave the wounded . . . attention . . . before being sent to the division hospital at Bushman's farm. To this place, when the fight was over, Sergeant Wright and three other men of Company A carried our young Colonel, (O'Rorke) and there laid him on the ground. I went with them. He had fallen instantly dead.[25]

Further on in the narrative it is stated that Colonel O'Rorke's body was buried on the Bushman farm. His wife came as soon as possible and took his body to Rochester, New York.

Lieutenant A. Peirson Case, 146th New York Infantry, wrote how the Bushman farm became a division hospital:

The Fifth Corps hospital had been made at the house and barns of J. Weikert on the Taneytown (Rd) . . . and during this cannonade (July 3, afternoon) many of the rebel shells came over the hill and struck our hospital, wounding some a second time. It was then moved to Lewis Bushman's, about a mile to the southeast.[26]

Colonel Strong Vincent, 83rd Pennsylvania Infantry, commanding the Third Brigade, First Division, Fifth Corps, was also carried to this farm, although two sources place him at a "Wm. Bushman's" and at "Diener's" farm. These two sites were probably not correct and may have been given due to faulty memories, etc.

The Lewis A. Bushman farmhouse was actually to the left of the telephone pole near a spring. The barn may be original. The house in the picture was built after the Civil War.

Colonel Strong Vincent. (MOLLUS-MASS)

Captain Carter, 22nd Massachusetts Infantry, said flatly: "Gen. Strong Vincent (sic) commanding our Second Brigade, was also mortally wounded and carried to Lewis Bushman's house, east of Round Top, and died July 7."

Oliver W. Norton, 83rd Pennsylvania Infantry, who was an orderly for Vincent, said in 1888:

"We did not know until the battle was over that Vincent was mortally wounded. When I went into the room where he lay, he seemed very pale and unable to speak, he looked the question he could not utter. I said to him, 'The boys are still there, Colonel,' and his face lighted up with a smile which showed his gratification." He placed Vincent at "Diener's". Later in 1913, Norton wrote that Lieutenant Colonel Norval E. Welch (16th Michigan) pointed out the Bushman place as the place where Vincent lay. Norton again:

Welch told me that Colonel Vincent was in that house. This was the Bushman farmhouse, where Vincent had been carried after receiving his fatal wound. . . . I entered the house, which was full of wounded men. I found Colonel Vincent in a room on the first floor.[27]

Vincent's wound was severe, the bullet passing clear through the left groin and then lodged in the right, with bones being broken in the process. He was tended to by Dr. James P. Burchfield, surgeon of the 83rd Pennsylvania, and Lieutenant John (or Daniel) Clark of the same regiment.

Colonel George L. Willard, 125th New York Infantry, wounded on July 2, was another well-known officer taken to the Bushman house. He also died there.

Just northeast of the Bushman farm was a place called the "Diener" farm, possibly the "Michael Dener" shown on the tax records of 1863 as a ten-acre farm. Henry Beitler actually owned this place in 1863. He purchased it from John Rodkey in December 1859. Dener may have been a tenant farmer in the year of the battle.

In 1987, I spoke to the eight-eight-year-old owner of this small brick farmhouse, Maebelle Sachs. She had lived there most of her life, and remembered stories about how the house was used by wounded soldiers during the battle. She also said that there were still bloodstains on the upstairs floors where they had laid. Mrs. Sachs told me about the original Lewis Bushman frame house and where it actually stood in 1863. "Miss Maebelle" remembered that in the 1940s a Mr. Sander who then owned this farm, discovered a skeleton of a Civil War soldier on the property.

The "Henry Beitler" farmhouse which is just northeast of the Lewis A. Bushman farmhouse.

 **THE GRANITE SCHOOLHOUSE**

83

It is very surprising to me that so few sources remain available which document the old Granite School. It was obviously a fairly important site for several days during and after the battle. In fact, in 1916, Captain Duncan of the U.S. medical corps, while compiling information on the corps hospitals at Gettysburg, stated:

The hospitals of (the Second Corps) were at first located in an opening of the woods, along the crossroad from the Taneytown Road to the Baltimore Pike, with headquarters at the Granite Schoolhouse." Also: "The division hospitals of the Second Corps were located July 2 at the Granite Schoolhouse but were soon removed to near Rock Creek. . . .

Possibly the Granite Schoolhouse as it appeared in 1863.

The Granite Schoolhouse Road. The school was to the left in what is now woods.

Surgeon Justin Dwinell said that the Third Division of that corps was at a barn forty rods to the right of the Sarah Patterson farm, and the First Division was located in the right rear of the Third, and near the *stone school house.*

There is a good possibility that the Artillery Reserve may have used this area for a while as a temporary aid station. Most accounts, however, place it "four miles to the rear."

Another source noted:

Lieut. Woodruff* (Battery I, 1st U.S. Artillery) was struck by a musket ball in the back, near the close of the action. . . . He was taken at once to the stone school house on the crossroad leading from the Taneytown road to the Baltimore pike where he was attended by Dr. H.B. Buck. . . . There he died, regretting to the last that it should have been his fate to be shot in the back and asking of his friends that it should be no reflection upon his reputation.[28]

What a sad commentary on the Victorian mores of that age.

*Lt. George A. Woodruff died July 4.

THE EVERGREEN CEMETERY GATEHOUSE (PETER THORN RESIDENCE)

84

Peter Thorn, keeper of the Evergreen Cemetery, had joined the Union army in 1862, serving in Company B, 138th Pennsylvania Infantry. His wife, Elizabeth (Moser)? Thorn, lived with her family in the gatehouse and cared for the cemetery during the war years while Peter was away. This historic site, still proudly standing on the Baltimore Turnpike, was the very center of the Union battle line on the evening of July 1 through noon of July 2. The gatehouse, sometimes referred to by people in the area as the cemetery "Gate-way House," naturally became a shelter for officers and men, both wounded and not. Mrs. Thorn, age thirty-one, who was pregnant, and members of her family, left their residence for safety on July 2. On July 3, they returned and Elizabeth recalled:

The Evergreen Cemetery Gatehouse in 1987.

When we got to the stable we could hear the wounded men holler and go on, laying around the house,—in the cellar too, and there is where we had carried our good things, that Gen. Howard had told us to leave there. We could not get near the house for wounded and dead (that) They had brought there from the first days fight. . . . My father got a man to take us into the cellar where six wounded men were, and they had our bed clothes spread all around. . . . The poor wounded men were crying and going on so that we did not want anything then. They called their wives and children to come and wet their tongues.[29]

After the battle, Mrs. Thorn helped to bury 105 soldiers. She said it took four days of washing to get the blood out of the families' bedclothes.

THE ABRAHAM SPANGLER FARM

85

Although owned by Abraham Spangler at the time of the Civil War, this 230-acre farm was occupied during the battle by his son, Henry and his wife Sarah, who were both in their early thirties. This very old farm, dating back to the middle of the 18th century, had a log house built on the land in 1744. In 1819, the house was enlarged by the addition of a fieldstone structure on the north side of the original farmhouse. Today, the barn and outbuildings are gone, but the house remains in its timeless and solid dignity along the old Baltimore Pike just south of Gettysburg.

The farm became an important field hospital for a portion of the Twelfth Corps (Second Division) on the evening of July 1 until probably July 4.

A young drummer boy, Bill Simpson, 28th Pennsylvania Infantry, wrote in 1913 about his experiences at Gettysburg. He recalled:

I had a good night's fun that evening (July 1). Dr. William Altman, surgeon of the regiment, gathered the drummer boys together to establish a field hospital. We went over to the Spangler house and camped in the barn all night. . . . The Spangler house was unoccupied. . . . During the battle, the drummer boys' place was to assist the physician, carry water to the wounded, and help load the ambulances. . . .

(Later) while the fight was at its hottest (I was told) to take (a) horse and go to Dr. Goodman at the hospital to get spirits. . . . Dr. Goodman called the steward as soon as I reached the hospital and my canteen was filled. I saw quite a few of our boys at the hospital. One especially I will always remember. He was a corporal and had been badly wounded. They wanted to amputate his leg. He said to me: 'Will, they won't do it, for I will shoot the first man who touches me. I am married and I won't go home to be a burden on my wife. . . .' When the surgeons went over to him the second time . . . he was dead.*[30]

Evidently the farm had an unusually large barn, because John Parker, 22nd Massachusetts Infantry, in writing about a comrade, stated:

Second Lieut. Charles K. Knowles,** a gallant officer, was mortally wounded, and (later) died on the field, it is supposed in Spangler's large barn on the Baltimore pike.

*He was Cpl. James O. Butcher of Philadelphia.
**He died July 11.

The Abraham Spangler farmhouse as it appeared in 1863. (G.N.M.P.)

The Abraham Spangler farmhouse in 1987.

Dr. Isaac Stearns of the 22nd worked in this barn. The regimental historian reported:

A temporary hospital was established near the Baltimore pike, where large numbers were cared for, many of them being powder-burned by the explosions of the caissons on our side. (On July 4) some of the worst wounded ones (were sent back from the Division hospital) to Spangler's barn, among them Capt. Rock, Lieut. Look, Lieut. Knowles, a lieutenant-colonel of an Alabama regiment, and others.[31]

One other possible eyewitness to the activities at this farm was Charles E. Benton, 150th New York Infantry. Benton, writing in 1902, recalled:

Early in the forenoon of July 3rd, our brigade was put in at Culp's Hill . . . our brigade and regimental surgeons established . . . their field hospital at the old stone barn on the Baltimore Pike, and I was assigned to their direction. . . .

There was room on the barn floor for some of the worst cases after their operations, but the others were simply laid on the grass. It was in charge of Dr. Campbell, the surgeon of our regiment. . . .

He set up his operating table, which was a portable affair, in the open field, and here we brought the most severely wounded, one at a time, and where we removed them, some minus a limb or arm which it had been found necessary to amputate.[32]

The burials located on Spangler's property alone would indicate a major field hospital. There were seventy-eight identified Union and five Confederate graves found here.

86

THE NATHANIEL LIGHTNER FARM

This farm stands on the west side of the Baltimore Pike about one thousand yards southeast of Hunt Avenue. Altogether much has changed here, and the stone house is all that remains of this site. Used by both the Sixth and Twelfth Corps including Mc-Dougall's and Shaler's brigades, and possibly some of the First and Eleventh Corps, it was in operation as a hospital for several weeks during and after the battle.

Two good eyewitness accounts remain. The first, written by Private Charles Muller circa 1900, 1st Minnesota Infantry, placed a hospital at the Lightner farm. He wrote:

(after being wounded in the leg on July 2) . . . our

captain detailed a man to conduct me to where our Dr. had established our hospital which was about a mile in the rear of our line in a nice apple garden and (there) was a nice spring. . . . Our doctor had our hospital established under an apple tree that thrust its branches over a stone fence along the Baltimore Turnpike. . . . When I got to that hospital I found our Colonel Colville, Lieutenant Colonel Adams, Major, Adjutant, some of the captains, Lieutenants and about 25 non-commissioned officers and privates . . . next morning some of our officers started off on foot in the direction of Baltimore, and in the afternoon some 20 or 30 ambulances came up to our hospital with orders to clear out our hospital. . . . About 3 o'clock in the afternoon I myself was put in a ambulance and carried off to our new hospital ground about a mile further to the southeast. . . .[33]

Muller said in his account that in 1897 he returned to Gettysburg and spoke to Mr. Lightner, "the farmer that owned the ground."

In 1904, Colonel William Colvill related his experiences in a statement saying that Captain Jasper Searles of the Division ambulance train helped to get tents set up at the abovementioned field hospital. Colvill continued:

. . . all the wounded were collected and taken to the field hospital by, say, 10 o'clock (p.m. July 2) (I) was placed on the surgeon's table. No operation was made. Ten days later, the bullet in (my) left shoulder was discovered and removed. . . . Lt. Col. (C.P.) Adams was taken to the same hospital, wounded in two places. . . . There were thirty amputations (made there). . . . The

rebel wounded were lying in great numbers on a hillside some thirty rods away.[34]

Mr. Lightner, a farmer and carpenter, also had memories of the battle. He had gone in to Gettysburg on July 1 to purchase some whiskey. Upon returning to his house at about four o'clock he saw,

. . . a red flag on the end of the house, and when I got nearer I saw my yard full of soldiers. Under an apple tree I found the surgeons with a man stretched out on our dining room table and cutting and sawing a leg off, and on the grass there lay a pile of limbs. I went around to the kitchen door and looked in. Horror of horrors! The floor was covered with wounded men. . . . My family had taken refuge in the stable . . . (A surgeon said) take your family and go to the rear. . . .

On the third day after the battle I got down to my house. . . . There stood the bare shop, the house full of wounded men, and the old barn where Gen. Slocum had made his headquarters. . . . We came back about a week later, and lived gypsy-like in the shop for six weeks . . . (when) they took the last of the wounded away, and permitted us to live in (our house) but it made us all sick. . . . Nine years afterward I took all the woodwork and plaster out and made the house new from cellar to garret.[35]

The Nathaniel Lightner farmhouse in 1987.

The Nathaniel Lightner farm as it appeared in 1863. (G.N.M.P.)

THE GEORGE MUSSER FARM

This small, approximately eighteen-acre farm was located on the south side of the Baltimore Pike, a short distance west of the bridge over Rock Creek. The barn is possibly original and still intact, the house which is now on the site may be postwar. Musser, aged sixty-nine at the time of the battle, lived there with his wife, Elizabeth. After leaving her home at the cemetery gatehouse for reasons of safety, Mrs. Elizabeth Thorn stopped here for a short while. As she and her father attempted to return to their home around midnight of July 2, she recalled that they passed through a room in the Musser home, "where the Union soldiers were sleeping, lying in two rows, with only one candle to light the whole room."

Another Gettysburg resident then living on the Emmitsburg Road, William Tawney, a small boy, had a similar experience. His father was a Union soldier, so Mrs. Tawney along with her four children, left home to secure a safe place during the battle. They first stopped at the Musser farm where William observed:

> This space was being used as a hospital and the porch was cluttered with arms and legs that had been amputated.[36]

The family went further on down the pike to Two Taverns and stopped at another farm until July 4.

The George Musser barn in 1987. The house on the site may not be original to the Civil War.

 THE ISAAC M. DIEHL FARM

This farm was located along Rock Creek about 1,500 yards south of the bridge on the Baltimore Pike. The farm buildings are no longer standing, but have been replaced by a huge quarry which has completely destroyed the area in ways a mere battle could never accomplish.

In a war damage claim filed by Mr. Diehl after the battle, he mentioned that his "house and barn were used for hospital purposes for four weeks," and that U.S. forces camped on his place throughout the battle and up until July 6. The farm was 150 acres large and he lost over six thousand fence rails, destroyed by the troops. During the 1840s, the Diehl place was described as having a two-story stone house, stone and log barn, with an orchard and small quarry on the premises.

 McALLISTER'S FARM AND MILLS

Just across the Baltimore Pike from George Musser's farm on Rock Creek stood a sawmill in the 1860s. North of this sawmill was the William McAllister farm and a grist mill, known far and wide, and not surprisingly so, as McAllister's Mill. Prior to the Civil War, this mill was locally spoken of as a "station" of the "underground railroad." From 1850 to 1858, the old mill apparently sheltered many fugitive slaves who were fleeing their masters in the South. The mill was built in 1790 near the site of an earlier and smaller one which went into operation about 1740. The McAllister family purchased the mill and surrounding land from Messrs. Gettys and Flemming in 1822.

The waterway which powered these mills, Rock Creek, has changed since those times. In 1906, William McClean, editor of the *Gettysburg Compiler,* wrote:

> (Rock) Creek is a pitiable caricative of what it was then. At that time McAllister's dam was unbroken. It was not then in the condition it has been for the last quarter of a century. High waters broke it and it was never repaired or rebuilt. . . .
>
> Those familiar with the story of the battle recall the number of wounded men found along the creek, those

who had crawled there to quench their hot thirst and cool their parched throats . . . (if) a survivor returned to the creek . . . (today) we would swear . . . the modern Rock Creek was not (there) in the days of 1863.

Today, the mills and other buildings are no longer standing, and the one hundred plus-acre farm is barely even a footnote in a history book.

There is little doubt that the grist and saw mills, as well as the farm, were large hospitals. The McAllister farm had nearly thirty-five identified burials, both Union and Confederate. And on the 1868 survey map drawn up by the U.S. Engineer Department under the direction of General Gouverneur K. Warren, both mills are labeled as "rebel hospitals." Also, a Union soldier, William Tallman, 66th Ohio Infantry, (First Brigade, Second Division, Twelfth Corps), wrote in a memoir that he was detailed to, "stay with our assistant Surgeon (who was acting Brigade Surgeon), and keep him informed of the (other) surgeons location on the field. . . ." On July 2, at about four o'clock, he reminisced:

I had left our line and gone down to the Baltimore Pike where a temporary hospital had been established at an old saw mill. . . . I lost no time in getting to the place . . . I done what I could toward washing and binding up the wounds of those who had been able to get to the rear. At one time there was quite a large number of Prisoners passed along the road those of them who were slightly wounded had their hurts attended to and moved on. . . .

Tallman mentioned too that on July 3 one of the line surgeons had established an aid station in rear of the brigade (which was near Culp's Hill) in a "bank barn" near the Baltimore Pike. [This may have been the Henry Spangler barn.]

Justin Dwinell, a surgeon in the Union Second Corps, wrote in a report after the battle that the First Division hospital of that corps moved to "near the saw mill on the Baltimore Pike," due to heavy shell fire from Confederate batteries. This division's hospital had initially been near the Granite School House.[37]

McAllister's grist mill as it appeared in 1863. (G.N.M.P.)

90

THE G. FLEMMING HOKE TOLLHOUSE

This small stone tollhouse is located on the north side of the Baltimore Turnpike, just across the Rock Creek bridge. An article in the *Adams Sentinel* in the middle of July of 1863, stated that a Union brigadier general who was wounded in the Battle of Gettysburg, had been in Hoke's tollhouse for a time. Interestingly enough, a staff officer, Lieutenant Josiah M. Favill, recalled just such a house:

> The General (Samuel K. Zook, mortally wounded on July 2) was in great pain, and Broom* told me he was shot through the bowels. I went ahead to find an ambulance, but before I returned they had fallen in with one, and were driven to the field hospital. Surgeon Wood . . . after examining the wound, told us it was fatal, and nothing could be done; there being no shelter here . . . we took the general on a stretcher, and carried him to a small house some distance in the rear on the Baltimore Road, close to a bridge crossing a small creek. The house was already filled with severely wounded men, and the sight was most distressing; the howls of pain from the men in the hall and front room were so dreadful that we moved the general back into a small room cut off from the others, and here we spent the night, doing what we could to make our dear commander comfortable. I went out several times during the night, and looked at the ghastly scenes on the floors of the hall and parlor. As many men as could lay side by side completely covered the floors, which were streaming with blood, and the poor fellows seemed to give way completely to their misfortunes. Over twenty of them died and

*Lt. Charles H.H. Broom, 57th N.Y. Infantry

were carried into the yard during the night.

Confirming Zook's whereabouts was John B. Linn who visited the battlefield from July 6–11. On July 9 he spoke to gate-keeper Hoke who said that General Zook had been wounded through the breast and was brought to the house in the evening of July 2. "He made the men who carried him put his blanket under him so that he would not bloody the bed, drank some coffee and said he felt more comfortable. . . ."

On July 3 Zook was moved to another house further away, where he died at five p.m.[38]

The tollhouse sometimes went by the name of "Hoke's gate," even as late as 1872.

General Samuel K. Zook.

G.F. Hoke's tollhouse on the Baltimore Pike south of Rock Creek in 1988.

91

THE ADAM WERT FARM

Just off the Baltimore Pike, where it crosses White Run, is a narrow lane which ran to the east past the small Wert farm. Although it was a somewhat secluded place, it still snagged its share of wandering, and wounded, soldiers.

Today the barn is gone, the house is a replacement, and the site is rapidly growing into a new housing development, as a new sewer line now cuts through the land. But when I lived across the pike from it between 1975 and 1981, it was still a quiet, lovely spot, untouched and pure, not yet raped by "progress."

The Adam Wert farmhouse site in 1988. The house is probably post-Civil War era.

My neighbor, Ms. Eva Schwartz, in her nineties then, who lived on the "Wert farm" with her brother often showed me a beautiful walnut table that was her great-grandmother's. It had been used as an amputating table at the Fiscel farm just west of the Wert homestead. Ms. Schwartz also told me how, as a young girl, she had actually known J. Howard Wert.

J. Howard, the son of Adam, was sixteen or seventeen during the battle, and spent hundreds of hours visiting the battlefield and hospitals, ofttimes aiding the wounded. In 1864, he joined the Union Army and fought as a lieutenant in the 209th Pennsylvania Infantry during the closing campaigns around Richmond and Petersburg. But on July 2, 1863, there were no *memories* of war, because it was presently in progress all around the Wert family household. Young Wert recalled their first wounded visitor:

On the evening of the second day's battle a United States regular, dripping blood, walked into my father's house and asked for a pair of shears and a basin of water. With the assistance of another soldier the sleeve of his blouse was cut off, and he began to lave his wounded arm with the cooling water. . . . (He said to my mother),

'Just see here madam, what a nice wound! What a beautiful wound! I never saw a finer one. The ball just went through, clean and neat and never touched the bone. Yes, indeed, it's a beautiful wound.'

The house was crowded, the entire night, with a surging mass of soldiers and civilians . . . (and) officers would come in precipitately to consult the map of Adams county on the wall. Other soldiers were coming in to have their wounds dressed.

So the regular soldier . . . extended himself on the bare floor beneath the dining table, his basin of water beside him (to avoid being tramped on). . . . The next morning he left to hunt up a hospital.

Wert goes on to explain the location of another hospital:

Across . . . from my father's house was a very large and time-worn log building, a century old and more when the battle . . . was fought . . . I had been aware . . . that there was a goodly number of soldiers in and around the old log building. . . . I knew, too . . . that many of these men were slightly wounded soldiers who were running a hospital on their own hook.

Wert said that one of these men was Colonel James L. Bates, 12th Massachusetts Infantry, who had been wounded in the neck and foot on July 3. After several days in this makeshift hospital, Bates was well enough to join his regiment.[39]

Another visitor to the Wert house was Leonard Gardner, a methodist minister, who stopped there on July 4. He recalled:

(After visiting the battlefield) . . . and as it was nearly dark I rode back to the house of Mrs. Adam Wirt (sic), where I was offered a place to sleep overnight. The house was filled with soldiers, but Mrs. Wirt managed to get me a good bed in which I passed a comfortable night.[40]

Mrs. Wert, locally known as "Aunt Katy", was very active in assisting the many wounded in and around the Second Corps hospital on the Schwartz farm. She became a favorite of the many Confederates at this hospital.

J. Howard Wert in about 1890.

79

THE DANIEL SHEAFFER FARM

A Gettysburg newspaper article dated April 19, 1905, stated:

The old brick house on the Baltimore Pike near White Run, once owned by Josiah Benner and later by Daniel Sheaffer, was in olden times a tavern stand. . . . The brick house still stands in its heavy age, and it was there that General Sickles' leg was amputated on the evening of July 2, 1863. . . .

This timeworn but sturdy old house was built about 1780 by Nicholas Mark, who had lost an earlier residence in another county when it was burned down in an Indian raid. It is said to be one the oldest brick houses in Adams County. Sheaffer purchased this farm from Josiah Benner in about 1845. In 1863, he lived there with his wife, Lydia Baublitz, whom he had married in 1838, and several children. The family farmed sixty-nine acres and operated a saw mill on White Run. In 1873, Daniel Sheaffer died near Williamsport, Pennsylvania, at the age of seventy.

In a damage claim filed after the war, Mrs. Sheaffer recalled:

(Our) farm was occupied by a portion of the army of the Potomac (Third and Twelfth Corps), and on the second day of July 1863 Maj. Gen. Sickles was carried to the house in consequence of a wound which resulted in the amputation of a leg—he remained over night; a number of wounded soldiers of the Army . . . were brought to the house and in consequence of which the family were ordered to leave . . . before the family left they had given bandages to the wounded men. . . .

From the above quote, it appears that General Sickles, one of the most important and controversial people who took part in the great Battle of Gettysburg, was indeed taken to Sheaffer's house where his leg was cut off. (This amputation, by the way, had very serious and interesting side effects on not only the general, but that of the battle story. *And* later, it affected the creation of the battlefield park, which some believe became a "personal memorial" to the man.) So, where the amputation took place is somewhat important and should take its proper place in history.

However, the problem is that no two people seem to agree on where the amputation occurred. In my files, I have at least ten different accounts of the affair. Eyewitnesses claim that the operation was performed, "in an ambulance," "in a wheat field," "behind a rock," "in a sheltered ravine," "in the Third Corps Hospital on the Taneytown Road," "then and there," "1/4 mile to the rear," "in an old Pennsylvania bank or stone barn," "that night," etc. John B. Linn writing on July 9 at the Hoke Tollhouse, said that "just below this house, at Mr. Bushman's General Sickles had his leg amputated."

Sickles, himself, quoted in 1882, said:

It was at a most critical moment in the turning of that eventful day. A projectile from the enemy's artillery did the work. . . . I lifted the crushed leg over the pommel of the saddle and slowly slid from my horse. . . . By this time I was losing blood rapidly. . . . I bound the leg close up to the body, (with an equipment tie down strap from a trooper's saddle) stationed a guard of twenty men about me . . . until the arrival of Dr. Calhoun. I felt if the leg must come off I would take my own choice of surgeons for the operation. . . . In a moment I was removed from the ground to the field hospital. On the Baltimore pike that night, in the gloaming, Dr. Calhoun cut off the useless limb.[41]

J. Howard Wert, approximately seventeen years old in 1863, lived on his father's farm about three hundred yards northeast of the Sheaffer homestead. In 1886, Wert published a handbook on the monuments erected until that time on the Gettysburg battlefield. On page 121 of that book, Wert eulogized:

Ever since that July afternoon when the writer watched, as best he could, a portion of this mighty contest, and saw, amid lurid flames of battle, brigade after brigade rush to sweeping fires of death's high carnival; and then saw the noble chieftain borne with shattered leg to the sombre brick house on the Baltimore pike, at that time occupied by Daniel Sheaffer, Daniel E. Sickles has been his personal ideal of the perfect hero and the fearless soldier.[42]

From this thrilling eyewitness prose it seems likely that Sickles still retained his soon-to-be-famous leg upon entering the Sheaffer dwelling. And we know for a fact that when he left the place he was missing that appendage. Because the Wert and Sheaffer families were such close neighbors, it would seem highly probable that J. Howard would know exactly where the leg was removed.

Several newspaper reporters also commented in various articles that General Sickles was carried to "a house on the Baltimore pike" and, "to the house of Mr. Shaffer, on the Baltimore road," but only *after* the amputation was performed in rear of the line of battle.

Elizabeth Thorn, who left her home at the Evergreen Cemetery gatehouse on July 2 with her family to find a place of safety further south, recalled in 1905:

We went down the Baltimore pike. It took us a long

The Daniel Sheaffer house in 1987.

The Daniel Sheaffer farm stables or carriage house in 1988. The double-log barn stood about 30 to 40 yards to the left of the rear of this building.

while to reach White Run for the pike was full of soldiers and wagons. When we got to the property in which Andrew Beitler now lives we smelt baking bread . . . a family by name of Sheafer lived there.

Her youngest son, George, continued the story:

. . . the house was vacant. (Our) family took possession and stayed there until Sunday, July 5th. A barnyard was used as a hospital and the wounded soldiers who required surgical attention were operated upon in the barnyard.

George Thorn and his elder brother later tried to see the sights and had their curiosity satisfied when they came upon amputations being performed on the wounded. George also said that, "General Sickles had his leg, shattered by a shell, taken off at that emergency hospital."[43]

Two accounts mention that Sickles was given tea during that long night. And interestingly enough, in 1952, an article in *The Gettysburg Times* said that a "Mrs. Christopher Young and family, whose farm was on the Taneytown Road, were forced to move out of their farmhouse during the battle, and went to the home of friends out on the Baltimore Pike. It was here, according to Mrs. Young, that the general was brought after being wounded, and where the leg was amputated. Mrs. Young made tea and toast for Sickles after the operation."

Evidently, Sickles had something else that was a bit more potent than tea. Another article written from an interview with the general on one of his visits to Gettysburg in the 1880s, told how Sickles was asked by his doctor after his operation, what he desired to make him feel better. He requested champagne. This, the doctor said, could not be gotten, but a bottle of wine was soon found in a baggage wagon.

The warm wine Sickles could not take, and refused to try, directing that the bottle should be sunk in a well for an hour to cool. The doctor chafed at the delay . . . but (the general) insisted on this process for a full hour. When the wine was brought at last, it was sufficiently cool, but after taking a single swallow he put down the glass . . . he declined to take another mouthful for five minutes, and . . . drank it this way—one swallow every five minutes. . . . During the night he was able to finish the bottle, and thus started on the way to recovery.[44]

For about seven years, my family and I owned and lived in this two-hundred-year-old house. The old stone-lined well was still there on the north side, the water just as cold as when it chilled the general's wine. There were bloodstains, too, on the ancient board floors, and even holes in the parlor floor which had been drilled into the floorboards to allow blood and water waste to run down into the cellar. I even uncovered an account of a Christian Commission nurse, Rowland, the brother of General O.O. Howard, who spent two nights there tending the wounded during the battle. He was another one who said in 1887 that he visited the spot where he saw Daniel Sickles immediately after the amputation—and, of course, it did not appear to be the Sheaffer house.

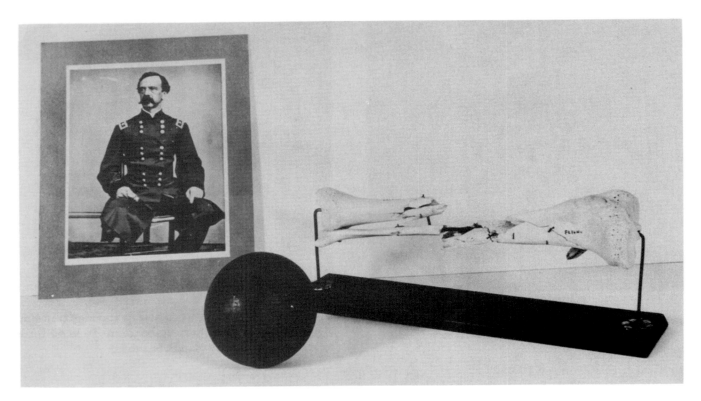

Photo of General Daniel Sickles, and his actual leg bone showing the effects of a 12 pdr. solid shot cannonball. (A.F.M.M.)

A bloodstain on a second-story floor of the Daniel Sheaffer house.

So, the search goes on. Just where did the famous leg, often visited by the general after the war and now held by the Armed Forces Medical Museum, come off? We may never positively know, unless we stop our search now and believe the general himself.

In 1988, this 208-year-old house still endures, its history older than the United States itself. Although the house is in excellent condition, and the old carriage house stands nearby, the barn, which was described as a "double-log" building, was destroyed probably before 1880. The sawmill, which provided lumber for bunks and coffins for the Third Corps' casualties, has long been washed away by the fickle waters of White Run.

MARK'S GERMAN REFORMED CHURCH "WHITE CHURCH"

In 1789, Nicholas Mark, the great-grandfather of J. Howard Wert, and a farmer and miller who had in 1780 built what became the Sheaffer house, permitted the twenty-eight-member Reformed congregation to erect a meeting house on his land. In 1863, it was locally known as "White Church" and was described as a "wood church, constructed of hewed logs, weather-boarded on the outside and plastered on the inside." It was about forty-five feet long, one-story, with a gallery at one end. It had no steeple, but had two doors in front, one to the main audience room and one to the gallery. The roof was shingle, the ceiling about seventeen feet high. The pews were common pine, and it had a "very fine pulpit."

Mr. Alexander J. Schwartz, who lived nearby, stated in the damage claim:

"The doors were taken off and used. One door was used for an amputation table. The pews were taken out, some of them, cut up and made bunks, tables (were) taken for beds for the soldiers to lie on. . . . They occupied that church about 5 weeks. . . . I do not know how many soldiers were there, but the church was full, and the lot, that was full." He also said that the floor was dirty and bloody all over.

Samuel Schwartz, who lived three-quarters of a mile from the church, stated:

"I went (there) on the morning of July 2nd, 1863. . . . When I come there, I saw quite a lot of wounded soldiers. They had some on the amputating table, which was right in front of the church. . . . I saw wounded soldiers. They were scattered around . . . some lying there and some sitting."

J. Howard Wert said that the First Corps hospitals were divided into the three divisions of that corps. He noted that the First Division had its hospital centered around this historic old church. He remembered that Surgeon G.M. Ramsay was in charge at this division.

Another surgeon, George W. New, 7th Indiana Infantry, who was Surgeon-in-Chief of the First Division, recalled:

"I took possession the evening of the 1st, of a small white church building on the Baltimore road, also the house and barn of Mr. (Isaac) Lightner and others convenient. Besides the men of our army, the next day 2d July, Gen. Patrick, Provost Martial of (the) Army of (the) Potomac, had placed in a lawn and grove near the church several hundred wounded rebels, who were fed and had their wounds properly cared for. . . ." New noted that eighteen barrels of flour were found nearby, and a thick soup was made in several large wash kettles and then served to the wounded.[45]

During the first week of July, Henry C. Marsh, hospital steward of the 19th Indiana Infantry, wrote home that,

"Most of the slightly wounded of our division were collected at White Church . . . and at a neighboring house and barn, and were suffering very much. . . .

"When our regimental hospital wagons came up, I took out the hospital tents, put them up together, and laid a floor in them, and made beds of hay and straw."[46]

Isaac Lightner, a nearby farmer, claimed in 1876 that a great amount of his hay and a large quantity of lumber was taken from his barn and used in the church as bedding. Lightner said that the boards were placed across the pews, hay was then laid on top and these makeshift bunks were occupied by the injured men.

The Medical Department of the U.S. Army reported 1,229 wounded in the First Division. And the Sanitary Commission mentioned that a "Mrs. Spencer" from New York was a volunteer nurse in that division.

Mark's church today is a replacement. J.H. Wert said: "A few years (after the battle), the Congregation erected a brick building, and the white church of many memories disappeared forever from the landscape."

Mark's "White Church" site in 1987.

THE ISAAC LIGHTNER FARM

The Isaac Lightner farmhouse in 1985.

"Sheriff" Lightner's* 115-acre farm, just across the Baltimore Pike from White Church, became the hospital for the Second Division, First Corps on July 1. Surgeon New mentioned earlier that when he took possession of Mark's "White Church", he also used the "house and barn of Mr. Lightner and others convenient." The Second Division surgeon-in-charge was C.J. Nordquist, 83rd New York Infantry.

In contrast, Captain Louis Duncan, in his 1915 (?) study of the U.S. Medical Department, published his view that the Second Division was at Peter Conover's farm, and the Third Division at that of Jonathan Young. The Sanitary Commission also listed these, the Young and Conover sites, as locations of the Second and Third Division, and the Lightner farm as the First Division, with headquarters at White Church. This makes more sense, because the church and Lightner's place were contiguous to each other.

A good account was left by a private in the 5th Maine Battery. He wrote:

> (After being wounded)** . . . I was taken to the First Army Corps Hospital. It was a farm owned by Isaac Lightner. . . . They laid me down beside the barn, where I waited three more days before my wounds were dressed. The surgeon let me lie there to 'finish dying'. . . . I (then) lay on the barn floor several days, and was taken into the house, where I stopped for a week. From there I was removed to Seminary Hospital.[47]

According to J.H. Wert, the commanding officer of this battery, Greenleaf T. Stevens, was also taken to this farm after being wounded.

In a damage claim filed after the war, Mr. Lightner stated that "all . . . buildings on (my) land were occupied . . for the first corps Army of the Potomac. The dwelling house is 40 × 31 feet, three stories including basement, containing ten rooms, cellar, and garret, three miles from Gettysburg."

Lightner mentioned, too, that hay from his barn was carried to White Church and used for bedding, and shingles and boards were taken from his land and used for crutches, tent flooring and bunks for the wounded, as well as coffins for the dead. Lightner claimed that his dwelling, barn and other outbuildings were used from July 2 to July 20 as a First

The Isaac Lightner farmhouse, east side view, in 1988.

*Isaac Lightner had served as sheriff of Adams County from 1857 to 1860. In 1863 he was fifty-three years old, and lived with his wife Barbara who was a year older.

** Private John Chase, though wounded forty-eight times, survived.

Corps hospital, and a large number of hospital tents were erected on his property. Furthermore, he stated that one of his outbuildings was occupied as a bakery where fires therein consumed great quantities of his rail fencing for firewood.

The barn is gone now, but the house still stands in its great Pennsylvania beauty. When I spoke to a gentleman who lived in that area, he told me that the barn, which was situated in the rear of the house, was approximately 25 × 50 feet in size and was dismantled about 1970. The structure was built entirely of wood and the main door faced the Baltimore Pike. The house, itself, is constructed of brick and was completed in 1862.

The bake oven on the Isaac Lightner farm.

95

THE PETER CONOVER FARM

The Conover farm is located south of the White Church, several hundred yards west of the Pike. The barn is original; one stone on the south side bears the inscription "P. Conover 1859." The house that stands on the site today was built years after the Civil War. The first house was probably located behind the barn and west of the present dwelling place. The old well also stood nearby.

This farm was most likely the Second Division hospital for the First Corps, and may have been used primarily by Stannard's and Paul's brigades. Eleven identified burials were noted here, four of them were Confederates from Mississippi and North Carolina. (The Second Division suffered 616 wounded at Gettysburg.)

On July 4, according to an army voucher signed by Surgeon A.J. Ward of the First Corps, Peter Conover sold the U.S. Government seventy-five gallons of milk and 510 pounds of meat which was used to feed the wounded of those hospitals.[48]

J. Howard Wert, who spent so much time in the hospitals and lived only a short distance from many of them, thought that the Conover place was the Third Division's hospital. Duncan, however, who may have done more research, placed the Second Division there. Actually, both divisions had wounded brought here.

The reader will note in the narrative of the following site that Captain James Hall visited a farm adjoining the Beitler place. This probably was the Conover farm he described. Hall found that, "In the stables (with) the cows were . . . wounded men who had hobbled four miles from . . . the ridges west of Gettysburg. . . . (They) had crawled in among the straw and litter to moan and lave their wounds with water. . . . (He) rounded up (fifty men and) had the wounded taken to an adjoining log building and placed on beds of clean straw. . . . In less than five minutes, . . . the wounded (were) removed and cared for."

Conover, fifty at the time of the battle, and wife Ellen, age fifty-one, had five children.

The Peter Conover barn—the house is not of the Civil War era.

85

THE HENRY BEITLER FARM

96

In 1863, the Beitler family owned at least twenty-four acres, located just south of the Sheaffer property at the intersection of Low Dutch Road, on the north side of the Baltimore Pike. However, the 1858 county map shows a "store" also present on this site, which may explain one reason for such a small-sized farm. This field hospital was mentioned in the account by Mrs. Elizabeth Thorn who said:

> . . . About three o'clock in the morning (July 3) we started on another journey, and went down the pike to the White Church . . . and we stopped a little bit there and . . . then we went into a big farm house (Henry Beitler lived here). They had there a big wagon shed where they brought the wounded and took off their limbs, and threw them into the corn crib, and when they had a two horse load they hauled them away. . . . The house was full of soldiers. In daytime we were watching the sick and wounded, and they were calling for water and screaming all the time.[50]

Mrs. Thorn also related that the Beitler family was absent, they had all gone to a friend's house in Littlestown.

J. Howard Wert claimed that an artillery lieutenant was buried in the Beitler garden on or about midnight of July 2, and that Hall's 5th Maine Battery camped here, in an apple orchard, on July 1 and 2. Wert said too, as seen earlier, that in the barn of "an adjoining farm" Hall found wounded men of the First Corps who had crawled into the stables. This farm was possibly the Peter Conover place. The Conover farm was part of the First Corps hospitals along the pike.

The Henry Beitler farm in 1987.

One additional remark concerning the Beitler farm: There is a very good possibility that General Alfred Pleasonton, who commanded all Union cavalry, used this house for his headquarters on July 2 and 3. It was listed as such on a Civil War period map. It also makes excellent sense, because the farm was on high ground with a good view of the surrounding countryside, and it was directly on the crossroad which the Federal cavalry used to move from the Baltimore Pike to the Hanover Road. In fact, the cavalry battlefield is only a short distance northeast of this house.

Henry Beitler, twenty-eight years old in 1863, was married to Matilda, twenty-six. They had two children. Four years later, in 1867, Mr. Beitler died.

THE SAMUEL DURBORAW FARM

97

The old stone home of the Durboraw family is still in fine condition just about a mile northeast of the village of Two Taverns. The barn is no longer standing. In 1863, the family farmed one hundred acres.

Lieutenant Isaac N. Durboraw, of Company K, First Pennsylvania Reserves, visited his home on July 2 after being in the fight near the Wheatfield. He remembered the circumstances:

> I now told Captain Minnigh I was going home, and that he should neither say Yes or No! I went back to the place where we had piled our knapsacks, the day before, but could find neither knapsacks nor (their guard). (This was at Rock Creek bridge on the Balti-

The Henry Beitler farmhouse in 1988.

more Pike.) I had only three miles to my home and soon reached it only to find it filled with wounded soldiers, General (Solomon) Meredith being one of the number. I slept on the floor that night, and next morning, with a knapsack well filled, I returned to the company. I did not find many of the people in the neighborhood at their homes and their houses were occupied by skulkers and shuysters absent from their commands.[51]

An interesting coincidence concerned the farmer, Squire Durboraw. On the night of July 1, a newspaper correspondent for the *Cincinnati Gazette*, Whitelaw Reid, travelling to Gettysburg spent the night at the Durboraw farm. He was very well treated while there. On July 2, as he continued his trip toward the battlefield, he found the injured and wounded General Meredith in a temporary hospital just south of Gettysburg, and there visited with him for a while. Later that night Lieutenant Durboraw recalled seeing Meredith at his father's home. Might not the possibility exist that Reid mentioned to Meredith about the Squire's home, the kindness received, and the safety it promised?

Whatever the case, it is an unusual and exciting possibility. It is not often that such a coincidence turns up in history.

Indiana military relief agent J.W. Monfort was in Littlestown on July 7, tending to the injured of his state. He had just visited Lieutenant Colonel William Dudley of the 19th Indiana and wrote in a letter to his agency headquarters:

"We arrived here one hour since . . . every house a hospital . . . General Meredith is at a farmhouse 4 miles distant—will see him today. . . ."[52]

This would place Meredith in or near Two Taverns,

The Samuel Durboraw farmhouse in 1988.

General Solomon Meredith. (MOLLUS-MASS)

just at Durboraw's farm.

Oddly enough, there were two identified Confederates buried on the Squire's property. These men belonged to the 22nd Georgia and 14th Virginia Infantry regiments. So it seems that there may have been some Southern wounded cared for at this hospital as well.

98

THE ARTILLERY RESERVE HOSPITAL

Although the Artillery Reserve of the Army of the Potomac's headquarters were located around the Michael Frey farm at some time between July 2 and 4, the batteries themselves were posted (when not in action) either just across the road from the Granite Schoolhouse, or just west of White Church. The hospital for this organization (five brigades under General R.O. Tyler) is not positively known at this time. Here are two descriptions of the site:

First, from the diary of an artilleryman of the Fifth Massachusetts Battery:

July 5, 1863. Sunday. Went to the hospital this morning and had my wound dressed . . . (Later) went to the hospital of the Reserve Artillery with all our wounded, p.m., hospital on the Baltimore turnpike about three miles from the battlefield. Hospital a good dwelling house and a barn. . . . Remained with the wounded till 11 p.m., with G. Trumbull, attending to their wants. . . .

July 6, 1863—The wounded men rested very quietly most of the time. Hard bread and coffee with a little beef steak for breakfast. . . . By request of M.J. Coleman* wrote to his father that he could not live. . . . Went to see some rebel prisoners in the hospital,—wounded,—p.m. Their hospital was a small church** and a cemetery, graves serving as pillows.[53]

The second source is a newspaper article written on July 10. The reporter spoke about the First Corps and White Church and then said:

At the hospital of the Reserve artillery, four miles from Gettysburg, in charge of Dr. Osborne, there are about two hundred patients, including Captain D.R. Ransom, of the Third artillery, and Lieutenants R.P. Eakin, First artillery, H.T. Scott, 5th Massachusetts battery, and E.M. Knox, 15th New York Independent battery.[54]

From all indications, the site was somewhere in the vicinity of White Church, at obviously a farm of some size. No other information is available as of this writing, except that one account did place this hospital at or near Two Taverns, which is only one-and-a-half miles from the church.

*died July 16.
**This church was probably the "White Church".

Two Taverns, Pennsylvania, in 1988, looking north along the Baltimore Pike.

99

THE JONATHAN YOUNG FARM

This farm was located across the Baltimore Pike and one mile northeast of Peter Conover's. In 1863, the Young family farmed 124 acres. Today, the barn is a replacement, while the house is very possibly the original building.

Frey's burial list made in the 1870s showed seven identified U.S. graves on the "Jesse" Young property and one Confederate from the 22nd Georgia Infantry. It is possible that this is an error, as I was unable to locate a Jesse Young farm in the area.

The Sanitary Commission report of August 15, 1863, stated:

"The First corps hospital was divided. . . . The First division was in and about the White Church and Lightner's house, the Second division in and about Peter Conover's house; and the Third division had Jonathan Young's house for the centre. There were in these . . . 2379 wounded of whom 260 were Confederates."

Duncan also placed the Third Division at Young's, but using a post-war map, he showed the Young farm as *south* of the pike, which is incorrect. Young lived north of the Baltimore Turnpike in 1863.

In 1887, a 847 pound meteorite was discovered in this area by Jacob Snyder. It was called the "Mt. Joy Meteorite" and is now on display in Vienna, Austria. It was one of the largest meteorites ever found in North America.

The Jonathan Young farm in 1987. The barn is a replacement of the 1863 era structure.

88

The Jonathan Young farmhouse in 1988.

A portion of the Mt. Joy meteorite photographed in 1988.

THE JESSE WORLEY FARM

100

This handsome farm, still carefully kept up by an obviously proud owner is located about three-quarters of a mile southwest of Two Taverns, Pennsylvania. The Worley farm was possibly the most remote Federal hospital from the actual center of the battlefield. Several sources show it was the Third Division field hospital of the Fifth Corps. Dr. O'Neal, in his 1863 physician's handbook, said it was the hospital for the

Pennsylvania Reserves (Third Division, Fifth Corps) with Dr. W.W.L. Phillips in charge.[55] Duncan wrote that this division was, "one-half mile west of Two Taverns, on Jesse Werley's farm" with a total of 181 at that place. This location is also given on the official government marker, which showed Surgeon Louis W. Read in charge of the Third Division.

Worley, and wife Ann, were both thirty-three. They had three children.

The Jesse Whorley farm in 1987.

THE J. BAIR FARM

100a

As of this time in 1988, I have been unable to locate this farm on any map of Adams County. The only information available is a notation that it was one of the farms associated with a division of the First Corps used as a hospital. Also, there were five identified U.S. burials at this farm which would indicate possible use as an aid station or field hospital. Since the name "Bair or Barr" is prevalent in the Two Taverns area, the farm may be situated in this part of the county, or somewhere between Two Taverns and Littlestown.

The closest name I found is "J. Barr" who owned a farm about two miles directly south of Two Taverns. The 1863 tax records of Mt. Joy township indicate a "James Barr" who owned 261 acres there. James W. Barr was a descendant of James Barr, Sr., an Irishman who came to America before the Revolutionary War and settled on a farm near Two Taverns. Barr, forty-five, and his wife Elizabeth, thirty-nine, lived on the farm in the 1860s.

The soldier graves buried on the farm are from

the Third Corps, but there appears to be no pattern to these burials and they do not fall into any one divisional organization.

THE ALEXANDER J. SCHWARTZ FARM
101

As a hospital site, this farm was unknown to me until I was reading, again, through my material on Mark's White Church. One of the churches' witnesses for damage claims, Mr. A.J. Schwartz, stated that he lived about one mile south-southeast from the church, and that he recalled the old building was occupied for about five weeks. He then said: "They were at *my place* about six weeks." Later in his statement, Schwartz mentioned again how, "the wounded left the church about a week before they left (my) farm." Mr. Schwartz purchased this farm only six months prior to the battle.

Unfortunately, as with many hospital sites, the above is all of the information which I have available at this time.

The Alexander J. Schwartz farm as it appeared in the late 19th century.

THE JANE CLAPSADDLE FARM
102

In 1863, this nineteen-acre farm was located just east of the "White Church road" and on the banks of Lousy Run.* On most maps the farmhouse appeared to be on the north side of the run. Evidently, by the year of the battle, Mr. Jesse Clapsaddle had died, and the farm was being worked by his widow, thirty-nine-year-old Mrs. Jane Clapsaddle and her three children.

Captain Duncan located the Second Division of the Fifth Corps as being "south of Mrs. Jesse Clapsaddle's house across Louzy Run." This must have been the "official" location, because the U.S. Government hospital marker prior to 1900, lists the Second Division hospital "near the Clapsaddle house."

Today, a portion of the old log Clapsaddle farmhouse still stands, nicely reconstructed by a family now living there. It sits about one hundred yards north of the small run and is one of the most uniquely built log houses I have ever seen. Instead of having plain mud as chinking between the logs, the original builder mortared stones into this space, making it almost a work of art. The current owners have done a beautiful job of restoration using the same technique.

*Lousy Run (or Lousey/Louzy) flowed southward into Little's Run, which was called Two Taverns Run in the 1870s.

The Jane Clapsaddle farmhouse in 1988. The stream, "Lousy Run," is to the right, just in rear of the house.

THE JACOB SCHWARTZ FARM I
The Second Corps Hospital

103

Abraham Lichtenfelter secured a land grant from the Commonwealth of Pennsylvania in 1797 for several hundred acres in Mt. Joy township in Adams County. Some time around the year 1812, this land was sold to Jacob Schwartz, Sr., who, born in 1783, later married Mary M. Geiselman in 1808. This couple raised twelve children, and both husband and wife died in their eighties during the Civil War.

One of their offspring, Moses Schwartz, purchased the family farm in February of 1849. After living and working there for about six years, Moses and his wife, Mary E. Duttera, moved to the Cashtown area where they remained. However, in April of 1858, a few years after this move, Moses and Mary sold the farm to his brother, Jacob, who occupied the farm during the war years.

During Jacob's ownership, the Schwartz estate consisted of a little over three hundred acres, and became the site of a few of the largest field hospitals established after the Battle of Gettysburg, including that of Union General Hancock's Second Corps.

Evidently, even as late as 1863, this farm was still locally known as the "Moses Schwartz" place. J. Howard Wert, who lived nearby during the battle, wrote several articles in 1909 concerning the field hospitals. In one article he related: "The central point of the Second Corps hospital was on the Moses Schwartz farm, but it lapped over on the lands of adjacent property owners."[56]

In any event, the Jacob Schwartz property quickly became the very center of Federal corps hospital activity on or about July 3, and remained so until the middle of August, 1863. Located north and south of White Run, and one-half mile southwest of the Pike, the farm buildings, ridges, hills, woods, and ravines of the Schwartz place were generally designated as the "Second Corps Hospital." They soon became filled with approximately 2,300 Union and almost one thousand Confederate wounded. (Many of these Confederates were captured during Longstreet's assault on July 3.) Surgeon Dwinell recorded 3,260 wounded here; of these, 952 were Southerners. On July 15, only a total of 532 men remained. This hospital was in close proximity to the First, Sixth, and Twelfth Corps, and actually spread over into parts of the Third and Fifth Corps. I consider this site the most important field hospital of them all, excluding Camp Letterman of course, which was a "general hospital."

During the actual battle, the Second Corps field hospitals and aid stations were set up along the Taneytown Road, at and near the Granite Schoolhouse, around the Lewis Bushman farm, and later along Rock Creek about five hundred yards east of the George Bushman farm. Dr. Justin Dwinell reported that at about one o'clock on July 3, due to heavy shelling by the rebels, the hospital of the Second Corps was moved, "into a piece of woods a mile and a half to the rear on the Farm of Mr. George Bushman." This was the first "Rock Creek" position of that corps' hospital. The First and Second Divisions occupied the north side of the creek, the Third Division was on the south bank. It appears that Thomas Livermore, the officer in charge of the ambulances of the Second Corps, actually picked this latter location. He wrote: "I selected a place (for our Corps hospital) removed from the range of projectiles . . . on Rock Creek about a mile and a half down the stream from the crossing of the Baltimore road . . . the left bank was a hillside, and the right bank was level and low. . . ."[57]

Livermore's chosen position became untenable when high water, brought on by the heavy rains of July 4 and 5, inundated the low ground of the hospital. It was soon moved eastward across the creek to high ground around and west of the Schwartz buildings. This move was due to the loss of nearly twenty men who supposedly drowned in the Schwartz and Sheely meadows along Rock Creek and White Run. Captain Azor Nickerson, 8th Ohio Infantry, said that the water was only about two feet deep in his area during the "flood," but to men who could not raise their heads, it meant certain death unless someone came to the rescue. Nickerson remembered several drownings very near him. He, fortunately, was saved as he happened to be raised off the ground on a homemade cot.* Later, on July 7, he saw and spoke to Miss Cornelia Hancock, of New Salem, New Jersey, a nurse who came by his tent to offer assistance. She was the first female nurse to enter this hospital.[58]

A Christian Commission delegate, Reverend Williams, reported the following situation during the first week of that hospital's operation:

> The men were in terrible condition. They were upon the damp ground, many of them with nothing under them . . . there was an unusually large number of amputations, the . . . stumps lying directly upon the ground. Many of the men, perhaps most of them, were in want of clothing. Suitable food was not to be had. The surgeons were overworked. . . . (The) Rebels, most of them severely wounded . . . (were) shrieking and continually crying for assistance. . . . Destitute of clothing, many of them naked, lying in the mud . . . cursing, praying, begging their visitors to put an end to their suffering.

*Surgeon Dwinell said that *no* men were "swept down the creek and drowned."

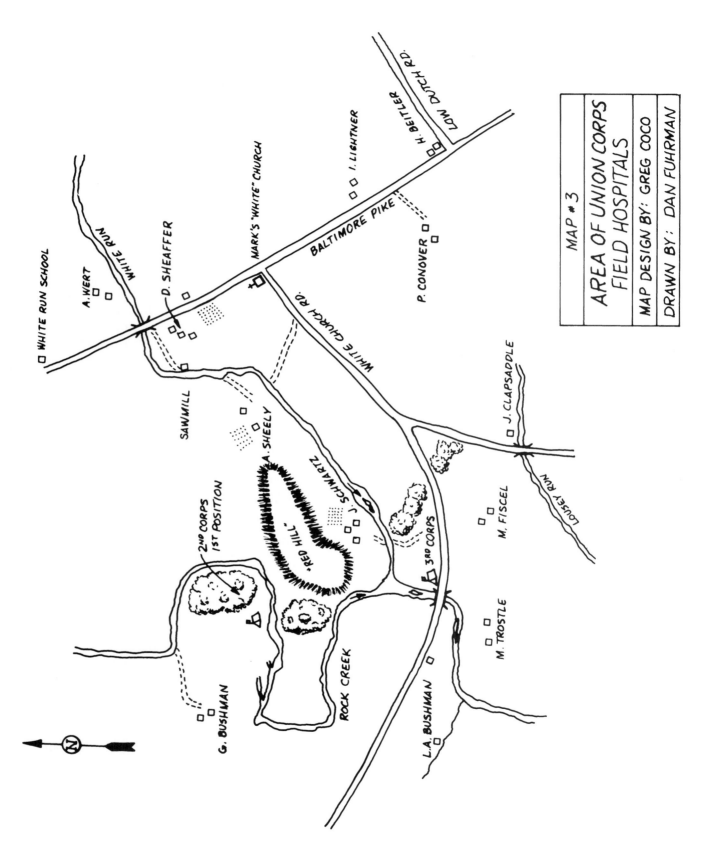

MAP #3

AREA OF UNION CORPS
FIELD HOSPITALS

MAP DESIGN BY: GREG COCO

DRAWN BY: DAN FUHRMAN

LOW DUTCH RD.

H. BEITLER

I. LIGHTNER

MARK'S "WHITE" CHURCH

BALTIMORE PIKE

P. CONOVER

WHITE RUN SCHOOL

A. WERT

WHITE RUN

D. SHEAFFER

WHITE CHURCH RD.

J. CLAPSADDLE

SAWMILL

A. SHEELY

2ND CORPS
1ST POSITION

J. SCHWARTZ

"RED HILL"

LOUSEY RUN

M. FISCEL

3RD CORPS

M. TROSTLE

G. BUSHMAN

ROCK CREEK

L.A. BUSHMAN

N

92

Confederate Lieutenant John Dooley, First Virginia Infantry, remembered the terrors of the night of July 4:

This is a horrid night, cold and wet and rainy. Groans and shrieks and maniacal ravings; bitter sobs, and heavy sighs, piteous cries; horrid oaths, despair; the death rattle; darkness; death. The Yankees (nurses) near me, instead of alleviating to some degree the fearful sufferings . . . are indulging in curses, the most ignorant curiosity, and obscene tales.[59]

Many of these wounded did not make it. Almost five hundred men died in this hospital, one burial list shows 140 identified U.S. graves, and 168 identified Confederates there in 1871. J. Howard Wert said that, "At one time the number carried forth each morning from the Second Corps hospital for interment in . . . trenches averaged anywhere from thirty to fifty." One surgeon reported 437 deaths in this hospital, of these 192 were Confederates.

The graveyard was located behind the barn and on a ridge or hill just north of the farm. During those war years, this elevated ground was known as "Red Hill" or "Slaty Ridge." It ran in an east-west direction, connecting the farms of Jacob Schwartz and Aaron Sheeley.

Wert added:

By the barn of Mr. Schwartz out in Mt. Joy Township . . . stood the amputation tables, and the work on them was incessant, sickening, and gruesome—until the legs and the arms were piled by cords and hauled off by wagonloads to be dumped in trenches where a century hence the plowman will unearth the moldening bones of those who fought at Gettysburg.

J. Howard Wert was almost correct in his far-reaching view of history as can be seen in this account by a volunteer civilian physician named Bushrod W. James. Dr. James, of Philadelphia, left an excellent picture of his medical work in or near the Second Corps field hospital on those fateful summer days.

Dr. James, who had also volunteered his services after the Battle of Antietam, arrived in Gettysburg shortly after the battle, with a large load of medical supplies. After distributing these much-needed items, he rode out of town on the Baltimore Pike, crossed White Run and then moved westward until he arrived at the Sheeley farm. From "Red Hill" or "Slaty Ridge," which ran west toward the Schwartz farm, James could see several thousands wounded men laying near the creek, in the woods, and out in the open on the slope of this ridge. He explained what occurred next after his arrival was announced to the surgeon in charge:

. . . he immediately placed me in charge of a row of hospital tents, (the hospital tents were run in rows along avenues on the level area to the north) the occupants of which had undergone the severe operation of amputation at the hip-joint or along the femur. . . . (Later) I spent my available time at the operating tables, which were situated in the woods on the crest of the slope which receded to White Creek. Every surgeon in the hopsital was kept busy nearly a week amputating limbs, probing for and removing bullets, or sewing, bandaging and dressing the wounds of those who were too badly mangled and shattered to be aided in any more hopeful manner. . . . We toiled nearly all day and night, snatching a few hours for rest only when we became too much exhausted to continue. . . . In fact only the power of will kept some of us at our post.

But Dr. James' "will" could be pushed only so far. After several weeks of this unrelenting duty, he succumbed to a "violent cholera morbus," and had to return home, his health completely broken down.

In 1895, thirty-two years after he had labored among the wounded in the field hospitals of Gettysburg, Bushrod James returned for a visit to the nightmarish haunts along White Run. The horrible scenes he had witnessed there were never forgotten. Dr. James recalled:

Driving to White Creek, and crossing the bridge, I immediately recognized the former location of the three hospitals, which were located within about a quarter of a mile of each other, close to the stream. . . . (Later) I came to the crest of the hill. This was the place where our hospital tents and operating tables were situated. . . . I went along . . . the flat area on the top of the hill where the rows of tents had been placed, and some of the depressions which had been made for the tent poles and posts were still visable. The hay and straw which we had used in the tents had enriched a growth of grass the following year, and, annually, this grass had gone on seeding, and springing up, and . . . the old tent lines and avenues are thus made visible or are marked out at the present day.

I recognized also the position of the commissary and culinary departments. . . . My next object was to ascertain the situation of the operating tables where I spent so many wearisome and fatiguing hours, with my sleeves rolled up, and with copious drops of perspiration covering my brow, in the sweltering days of that fearful July; and taking the markings of the rows of tents as my guide, I speedily ascertained the exact location; and the depression in the ground which we made for the blood and water to run into was even visible, while some two or three little elevated, mound-like spots indicated the places where we buried the many limbs which we were obliged to remove. . . . I turned to see if I would not find some relic from this point to carry home. . . .[60]

One officer who watched the work of men like Dr.

James was Captain John Adams, 19th Massachusetts Infantry. Adams, who incurred three serious wounds at Gettysburg, was eventually taken to the Second Corps hospital. He vividly remembered:

> Directly in front of us were two amputating tables which were always busy. We saw several men whom we knew placed on them and removed, minus a leg or an arm. The groans of the wounded were constant . . . I remained here six days, and my wounds received no attention. . . . Do not think I blame the surgeons. No nobler men ever lived than composed the medical staff of the Army of the Potomac; but there were twenty thousand wounded men . . . on the field of Gettysburg.[61]

As a summary of the locations of the Second Corps hospital after it was moved to Rock Creek, sources show: It was first situated east of George Bushman's farm buildings (on his property) in a bend of the creek. (July 2) Due to dangerous artillery fire it was moved a second time (on July 3) to "the bank of Rock Creek, at its junction with White Creek." Due to the flooding of this area on (July 5) a third place was selected which was south-east of Bushman's (but on Schwartz's farm) *across* the creek "on a steep hill covered with woods, and encircled by Rock Creek." The forth and last location was "on an open grassy slope," the three divisions united on the three sides of the slope. This last move (July 23) was the "clover field" which will be mentioned later in this narrative.

The main buildings of the Jacob Schwartz farm were a two-story brick house and a barn made of both brick and wood. The other buildings consisted of a wagon shed, corn crib, carriage house and smokehouse.

A Christian Commission nurse who served the injured men in the barn wrote in 1887:

> The old farmhouse (was) occupied by the men of Hancock's corps. . . . Its every room was a chamber of death and the boards of the shambling porch . . . were stained with the blood of the men for whom there was no room inside. . . . West of the farmhouse . . . stood the old barn. This was devoted exclusively to the wounded of the Confederate army. . . .*
>
> The smaller of the barn doors had been unhinged to serve as surgeon's tables. . . . Every available inch of space was occupied (eighty men were in the barn). The men lay close to each other, side by side in long rows. . . . The cattle pens, too, still reeking with the litter of the barnyard, were densely packed with victims as (was) the threshing floor above, and I noticed with horror, as I assisted the dressing of a bleeding wound, that the blood of the patient (above) filtered through the cracks . . . and dripped upon the sufferers below.[62]

*Schwartz's barn is mentioned often as a "Rebel hospital." A Third Corps account says it was one of their facilities.

Captain Benjamin Thompson, 111th New York Infantry, who was wounded and brought to this hospital, commented that the doctors and nurses in the Second Corps hospital worked very hard. He said, "There were no shirkers there." But he had other words for the local farmers:

"The patriotism of the neighboring farmers did not shine very brightly. A well-to-do farmer near us refused us straw for our men . . . not a man or woman in the vicinity offered a hand to help or a drop of milk for the poor sufferers. I employed one of them to take the men of my company to the depot. He . . . charged twenty dollars for the service."[63]

Another eyewitness who visited this hospital about July 15, related:

> . . . the Hospital of the 1st and 2nd Divisions of the 2nd Corps is (on) a steep hill covered with woods . . . under the charge of Surgeon (Justin) Dwinell (106th Pennsylvania Infantry). . . . The 3rd Division (is on) an open hill half a mile further south. . . . The location of this hospital was not the most desirable. The trees kept out the sun and obstructed the circulation of the air. The space was too small, rendering it necessary to crowd the tents and narrow the streets, and the ground continued wet after the rains. . . . (Later), a fourth position was selected on an open grassy slope, and the three Divisions (were) united on the three sides of this slope. . . .

Cornelia Hancock, the civilian nurse mentioned earlier, reached the Third Division, Second Corps hospital on July 7. One of the first sights which greeted her was,

> a collection of semi-conscious but still living human forms, all of whom had been shot through the head, and were considered hopeless. They were laid there to die. . . .
>
> A long table stood (nearby) in the woods and around it gathered a number of surgeons and attendants. This was the operating table, and for seven days it literally ran blood. A wagon stood near rapidly filling with amputated legs and arms. . . .

She recorded that on that date there were about five hundred patients in that particular division. She also noted that surgeons were in great demand, and that on July 7 four surgeons amputated all day, "none of whom were idle fifteen minutes at a time." Later she explained: "It took nearly five days for some three hundred surgeons to perform the amputations that occurred (at Gettysburg)." She wrote home on July 26 that the Second Corps hospital patients were being moved to the new General Hospital east of Gettysburg. On this date she still had, "eight wall tents full of amputated men. The tents of the wounded I look right out on—it is a melancholy sight. . . ."

Even as late as July 20, food and bandages, and other essentials were scarce in this very large and important hospital. Another nurse, Mrs. Emily Souder, recollected that even late into the month of July the Rebel section within this corps hospital was still in poor condition, as even were the Union wounded. The diet here was "corn-starch and farina, eggs in various shapes, and nicely made tea and coffee." Evidently, bread too was scarce, for on July 22, Souder mentioned that not a loaf could be found anywhere. Condensed milk and canned meats were used—fresh meat was unavailable. Milk punch flavored with corn-starch and brandy, along with toast, were considered highly prized luxuries, although attendants were able to furnish the mixture often enough. She concluded that, "No one can estimate the value of pieces of old sheets . . . (even) the smallest rag, who has not been in such a place as this, and the poorest shirt, drawers, or pantaloons, is a real blessing."

Mrs. Souder recalled that on Thursday, July 23, the whole camp of this hospital was moved to a clover field one-third of a mile away due to the unhealthy conditions present at the old site. The move was "across a run" and was very serious for many of the badly wounded, who knew the moving might bring death to some of them. On July 25, she noted:

The hospital is now located on a beautiful ridge, open to sun and air, and forms a hollow square. . . . It is a lovely spot. A bright stream flows close to the encampment, and the water is good.

But on July 27, she concluded:

At all events, the Second Corps is being moved to the General Hospital. . . . The Third and Fifth are being brought (in now). The Twelfth Corps is entirely removed; the Eleventh nearly so.[64]

Dr. Dwinell said of this move: ". . . fearing the bad effects of too much dampness . . . I was induced to move the Hospital into a large clear field of second growth clover where a number of circumstances combined to make it every way desirable for Hospital purposes." Dwinell added that the last man left this site on August 8, and the hospital was closed.

In 1988, the Schwartz estate, now reduced in size to approximately 156 acres, remains mostly intact and in relatively good historic condition. The original house is gone now, replaced by another brick structure which could possibly be seventy-five or more years old. The beautiful barn, where so much human suffering took place, is in terrible disrepair and will probably never see the 21st century. Just to the east, where the old Aaron Sheely farm stood (much of that land is for sale at this time) a new sewer plant has been installed which has paved the way for development in

the near and foreseeable future. As Richard Ben Sapir has written, "What a price to pay for so little in return."

Schwartz's wagon shed sheltered its share of wounded, but the house pictured is post-Civil War.

The Schwartz barn, looking southeast from "Red Hill."

The Second Corps hospital's final site on the Schwartz farm from "Red Hill" in 1987.

The Second Corps hospital several days after the battle. (MOLLUS-MASS)

Below is an enlargement from the above photo with Dr. Justin Dwinell standing to the left of the tree.

The Jacob Schwartz barn in 1987.

Dr. Justin Dwinell, courtesy of Todd E. Meisenhelter.

Remains of the "sinks" or latrines near Rock Creek at the Second Corps hospital. The creek is off to the right.

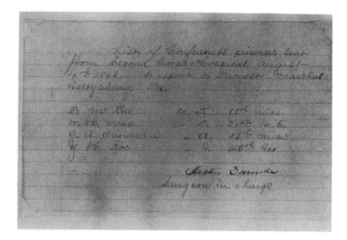

A receipt for wounded Confederate prisoners of war at the Second Corps hospital, August 4, 1863.

"Red Hill" looking west from the Aaron Sheely farm to the Jacob Schwartz farm.

THE MICHAEL FISCEL FARM

Today, this 162-acre farm is located along Goulden Road about one mile southwest of White Church. In July of 1863, it was just east of the Sixth Corps hospital (at the Trostle farm) and about three-quarters of a mile directly south of the Second Corps hospital which partly occupied the Schwartz farm. Fiscel's farm, like the Third Corps site, seemed to be a medical mixture; with parts of the Fifth, Third, and Sixth Corps' wounded within its boundaries. Fiscel, who owned this land, was forty-one. He and his wife Matilda, thirty-seven, had eight children in 1860.

The earlier field hospitals and aid stations of the Fifth Corps were mostly located along and near the Taneytown Road, as reported in previous descriptions, such as the Weikert and Bushman farms. In fact, the First Division's wounded were deposited on July 2 in a field in rear of Big Round Top, about a half mile from its base.

Historian Louis Duncan wrote that on July 3 the hospitals were moved to a new site, "a large grove of trees, entirely free from underbrush, on the banks of a little creek, about a mile from the Baltimore Pike."

On July 5, there were eight hundred wounded in this hospital, with only seventeen tents available. Eleven surgeons were on duty there, and of these, eight became ill. The hospital continued in operation until August 2. Duncan said that the First Division was on "Little's farm," "north of the house and south of White's Run. (The) Second Division, south of Mrs. Jesse Clapsaddle's house, was across Lousy Run, and one hundred rods south of White's Run. The Third Division, one-half mile west of Two Taverns, was on Jesse Whorley's farm. The three hospitals are said to have sheltered about (1,600) patients." Seventy-five Confederates were included in that total. The "Little" house he mentioned was probably the Fiscel place, as there does not appear to be a family by that name in the area during the 1860s. However, in 1857–8 there was a "D. Little" farm about one mile southeast of Fiscel's. David Little was one of the original members of Mark's German Reformed Church in 1789. No damage or hospital claim was ever filed by this family with state or federal authorities.

J. Howard Wert recalled that the Fifth Corps hospital was "somewhat to the south and east of the Third Corps . . . bordering at one point on the Two Taverns Run, extended on either side of a public road, through long stretches of forest. . . ."

A New York relief agent reported that the Fifth Corps hospital was east of the Sixth Corps hospital (the John Trostle farm), one-half mile along the road then turn right through the woods, and on the banks of Little's Run. He said that the policing was good in this camp, and it was filled with U.S. regulars and Pennsylvania reserve troops.

One of the best accounts of this hospital was written by Private James B. Wescott, 20th Maine Infantry (Fifth Corps) who was ordered, on July 3, to assist the wounded of his regiment. He left an excellent description in 1896 of the hospital at what he said was the Trostle Farm. Wescott probably meant the Fiscel farm. Both the Fiscel and Trostle farms were very close together, and Wescott commented that he did not keep a diary and, "whatever I may write will be wholly from memory." Here is part of his letter:

. . . I was detailed to go to the hospital and care for Lieutenant Arad Linscott . . . (on July 3) and . . . (the wounded were) removed to the Trostle(?) farm about three miles to the left of the battlefield of the day previous. This place consisted of a *very small house* and a *very large barn*. Several rooms of the house were cheerfully given up by its ocupants (sic) and were soon filled with wounded men. There the barn which was a large structure with floor running through its entire length with hay bays on either side was filled to its utmost capacity. Beds of hay were arranged on both sides of the floor, also in the bays.

Here many of the severely wounded were made as comfortable as circumstances would admit. Others were carried beyond these buildings . . . and arranged on the ground in long lines. . . . Among those belonging to the 20th Maine were Capt. Billings . . . Lieut. Kendall . . . Lieut. Linscott . . . Sergt. Hiscock . . . J.M. Kennedy . . . and many others. . . . (Due to) unsanitary conditions surrounding the barn . . . hospital tents were procured . . . and pitched in regular order. The wounded were not comfortably sheltered. . . . The medical officer in charge—Dr. Porter, surgeon of the 5th Corps who visited the hospital every few days was ably assisted by Dr. True (sic) of the 83rd Penna. (Dr. Free) (and) Dr. VonTeague of Philadelphia. . . .

About the last of Sept. or the first of Oct. the last of the wounded men were transferred to the Gen. Hosp. . . . G.M. Baker was Hosp. Stewd. . . .

H.B. Hackett, a Christian Commission delegate who was at the Fifth Corps hospital for two weeks, wrote in 1864 that, ". . . a captain (Billings) from the . . . 20th Maine Volunteers . . . was brought into that old barn, where (there) were sixty-five of the worst cases in the whole corps. Oh, they were all sadly wounded! The brave fellow had some of his own men lying on the floor not far from him . . . with great difficulty we got him away from his men who were dying—into a room by himself. . . ."

The "old barn" he mentioned may have been the Fiscel barn, which is still standing. By the looks of the

The Michael Fiscel barn in 1987. Many of the hospital tents were erected in these fields.

style of it today, it was an old barn even in 1863. The architecture suggests its age as dating possibly back to the late 18th century or early 19th. Unfortunately, at the time of this writing, this beautiful memorial to history, both in aesthetics and humanity, will be fortunate to live out the century.

Dr. Augustus Milton Clark, a U.S. regulars surgeon, recalled this farm in 1869 when he wrote:

At the time of the battle I was Acting Surgeon in Chief, 1st Div. 5th A.C. and . . . assumed charge of the 5th Corps Hospital. In order to avoid the artillery fire of the enemy, it became necessary to remove the several Division Hospitals of the Corps several times . . . and I finally concentrated them in a large grove between the Baltimore and Taneytown roads, about 1 1/2 miles in rear . . . and near the house of a Mr. Fissell (sic). Engaged in this duty, I remained on the field until August 3d when . . . I broke up the Hospital, and transferred the remaining patients to Camp Letterman . . . it contained some 1780 patients (when first established).

During the battle, it became my melancholy duty to attend . . . the last moments of Generals Weed and Vincent. . . .[65]

The hospital plaque on the site tells us that the, "1st Division (was) south of White Run on the Fiscel Farm. 2nd Division 100 rods south of White Run near the Clapsaddle house. 3rd Division one-half mile west of Two Taverns and near the Pike."

William Clark, 140th New York Infantry, was wounded on Little Round Top July 2. On July 3, he said that an ambulance "took us back about a mile and a half (from the Weikert farm) to a farm house they had fixed up as headquarters for the wounded. I got out of the ambulance but I couldn't see any place to lay, there were so many wounded already around

. . . the yard was so full and no room in the farm house or barn or anywhere. . . . I just crawled over into a wheatfield and lay there all night."

Later he moved to "a piece of woods" and stayed there thirteen days with a few of his comrades. There was a creek nearby.[66]

On July 21, nurse Jacob Shenkel, 62nd Pennsylvania Infantry, who was serving in the First Division hospital of the Fifth Corps, reported only fifty patients remaining in that division. Just a few days earlier he wrote in his diary that Governor Curtin of Pennsylvania visited their hospital, but did not remain long.[67]

Dr. Cyrus Bacon, another U.S. regulars surgeon, was stationed with the Fifth Corps hospital. He noted in his diary on July 4 that he was collecting and operating on the wounded of the 2nd and 14th U.S. Infantry. This section of the hospital was evidently in an open area near a stream. He mentioned sleeping on the lid of his operating table and also in the rear bed of an ambulance. Bacon is another who noticed the lack of help extended to the soldiers by the local farmers. He said:

"Thousands visited the battle(field), yet for days I did not see the first act of charity from the people. Finally, Secretary Cameron did bring and distribute six lemons to the men of the hospital. . . ."

Bacon said, too, that the rains had continued for days, and the straw in the tents of the men was wet. "Men (and doctors) lie on the ground and the rain soaks all nearly without exception."[68]

What must have been a sad duty, indeed, fell to the brother of Thomas Hunt, 44th New York Infantry. Hunt had been wounded on July 2 in the left leg and lost it by amputation several days later. His brother, Mark, sent from home to locate him, visited the Fiscel farm on or about July 23. Mark Hunt's letter home on July 24, 1863, explained to the family that Thomas was dead. In searching for the grave one evening, he was directed to a white-framed house which had been pointed out to him as part of the hospital of the Fifth Corps. Just after dark, a civilian who was working in a field by the light of a lantern, directed him to the hospital's graveyard at the edge of a woods. In that lonely spot, a crudely-carved headboard was found which marked the spot where Thomas Hunt's body was buried. Afterward, Mark followed the deep ruts made by artillery pieces and wagons to a brick house where he was given instructions on how to reach the Baltimore Pike. He crossed a small stream and passed through an area where a ghostly phosphorescent light hovered over the many scattered graves along the route. Hunt finally reached the pike and, later that night, walked to Gettysburg, his heart-rending mission completed.[69]

The Fiscel farm is listed as having 179 identified Union and seven Confederate burials, indicating a major field hospital, especially when the reader will note that two out of three graves counted were *unidentified.*

THE JACOB SCHWARTZ FARM II
THE THIRD CORPS HOSPITAL

105

It is evident from looking at the known sources on the Third Corps hospital that it and the Second, Fifth, and even part of the Sixth Corps hospitals, which all finally rested along Rock Creek or White Run, were not only very near each other, but all four even "overlapped" in some way. The Third was the most conspicuous in this matter. Being near the center of the rest, and due to the quick and large growth of all of these hospitals, the Third naturally became intermingled with the others. The main portion of this hospital, however, occupied a section of the Jacob Schwartz farm, south of White Run.

The official U.S. War Department hospital marker places this hospital in "houses and barns along the Taneytown Road from the School House Road to the Mill Road on July 2. During the night they were removed to the south side of White Run, three hundred yards from its junction with Rock Creek."

Several accounts mention that the first Third Corps field hospital was, ". . . in a grove about half a mile to the left and rear of where we (were in position)." This "grove" was named in at least three different sources. Its location was never pinpointed and is today, therefore, unknown. On July 2, the estimate of wounded in this grove was about three thousand.

On July 16, Dr. Theodore Dimon wrote this to the New York Sanitary Commission agent about the Third Corps hospital:

> Leaving the 2d Corps Hospital, and crossing White Creek at its junction with Rock Creek, and following the stream south, the cross road running from the Baltimore Turnpike west, across the left of the battlefield is reached.
>
> On the left of this road, as you face the east at this point, is the Hospital of the 3d Army Corps, and on the right, the Hospital of the 6th Corps. The three Divisions of the 3d Corps have separate encampments in the same field, on a dry, airy hill, well-policed, and the tents at proper distances from each other.[70]

A New York newspaper article on July 24, 1863, however, described the new location as eastward across Rock Creek, "(on) a high hill, (we) find the hospital of the Third corps, in a delightfully airy and shady

situation, now under charge of Dr. (Thaddeus) Hildreth of the Third Maine. It was here that General Sickles' leg was amputated. . . . The hospital tents are sweet, and the air pure compared with the atmosphere of town hospitals."[71]

In his book *"The Medical Department of the U.S. Army in the Civil War,"* Louis Duncan, in about 1915, noted:

> (The) last move (of the Third Corps Hospital) took it across Rock Creek to an excellent site on a slope with a fine stream of running water at hand. The operating tables were again set up; all were busy that day (July 3) the succeeding night, and the following day. The records show 813 treated in (the First Division) hospital. There were 97 operations, 53 being amputations. . . . Many slightly wounded were dressed and sent away with no record. . . . The hospital of the Second Division also appears to have been near the front on July 2 . . . when moved back next day the two hospitals were brought together. They were finally located east of Rock Creek, on the Schwartz farm, and southeast of the Second Corps hospitals.
>
> This place is on the north bank of White's Run and 300 yards east of Rock Creek.

Evidently, this hospital was well organized, because as early as July 6, a nurse, Lewis Schaeffer, 68th Pennsylvania Infantry, was put in charge of "Ward 20" of the First Division hospital, which had nine amputation cases. Schaeffer stated in his diary that Doctor (William) Hays was working at this hospital, and that Dr. James T. Calhoun was the Corps Medical Director.[72]

An interesting comment was made on July 15 by an agent of the Christian Commission. He said that, "The men in this corps, though very great sufferers, did not appear to have been so severely wounded as many in other corps. . . ."

He continued:

> Connected with the hospital of the Third Corps was a barn,* full of wounded rebels, who were in a most destitute condition. Some (were) half buried in the dark, filthy water concealed under the hay. . . . Others were on the ground—floor of stables, others in sheds, and some lay in the shadow of the fences which lined the narrow lane on which the barn stood. . . . They were aided by a young lady from Chelsea, Massachusetts, who cooked and distributed food.

A Sanitary Commission report on August 15 chronicled: "The Third Corps hospital was on high ground south of Schwartz's house, about one hundred rods above the junction of White's Creek with Rock Creek, on Schwietzel's (?) farm. It contained 2,550 wounded;

*This barn always "filled with wounded rebels," is mentioned in several sources. It is very likely Jacob Schwartz's building.

A portion of the Third Corps hospital site. The tree line in the distance (shown below Round Top) is along Rock Creek.

of these 259 were Rebels. Dr. Hildreth was surgeon in charge."

J. Howard Wert gave *his* location for this hospital in 1907:

"South of the Second corps . . . began the hospital of Sickles' Third corps. Running through thick forests and along the bluffs of Rock Creek, White Run and the Two Taverns Run,** it occupied not only the large farm of Michael Fiscel, but lapped over on several contiguous properties."

Surgeon Jonas W. Lyman, 57th Pennsylvania Infantry, reported: "(Our First Division hospital was on a) finely wooded and shady slope, (and) had a fine stream of running water . . . there were 97 cases operated upon. . . . 53 amputations, the whole number of wounded being 1,458 (in this division only)."

On July 4, Captain Richard W. Musgrove, 12th New Hampshire Infantry, helped to carry a comrade, Jon Leavitt, from the Sixth Corps hospital, to that of the Third, to secure help. He noted that Dr. H.B. Fowler was at the Third Corps hospital, and was very short-handed. Fowler was on duty at the amputation table and immediately performed the operation with the use of ether. Leavitt, who had both feet and ankles crushed by a cannonball, died on the table.[73]

Another surgeon who actually worked in this hospital, William Watson, 105th Pennsylvania Infantry, wrote in letters home of his experiences while at Gettysburg from July 7 through August. Here is a portion of what he saw in the hospital of the First Division, Third Corps:

Day before yesterday (July 5) I performed fourteen amputations without leaving the table . . . I have performed at the least calculation fifty amputations. . . .

**Two Taverns Run is today called Little's Run.

There are many operations yet to be performed . . . I am detailed as operator for the Division . . . most of (the wounded) are lying on the wet ground without any shelter whatever. The people in this district have done nothing for them. I have yet to see the first thing brought in for the comfort of the wounded. Some farmers brought in some bread which they sold for 75 cents a loaf.

On July 9:
We have eight hundred wounded in our Div. Hospital and only eight Medical Officers to attend them. (Soon) I will (be able to) turn my attention to wounded Rebels. There are about 100 of them in a Barn near us in a most distressing condition. . . . All slightly wounded are being sent off—it is impossible to remove the serious cases. Dr. Letterman . . . intends establishing a general Hospital in Gettysburg.

On July 11:
My Hospital is located just in rear of the place our Corps fought. This was on the extreme left . . . about 3 miles from Gettysburg. Dr. Hildreth, Surgeon in charge of (the) Corps Hospital, thinks we will remain about 8 or 10 days longer.[74]

106

THE JOHN TROSTLE FARM

About four-tenths of a mile east of Fiscel's farm and below the mouth of White Run, stands the old Trostle homestead, consisting of 176 acres in 1860. Several maps designed both prior to and after the Civil War, list this farm as "John Trostle's." However, the 1858 Adams County map, and the post-battle damage claim, give the name as Michael. John will be used in this study, because the 1860 census lists him as owning 165 acres. Michael Trostle, however, was recorded as being a "Wagonmaker" and did not own land in Mt. Joy township. So it appears that John may have been the farmer of this property in 1863. In that year, John was thirty-five, and married to Suzannah, thirty-one. They had two children. Michael, who could have been John Trostle's father, was sixty-two, and was the husband of Ruffine, age fifty-four.

This site is generally and officially referred to as the Sixth Army Corps hospital. Inasmuch as the Sixth Corps was not heavily engaged in the battle, there were few casualties. Therefore, several other corps, the Second, Third, and Fifth, used the medical facilities situated there.

On July 24, the *New York Herald* reported that the "hospital of the Sixth Corps (is) under the charge of Dr. (C.N.) Chamberlain, (U.S. Volunteers) and Dr. L.W. Oakley, (2nd New Jersey Infantry). Their pa-

The Michael Trostle farmhouse in 1987.

The Michael Trostle barn in 1987.

tients number but about two hundred. . . .

"The hospital is in fine order, however, and the cases doing well."

The Sanitary Commission report said that the three divisions of the Sixth Corps hospital, "were the first, about the house of John Frastle (Trostle) . . . and the Second and Third divisions in tents nearby. There were 300 inmates. Dr. Chamberlain, surgeon in charge."

A Confederate, Captain Benjamin Little, 52nd North Carolina Infantry, wrote after being wounded in Pickett's Charge on July 3, "(the) . . . next morning (I) was taken in (an) ambulance to (the) hospital of (the) sixth corps, where Drs. Oakley and Chamberlain gave me every attention and through that, saved my life. It was at John Trostle's house. I took the names of men I hope to see."

The U.S. Government hospital marker at the site says that, "The Division Field Hospitals of the Sixth Corps were established July 2, 1863, near the Trostle

House east of Rock Creek and 200 yards southwest of this point. These hospitals cared for 315 wounded."[75]

Fifty-eight identified U.S. soldiers and eleven Confederates were buried on this farm near an area known as "Walnut Row."

THE GEORGE BUSHMAN FARM

107

Just west of Rock Creek and about a mile south-southeast of the George Spangler farm stands what is left of the old Bushman farm.* The stone house which remains on the property today was actually built in two parts. The north section was the oldest, constructed possibly as early as the late 18th century. A bake oven was attached to this section. Years later, a second stone portion was added to the south end of the house, making the total building about seventy feet long. A fire destroyed much of that new section some years after the Civil War, but that damage was repaired. Throughout its history, a large barn was part of the farm, as was the norm. This original structure was destroyed after 1863 and was replaced by a second large barn which burned to the ground several years ago. The new metal building, standing adjacent to the ancient stone house, looks out of time and place, and unfortunately, leaves the farm, now sitting on busy U.S. Route 15, with a more modern, but, mostly forlorn, look.

Bushman's farm was the site of the Army of the Potomac's Twelfth Army Corps hospital, an important medical facility which cared for about 1,200 wounded (125 Confederates) from July 2 to its closing on or around August 5, 1863. Both divisions of this corps were near and north of the Bushman house, with the hospital establishment extending over onto the land and buildings of Franklin Swisher's ninety-four-acre farm which stood just across the road and west of the Bushman place. The reader may also remember that the first position of the Second Corps' field hospital along Rock Creek, was on land in an eastern section of the Bushman farm.

The New York Herald, on July 10, stated that at this hospital, "under charge of Dr. Chappell (sic) . . . there are 460 wounded. Over 100 amputations have been performed there."

Another newspaper story, written on July 26, commented that the hospital of the Twelfth Army Corps was under the care of Dr. H. Earnest Goodman, (28th

*George Bushman was fifty-three in 1863, and married to forty-nine-year-old Anna. They had three children.

Pennsylvania Infantry), and had numerous cases with, "the operating table in almost constant use." The article also related that the site was a good one, with medical supplies abundant. It should be remembered though that this corps was the only one in the Union Army which had its medical trains along with it, and not left miles in the rear.

The New York relief agent reported in 1864 that the Twelfth's hospital at Gettysburg was, "a farm house and large barn . . . occupied by wounded, but the great body of them were under hospital tents. The wounded looked cheerful and hopeful, and spoke gratefully of the care taken of them."

The best account of this site was left by Dr. John Love, 13th New Jersey Infantry, written in 1888:

The Twelfth Corps Field Hospital was first located in rear of Power's Hill, but after being shelled out . . . was permanently located on a farm owned . . . by G. Bushman. . . .

The farmhouse was used as a dining place for the surgeons and attendants, and the female portion of the farmer's family were kept busy in the preparation and serving of food. The large barn was utilized for shelter for as many of the wounded as it would hold, and hospital tents were put up in rows on each side of an imaginary street running up in the field north from the barn. The tents on the west side of the street were allotted to the Second Division, and those on the east side to the First Division. [Records indicate that about six hundred wounded were brought to this hospital.]

During the evening of July second the wounded began to arrive. . . . These (men) were sheltered, their wounds dressed, all necessary operations performed, and everything fixed up in good condition by . . . July 4. Then the army having left . . . Surgeon H.E. Goodman with twelve assistant surgeons and the necessary number of hospital stewards and nurses were detailed to take charge of the hospital. . . .[77]

A Fifth Corps soldier, Richard C. Phillips, 44th New York Infantry, wounded in the arm on July 2, recalled a visit to this hospital:

. . . I saw a red hospital flag in the distance and started for it. It proved to be the Twelfth Corps Hospital and I went there, and asked a doctor to dress my wound. . . He proved to be the Corps surgeon . . . he told me to lay down on the amputating table. . . He then took a knife and cut the ball . . . out, and told me to go and lay down in a barn that was nearby. I found the barn floor nearly covered with two rows of men nearly all with either a leg or an arm off . . . when I awoke in the morning there was a man dead on each side of me. As I stepped to the door there lay twelve nice looking officers on a bench, all dead, and the amputating table nearby with a large pile of legs and arms near it.[78]

Chaplain Lyman Ames, 29th Ohio Infantry, who worked in this hospital from July 2, wrote in his diary that by July 25 the wounded had mostly been moved to the General Hospital. He also made this interesting comment: *"Friday 24, July.* settled and paid Bushman for three week board $10.50."[79]

Confederate Captain Decimus et Ultimus Barziza, 4th Texas, left a good account of this Union hospital:

(After being wounded on July 2) I was taken to the Field Hospital of the Twelfth Army Corps . . . It consisted of the barn and other out-houses of a farm, sheds etc., besides a great quantity of hospital tents, which were afterwards pitched. . . . Our wounded were generally well treated, and were put side by side with the enemy's. Every shelter in the neighborhood was crammed; even hay-lofts were filled with the bleeding, mangled bodies. The surgeons, with sleeves rolled up and blood to the elbows, were continually em-

The George Bushman farmhouse in 1988. The barn stood just to the left, in the foreground.

The George Bushman farm as it probably looked when it was used as the Twelfth Corps hospital.

ployed in amputating limbs. The red, human blood ran in streams from under the operating tables, and huge piles of arms and legs, withered and horrible to behold, were mute evidences of the fierceness of the strife. . . . And then the dead are laid out in long rows, with their naked faces turned up to the sun, their clothes stiff with the dried blood, and their features retaining in death the agony and pain which they died with; and presently they are dragged forth and thrust into a shallow pit, with, perhaps, the coarse jest of a vulgar soldier for their requiem, and bloody blankets for their winding sheets.[80]

Such is the "glory" of war.

Nine-year-old Sadie Bushman was sent from Gettysburg to her grandparents' farm on July 1. There at the Twelfth Corps hospital she helped with the wounded for two weeks. One of her first duties, she said, "was to hold a cup of water to a soldier's lips while one of his legs was sawed off."[81]

The identified burials at this site were fairly close in number—U.S., fifty-two, and C.S., thirty-one. Several years ago, human bones were uncovered near the area previously mentioned where the bake oven stood. It is unknown whether these were amputated limbs or the remains of an entire gravesite.

Mrs. Margaret E. (Hawbaker) Nett, who lived on this farm in the 1930s, recalled a bloody footprint which was visible in a corner on one of the floors of the house. Mrs. Nett was kind enough to give me several interesting bits of information concerning her old homeplace.

Surgeon John Love.

Volunteer Nurse Hattie A. Dada, who worked in the Twelfth Corps hospital.

The fields behind the tree (looking north) were the area where hospital tents stood behind the barn.

The Frank Swisher farm which was west of George Bushman's (Twelfth Corps hospital) and handled a portion of the wounded.

104

THE GEORGE SPANGLER FARM

Spangler's 156-acre farm was located between the Taneytown Road and the Baltimore Pike, just south of the Granite Schoolhouse Road. The house was stone, as were other outbuildings. The large barn, with a wagon shed attached, was a typical Pennsylvania bank barn. This farm is still almost wholly intact and mostly unharmed by modern encroachments. It stands as the best example in the entire area of an Adams County Civil War era farm used as a major field hospital.

George Spangler was born in 1815, and married Elizabeth Brinkerhoff in 1841. They had four children, one, a son was named Beniah J.

The official government medical sources stated that this farm was taken as the Eleventh Corps hospital on July 1. There were a total of 1,400 wounded of this corps who were cared for in this hospital as well as at the Almshouse, Pennsylvania College, and other sites in the town itself.

The New York General Agent of the Sanitary Commission reported that he found this hospital,

> on a dry, airy knoll, consisting mainly of well-arranged hospital tents. A few of the wounded were deposited in a large barn. There was a sufficient detail here of surgeons . . . also a regular supply of hospital attendants. . . . Several good women were encamped here, cooking for, and nursing the wounded, and (some) relatives of the soldiers . . . were each caring for . . . brother or son. The wounded lay upon stretchers, or upon ticks filled with hay or straw.

Another Commission agent, J.H. Douglas, said that the, "Eleventh corps hospital occupied the house and farm of George Spangler. The (three) divisions were consolidated under the charge of Dr. James Armstrong. It contained 1,900 wounded, of whom 100 were said to be Confederates."

A Christian Commission delegate, Reverend J.B. Poerner, "carried out pieces of broken boxes from town, and barrel staves, and, with little assistance from any quarter, succeeded in raising all the men from the bare ground on which they had hitherto lain." Poerner, who spoke German, was also able to converse with many men of this corps who only spoke this language, and this way was even better able to serve the soldiers under his charge.

On July 2, Private Luther Mesnard, 55th Ohio Volunteer Infantry, ". . . found our 11th corps hospital, where I found some thirty or forty boys from our regiment, and thousands from the corps. I spent several hours helping comrades and watching the surgeons at the operating tables of which there were three."[82]

Another soldier, Justus M. Silliman, 17th Connecticut Infantry, wounded on July 1, wrote home on July 7 from the Spangler farm hospital that:

> all the hospital tents have been put up and are filled, the barn is also crowded and hundreds of shelter tents (are) occupied yet the wounded are so numerous that some have yet to lie out in the open air. Hundreds of wagon loads of delicacies for the wounded are on their way and have arrived . . . these are mostly gormandized by the gluttonous surgeons in charge who gorge themselves while many a poor fellow is lying in want.
>
> The rebel Gen. Armstead* (sic) who was wounded and a prisoner was taken to this hospital and has since died. he was rather past middle age. he is from Va. . . . he was wounded in the breast and leg. (he lay in the kitchen on the night of July 3.) There were at first 3,000 wounded in our hospital, hundreds have had limbs amputated. the barn more resembled a butcher shop than any other institution. one citizen on going near it fainted away . . .[83]

Reuben Ruch, 153rd Pennsylvania Infantry, acting hospital steward, remembered the barn at the George Spangler farm also. He reported on July 4: "This barn was full of wounded from one end to the other . . . The hay mows, the feed room, the cow stable, the horse stable and loft . . . I was the first 'doctor' that had come to the barn. . . . and I soon went to work dressing wounds. Sergeant Lantz was the first patient . . . Sergeant Lilly of Co. D was the next . . . Wm. Riehl was the third. He was shot in the shoulder. . . . Three of us sat on him while the surgeon cut out the ball. I dressed wounds until I got out of bandages."

Another 153rd man, S.C. Romig, said that on July 3, he,

> was laid on the threshing floor of the barn used for a hospital (on the George Spangler farm) . . . near the big door. There I had a fine view of the bursting shells coming in our direction (during Pickett's Charge). There were at one time six explosions of shells in one moment. . . . The danger was becoming so great that every man was removed excepting myself and an old German. . . . The surgeon who had been in shortly before looking at my wound ran for his life. . . . As he passed the door he called . . . 'get out of there as soon as you can,' . . . knowing that I could not move. He soon sent two men to carry me away. . . . They placed me in the lower part of the barn, in a building called a wagon shed. This place was occupied mostly by wounded Rebels.[84]

General Carl Schurz, a division commander in the

*Gen. Armistead's body was removed to St. Paul's Churchyard in Baltimore.

The George Spangler farm as it probably looked in 1863.

Eleventh Corps, recalled visiting the corps hospital on July 4:

> I saw long rows of men lying under the eaves of the buildings, the water pouring down upon their bodies in streams. Most of the operating-tables were placed in the open . . . partially protected against the rain. . . . There stood the surgeons, their sleeves rolled up . . . their bare arms as well as their linen aprons smeared with blood . . . around them pools of blood and amputated arms or legs in heaps . . . a surgeon, having been long at work . . . put down his knife, exclaiming that his hand had grown unsteady, and that this was too much for human endurance, hysterical tears streaming down his face.[85]

Reverend F.J.F. Schantz, who visited the Eleventh Corps hospital several times, recalled that one of the surgeons had been using material that was donated to the wounded. He questioned this man but got no results. Later, on July 26, he saw the items in question at the "Surgeon's quarters in a small wagon shed by the side of a barn. . . ." Evidently, this was the shed where the Rebel wounded were first placed during and right after the battle. He also noted that there were several civilians, including two or three women, who

General Lewis A. Armistead. (MOLLUS-MASS)

The George Spangler farmhouse and outbuildings in 1988.

The George Spangler barn in 1988.

were at this hospital assisting the sick and injured men.[86]

Dr. Daniel G. Brinton, Surgeon-in-Chief of the Second Division, Eleventh Corps, wrote in his diary that,

from the 1st of July till the afternoon of the fifth, I was not absent from the hospital more than once and then but for an hour or two. Very hard work it was, too, and little sleep fell to our share. Four operating tables were going night and day. On the 4th . . . the number in the hospital was 1,000. A heavy rain came . . . and as we had laid many in spots without shelter some indeed in the barnyard where the foul water oozed up into their undressed wounds, the sight was harassing in the extreme. . . . On one day I arose at 2 AM and worked incessantly till midnight. . . . On . . . July 3rd we were exposed to a sharp fire of shells . . . (which) fell within 20 ft. of the room where we were, and we were much in fear that the barn would blaze. . . . Among our wounded were three Colonels, Gen. Barlow, and Gen. Armistead of the rebel army a

fine man, intelligent and refined.[87]

Dr. Robert Hubbard, 17th Connecticut Infantry, wrote home on July 9 that the, "wounded (of the Eleventh Corps) are fast being sent to Baltimore and other places. The wounded (of this Corps) will number I think between 1,600 and 1,700. Of these I have already sent away 800 and shall send more today."[88]

The hospital at this farm was closed during the first week in August, 1863.

THE CAVALRY CORPS HOSPITALS

The first hospitals of Buford's First Cavalry Division, as we mentioned earlier, were located in the railroad depot, the Presbyterian Church and two schoolhouses nearby.

The location of the hospitals of the Second Cavalry Division (General David Gregg's), a portion of the Third Cavalry Division (General Judson Kilpatrick's) and probably including the Horse Artillery were noted by J. Howard Wert in 1907:

The cavalry hospital was scattered over the fields and amongst the barns in the immediate vicinity of the terrible combat between Gregg and J.E.B. Stuart. One of the principal points was the farm and large barn of the grandfather of Congressman (James A.) Tawney, of Minnesota. . . .[89]

This was the farm of Abraham Tawney, which stood just southwest of the intersection of the Hanover and Low Dutch Roads. The entire farm is completely gone now, however, several maps showed the barn to be quite large. It was also General Gregg's headquarters for a time. One Confederate burial, a man in the 1st Virginia Cavalry, was found here.

Another farm, located in the center of what is now the East Cavalry Battlefield, was also used as a temporary hospital. This was the John Rummel* farm, owned today by the Hoffmans, a fine family who respect and care for the treasure that is in their safekeeping. The barn here is original, but the stone house was rebuilt in a slightly different area in the 1870s.

Just after the afternoon cavalry fight at this farm on July 3, the barn and other buildings were made available to the wounded. An eyewitness, T. Eliason, stated in a letter written in 1885:

*Rummel, fifty-six and Sarah, fifty, had two children.

The John Rummel farm, some years after the battle. The house was replaced in the 1870s.

The John Rummel farm, one of the cavalry hospitals, in 1987. The house in the photo was rebuilt on a slightly different site in the 1870s.

. . . after the fighting ceased as late as 7:30 or 8 o'clock, I took wounded from the fields around the barn you refer to (Rummel). . . . Nearly all the men brought away were Yankees our men having been removed. I remained all night at a farm house about a mile distant from that barn. . . . I had sent my horses away intending to remain with the wounded. Asst. Surg. Wilson, 1st Va. rode up. I put him in charge, and rode his horse away.

A soldier of the First South Carolina Cavalry, P.J. Malone, said in a letter in 1867 that Surgeon Joseph Yates set a temporary hospital "on the field." Later, many of the wounded were moved to shelter.[90]

Evidently, there must have been another hospital for this Corps on or near Wolf Hill. A museum in Gettysburg in 1938 reported it had a photo in its collection of the "Cavalry Hospital at Wolf Hill." No other information is available on the site at this time.

It must be remembered that many cavalrymen wounded in and around Gettysburg, ended up in regular infantry corps hospitals, whether Union or Confederate. Elsewhere in this book the reader will find additional information on the cavalry hospitals set up after the Hunterstown and Fairfield fights of July 2 and 3, respectively.

In the same area, the J. Brinkerhoff farm may have been an aid station or cavalry hospital, as it lists two burials. One was a lieutenant in the 4th Virginia who had a leg amputated and evidently died at this farm.

Another farm possibly used for medical purposes, was that of "J. Lesse" or Joseph B. Leas, located four miles from Gettysburg in Straban Township. That site indicated the burial of five mortally wounded cavalrymen from the battle on July 3. This place was very likely a temporary field hospital.

Presumably one other cavalry hospital in the area was the Isaac Miller farm directly north of the Rummel buildings. This farm was just in rear of Stuart's Confederate corps on July 3 during the fighting on what is now called East Cavalry Field. Mrs. Sarah B. King, who stayed with friends and family at Mrs. Jacob (Rebecca) Rinehart's house nearby, remembered:

We stayed in the cellar while the skirmish fight was taking place. Whenever there was a lull we went up to look around. The lot west of her house had many riderless horses, wounded and in agony.

The Rebs brought a wounded Michigan soldier by the name of Smith and laid him down on the porch, saying he was a wounded Yank. Mother was a good person at such work and . . . we had him in comfortable shape very soon. . . . Mr. Smith was (then) taken to Miller's where there were other wounded. Afterwards he went to Aunt Polly Culp's . . . and was cared for by her until he returned to his home. . . .[91]

THE HUNTERSTOWN HOSPITALS

On the afternoon of July 2, while the Battle of Gettysburg raged eight miles to the southwest, an interesting little cavalry action took place at Hunterstown, Pennsylvania, between portions of Kilpatrick's U.S. division and Hampton's Confederate brigade. There were about 3,500 Federals and 2,000 Confederates in the area, but not all took part in the small fight. The casualties numbered approximately one hundred for the Southerners and thirty-two for the Union force. Participants recalled that the wounded were taken to the Great Conewago Presbyterian Church, the Jacob L. Grass Hotel, the Abraham or Hugh King house and store, the J.G. Gilbert farm, and the Methodist Church. (Since Abraham King was eighty years old at that time, his son Hugh must have operated the grocery store.)

One of those horsemen, William Baird, 6th Michigan Cavalry, wrote in his memoirs:

". . . while we were supporting the Battery . . . Comrade Charles Cox* . . . was shot through the Bowels and after the Rebels had left I carried him to a Barn where the Surgeons were caring for the wounded and then went to the telegraph office and sent a dispatch to his father. . . ."[92]

Jacob Taughenbaugh, who celebrated his 100th birthday in 1949, lived about a mile south of Hunterstown in 1863. He recalled:

I saw the wounded coming back from the battle. In some cases a man was leading two or three horses, with one or two wounded men on each horse. Some of these men had an arm in a sling, some were flung on the horse's back like sacks of meal. . . . Two of the brick houses in Hunterstown were taken over as hospitals for the wounded soldiers. Down at Ed Taughinbaugh's house were the Confederates, and the Union men were across the street in the building Bob Deatrick now uses as a store. . . .

When I went into the place where the Confederates were I saw a good many men ranged around on the floor, some badly hurt and some not so badly. The doctor was tending to those in the worst condition. . . . The Union doctor had a lieutenant who had been shot through the chest. . . . (The Confederate surgeon was called in to assist.) (He) took off the bandage and opened the wound in the lieutenant's chest and began pouring in (warm) water, a little at a time from (a) coffee pot. He said he wanted to pour it in until the water came through and dripped out the back. It did, too, for I saw the bloody water first start a trickle and then pour through to the floor.[93]

The dead of the battle were laid out in a row in front of King's store. They were prepared for burial by an undertaker named Deatrick. The burial list for Hunterstown named seven identified Confederate graves. Three of them, were Lieutenants Pugh, Chesseboro, and Brooks, who were taken to the old hotel on the corner and died soon thereafter. It was said that everyone did everything possible for their comfort.

*Sgt. Cox died on July 3.

The Great Conewago Presbyterian Church in Hunterstown, Pennsylvania, in 1987.

The J.L. Grass Hotel in Hunterstown, Pennsylvania, in 1987.

The store and post office in Hunterstown, Pennsylvania.

109

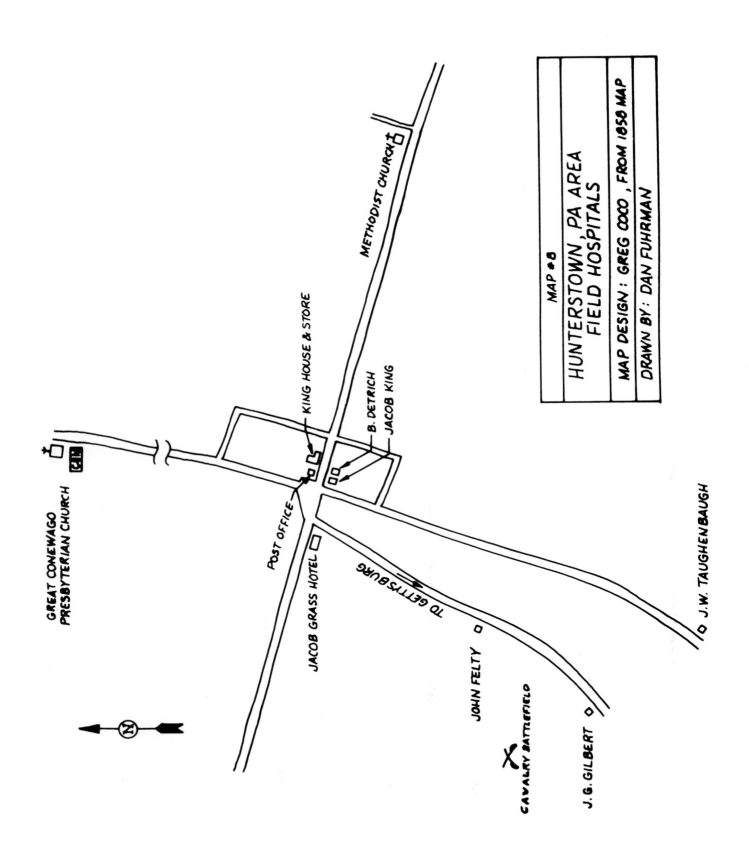

GREAT CONEWAGO
PRESBYTERIAN CHURCH

KING HOUSE & STORE

B. DETRICH

JACOB KING

METHODIST CHURCH

POST OFFICE

JACOB GRASS HOTEL

TO GETTYSBURG

JOHN FELTY

CAVALRY BATTLEFIELD

J. G. GILBERT

J.W. TAUGHENBAUGH

N

MAP #8

HUNTERSTOWN, PA AREA
FIELD HOSPITALS

MAP DESIGN: GREG COCO, FROM 1858 MAP

DRAWN BY: DAN FUHRMAN

The J. Gilbert farm, southwest of Hunterstown, in 1988.

Some wounded were cared for at the John A. Felty farm on the Hunterstown battlefield.

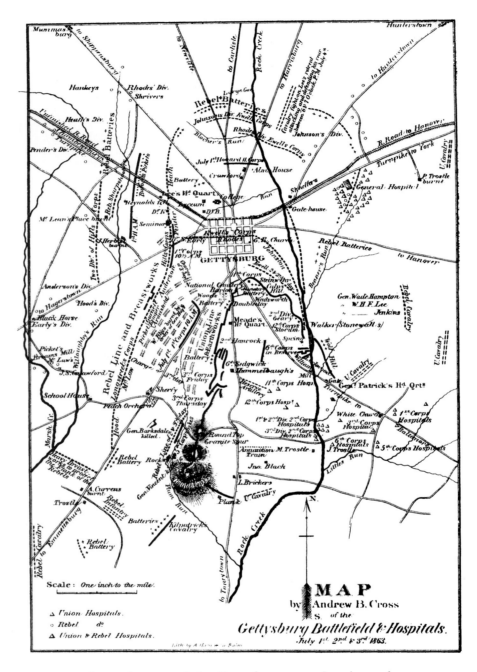

An early map of the Gettysburg area showing a few
Union and Confederate hospitals.

PART III
The Confederate Army Controlled Area Hospital Sites

"I thought I was fighting for liberty, and here I am dying like a dog."

Unnamed North Carolina soldier found in a Gettysburg field hospital

". . .and there was no end to the wounded."

Jacob Click
5th Virginia Cavalry

The many Confederate field hospitals were apparently not as well organized as their Union counterparts. In Part III, we shall examine sites which were easily ten miles apart, from farms located along the York Pike and Hunterstown Road in the east, to the villages of Fairfield and Cashtown, miles west of Gettysburg. The very extended battle lines of the Southern Army prevented these hospitals from being concentrated in one single geographic area. This circumstance made it difficult to supply and adequately arrange these hospitals for maximum efficiency.

It will also become apparent as you turn these next pages, that less source materials were available to the author in preparing the descriptions of these sites.

Very soon after the retreat of Lee's Army of Northern Virginia, the Federal medical authorities took control of the recently abandoned Confederate hospitals. Since so few Rebel surgeons were left behind, the formidable duty of caring for these wounded was left to the U.S. medical corps, local citizens and other volunteers.

The S.A. Felix house site in 1987. (depression)

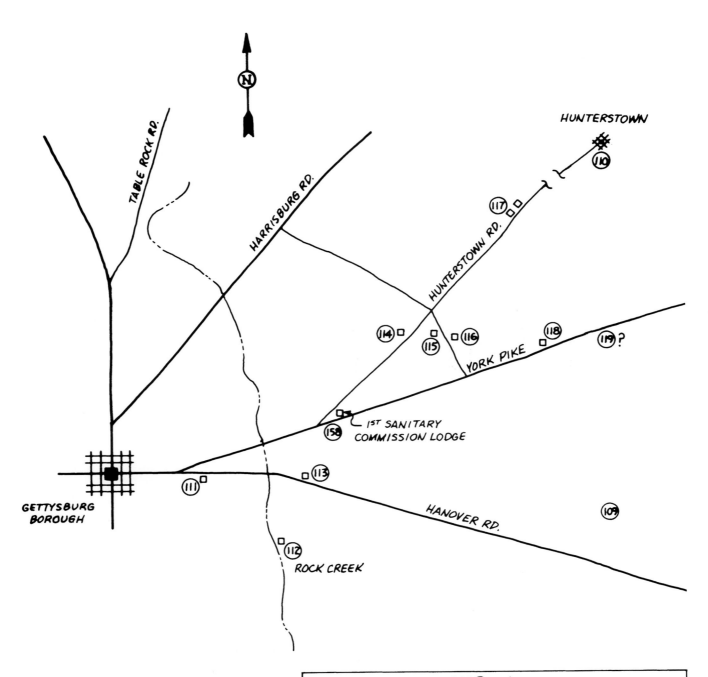

N

TABLE ROCK RD.

HARRISBURG RD.

HUNTERSTOWN

HUNTERSTOWN RD.

110

117

114

115

116

118

119 ?

YORK PIKE

158

1ST SANITARY
COMMISSION LODGE

113

111

HANOVER RD.

109

GETTYSBURG
BOROUGH

112

ROCK CREEK

MAP #4
CONFEDERATE ARMY CONTROLLED AREA FIELD HOSPITAL SITES
MAP DESIGN BY: GREG COCO
DRAWN BY: DAN FUHRMAN

The W. Henry Monfort farmhouse in 1987.

The W. Henry Monfort barn in 1988.

Henry Monfort then fifty-three and married to Catherine, fifty-two, had one child. In the 1860s they farmed well over 125 acres along the west side of the Hunterstown Road just northeast of the York Turnpike. Sometime in the 1870s the family sold their Pennsylvania holdings and made the great overland trek to California.

During the battle, the Monfort place was taken as a hospital for a part of General Johnson's Confederate division. Captain Duncan wrote: "The hospitals of this (division) were about the W.H. Monfort house, on the Hunterstown Road, about one mile east of Rock Creek. When abandoned, they contained 446 of the 1,300 wounded of this division. General Johnson says in his report that fewer wounded were left behind by his division than by any other; which does not appear to be the case. Dr. Whitehead was in charge of this hospital."

Also, a July 1863 map drawn by the Sanitary Commission, showed a C.S. hospital at this site.

A letter written in 1873 by C. Shambaugh in regard to Monfort's damage claim stated:

"In regard to the claim of Henry Monfort, . . . his house, outbuildings and barn were occupied as a Hospital . . . and considerable of damage done by the rebels while using the buildings as Hospitals."

After the war, only five identified Rebel graves were found on the property, most of the dead men were possibly moved to a larger burial grounds near or on the Picking, Shealer or Weible farms. These particular five were 44th Virginia and 1st, 2nd and 14th Louisiana Infantry soldiers.

THE MARTIN SHEALER FARM
115

Located just across the road from Elizabeth Weible's farm, was the Shealer farm, which in the 1930s was called one of the oldest farms in Adams County. The ancient and historic barn was still covered with a thatched roof when it was torn down fifty-six years ago. This location is at the southeast corner of the Hunterstown and Shealer Roads. A white building is on the site of the original barn.

Martin Shealer was a soldier in Company F, 165th Pennsylvania Infantry, at the time of the battle, and was discharged on July 28, 1863. (The 165th did not serve in the Army of the Potomac.) He returned home to find, ". . . his home occupied with men who fought against the Union. (He) immediately joined his wife in nursing the sick, and making the dying comfortable. They also furnished food for the wounded until all were removed." Shealer was fairly old for a soldier—he was forty-two that year. His wife Amanda, thirty-six, had cared for the farm and five children while he was away.

A 1932 newspaper article reporting the destruction of this barn said it was 114 years old, which means it was built about 1818. The article noted:

During the battle and for four weeks after . . . the building was occupied by the Confederates as a hospital, the mows, stables, and floor being filled with wounded . . . while timbers are stained with human blood, the marks of which are yet visible.

Forty-four Confederate soldiers, members of Johnson's brigade, (sic) died in this building, and their bodies were buried within 100 feet of the structure.[3]

The Pennsylvania claim listed Shealer's house as a Rebel hospital, much abused, with damage done to crops, fourteen animals killed and other property taken or destroyed.

There were thirteen identified Confederates buried on this farm in a meadow next to Weible's place. Most of these men were in the 37th Virginia, and the 1st and 3rd North Carolina Regiments.

The Shealer barn as it appeared in 1863. (G.N.M.P.)

The Martin Shealer farm in 1987. This barn stands on the site of the original "thatched roof" structure.

THE ELIZABETH WEIBLE FARM

There is little doubt that "Widow" Weible's home and barn served as a hospital for portions of Early's division, specifically, Hays' and Avery's brigades. However, on the Sanitary Commission map mentioned previously, this farm is *not* shown as a hospital, but another "J. Weible," located *on* the Hunterstown Road *is* so marked. Also, a burial of a Confederate named Goldsboro is shown on "Capt. Wibles farm." Since Mrs. Weible was a fifty-five-year-old widow in 1863, it is possible "J," or "captain" was her husband and the farm was still marked on maps with his name. Her farm was evidently owned by a family named "Walters" some time prior to the battle, because the place is sometimes listed by this name even as late as 1866.

Mrs. Weible's small farm is, however, still situated on Shealer Road, just south of the Hunterstown Road. The barn is gone now, but the brick house is intact and in relatively good condition. In her Pennsylvania damage claim she stated:

> The house and barn was occupied for a hospital for rebels wounded in the battle July 2, 1863 and the hospital was continued there until about the middle of August. The house was much abused by them and provisions, bedding and other property in, and about the premises was appropriated, damaged, destroyed or carried away.

A relative, Mr. William Weible, supported her claim and stated that "she lost all she had in the House. She had more property than she claimed for." J.M. Silliman, 17th Connecticut Infantry, was wounded

The Elizabeth Weible farm in 1987.

and captured on July 1 near Blocher's Hill (Barlow's Knoll) and said he was carried about three miles to the rear, which would have been in the area of Weible's. "Here we had every attention shown us, our wounds promptly attended to and received kind treatment . . . (the rebels) assisted our wounded, bringing them water, crackers etc.

"The hospital to which I was taken belonged to Hays' brigade called the La tigers of Early's division. The rebels occasionally came in bringing sheep, chickens, etc. captured at the neighboring farm houses."[4]

Burials of Confederates on this site totalled twelve, mostly from Louisiana, North Carolina, and a few from Virginia.

THE HENRY A. PICKING FARM AND SCHOOLHOUSE

117

A short distance northeast of the Monfort farm stands the school and farm of the Picking family. The barn does not date to the 1860s, but the mostly-brick house, although slightly altered, still stands along the Hunterstown Road. The current residents, Mr. and Mrs. John Lott, are fine and knowledgeable folks who understand and value the Civil War era jewel that they own. Mr. Lott's father actually purchased the farm from Mr. Picking himself.

The Sanitary Commission map of 1863 indicates a hospital at this location, but only at the schoolhouse. However, we know that Picking's farm was in use by Walker's brigade (the old "Stonewall brigade") of Johnson's division. Although a schoolhouse stands on the site today, it is constructed entirely of wood, while several 1863 maps show the schoolhouse as being built of brick.

Major Henry K. Douglas, who had been a staff officer with General T.J. Jackson, was wounded in the left shoulder on July 3, while serving as assistant adjutant general on the staff of General Edward Johnson. He gave an interesting account of his stay at this farm:

When I was carried to the rear I was taken several miles . . . and placed in a house which seemed to be vacated. I was laid on the floor of the parlor and during the day not less than half a dozen surgeons came to see and examine me . . . among them . . . my friend, Dr. Hunter McGuire.

During the day, I found the house not vacated, for Mr. Henry Picking, the owner, entered and spoke a few kindly words. As the shades of evening fell, a tall,

slender, young-looking woman . . . came softly into the room. It was Mrs. Picking. . . . She disappeared and in a little while was back again with a bowl of the best chicken soup that culinary skill ever devised. A bed and mattress and equipment followed . . . God, every now and then, does make such people as (these) and breathes into them his spirit of christian charity, beneficience, and unpretentious nobility, to let the world know to what a high plane he could lift up mankind—. . . But he doesn't make such often.

. . . my nurse Smith Shepherd of my old Company B, had remained behind, a prisoner, to look after me. Mr. Picking showed like kindness to the wounded in the barn. . . .

In a few days I was visited by a Federal Major, S.B.M. Young of the Fourth Pennsylvania Cavalry, who admitted me to parole with the soldiers in the

Major Henry K. Douglas.

The Henry A. Picking farm in 1987. The barn is post-war.

119

barn . . .

After the middle of July I was taken into Gettysburg and put in the Theological Seminary, which was used as a hospital.[5]

Major Douglas does not mention it, but Picking's attractive and kind wife was named Charlotte. She was thirty-eight at that time, with four children. Henry was forty-six years old in 1863.

Later, many of the Confederates assisted Mr. Picking with the harvesting of some of his crops.

Seventeen identified Southerners were buried on the property of Picking and near the school. Most were members of the 2nd, 5th, 27th and 33rd Virginia Infantry regiments.

The schoolhouse on the Picking farm. This building is probably a replacement of the 1863 building.

Dr. Hunter McGuire. (MOLLUS-MASS)

118

THE ALEXANDER D. BUEHLER FARM

During the war years, Mr. Buehler was in the merchandising business in Gettysburg which he had taken over in 1856 upon the death of his father, Samuel. Buehler was also on the Gettysburg Borough Council in 1863, and owned a farm in Straban Township. This farm, leased to tenant, John Z. or S. Hartzell, was probably located along the north side of the York Turnpike, about three miles east of Gettysburg.

The Pennsylvania damage claim filed by Hartzell after the battle stated that, "the premises were within rebel lines during the battle and was entirely overrun and crops trampled down. The house was appropriated as a hospital." A neighbor, Samuel Bucher, said that Hartzell was "driven out of his house by the rebels who took it for a hospital during the battle and used it for some time afterwards."

This hospital was likely used in conjunction with the other sites of Johnson's division which were nearby and along the Hunterstown Road.

This is possibly the Alexander D. Buehler farm on the York Pike in 1987.

THE DAVID JAMESON FARM

119

A book on Adams County history published in 1886, stated that David Jameson, son of James Jameson, lived with his wife and six children, one-and-one-half miles east of Gettysburg. The history reported that, ". . . their brick barn was used as a field hospital by the Confederates during and after the battle of Gettysburg."[6]

One of his sons, James B., was a lieutenant of an Ohio cavalry unit during the Civil War. The writer said that his duties included being the commander of the bodyguard of President Lincoln and Andrew Johnson.

This site was probably in the area used by Johnson's division on July 2 and 3. As of this book's publication, the Jameson place could not be located on any of the maps in the author's files.

A notation in the records of the Adams County Historical Society indicates that David Jameson died in 1874 near New Chester, Pa., at age seventy-two.

THE JOHN S. CRAWFORD HOUSE

120

Formerly the home of Henry Baugher, and rented to John S. Crawford in 1863, this brick two-story building was once a most attractive example of the classic "Pennsylvania German Farmhouse." Located on the old Harrisburg Road, it is now a "townhouse" and can hardly be recognized for its original and intended purpose.

During and after the battle, it sheltered several wounded men, including one general. Crawford was the son of Dr. William Crawford, a native of Scotland who, in 1789, settled near what is now Gettysburg. John Crawford was admitted to the Adams County bar in 1823. In the 1860s he also owned a large farm west of the borough. A daughter, Annie, was married to the Honorable Edward McPherson.

General Francis Barlow, a wounded division commander of the ill-fated Eleventh Corps, was carried to this house after spending a day or so at the residence of Josiah Benner. He wrote home in a letter on July 7, 1863:

On Thursday morning (July 2) I moved up into an-

The John S. Crawford house just northwest of Gettysburg as it appeared in 1863. (G.N.M.P.)

The John S. Crawford house in 1988.

other house just inside of the town where an elderly lady and her daughter were very kind to me. (Present in the house were Mrs. William Smith [Mrs. Crawford's mother], Mrs. Smith's other daughter, Jane, [Jennie], and a servant. The other family members including Mr. Crawford, left to find a place of safety.) I found some books there and passed Thursday and Friday very comfortably under morphia. I read and talked a good deal. I (ate) only some coffee and toast and cherries in those days. The ladies and some of our own wounded in the house did what nursing I required. . . . Some of the staff officers of Ewell and Early came to see me. . . . They were pleasant fellows.[7]

Jane Smith kept a diary during the war, and wrote this on July 2:

A night spent in attempts to alleviate the suffering of the soldiers of the Union. One immortal spirit from the little band under our care has exchanged

121

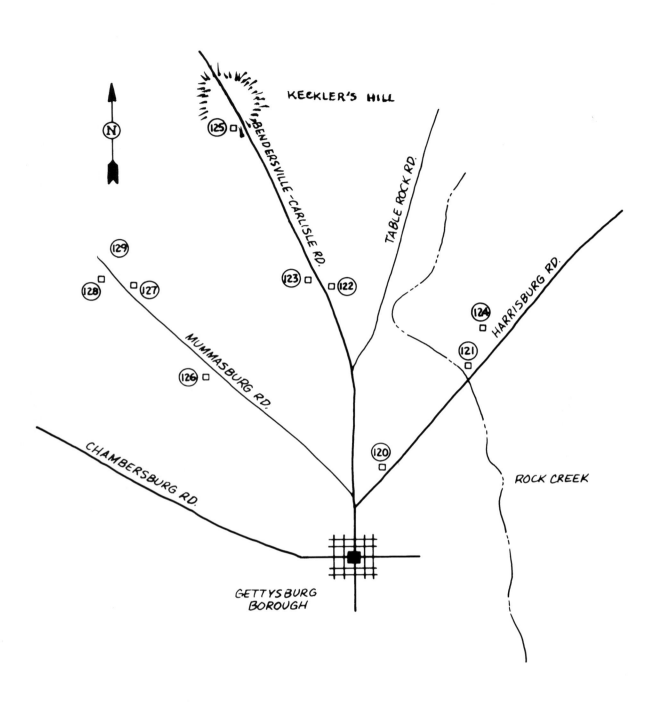

KECKLER'S HILL

N

⑫⑤ BENDERSVILLE-CARLISLE RD.

TABLE ROCK RD.

⑫⑨

⑫⑧ ⑫⑦

⑫③ ⑫②

HARRISBURG RD.

⑫④

⑫①

MUMMASBURG RD.

⑫⑥

CHAMBERSBURG RD.

⑫⓪

ROCK CREEK

GETTYSBURG
BOROUGH

| MAP #5 |
| CONFEDERATE ARMY CONTROLLED AREA FIELD HOSPITAL SITES |
| MAP DESIGN BY: GREG COCO |
| DRAWN BY: DAN FUHRMAN |

122

worlds. . . . The day wears on, still only skirmishing. The family except for Ma and myself (have) gone. . . . Maj. Gen'l Ewell who with his staff, took tea and breakfast with us last night and this morning. . . . Brig. Gen'l Barlow brought in this morning wounded in yesterday's fight.[8]

Anna Mary Young, a cousin of the family, who was present in the Crawford house for a while, corresponded with a friend on July 17:

About four o'clock in the afternoon, (July 1), the Rebels had possession of us. They made a charge through our hall. We were obliged to open our house for the wounded. Near dark, some of our wounded came staggering into the cellar, covered with blood; the cellar floor was muddy with blood and water, the latter of which had been poured on their wounds. . . . (That evening) The Rebels took their wounded from our house, to the rear of their army; so we went to work and took up carpets, brought down beds, and tried to make our wounded as comfortable as possible. . . . Our troops paid respect to the (hospital) flag that floated over our house. . . . General Ewell wanted to make his quarters with us; but, as we could not, or rather would not put ourselves (to) any trouble to give him two private rooms, he went elsewhere to sleep, but came for breakfast, bringing with him Generals Early and Rhodes.[9]

An unidentified line officer of the 82nd Ohio Infantry who was also wounded on July 1 related:

I was carried in and laid upon the floor (of a large brick mansion near the railway station), the carpets having been taken up and the furniture removed. Already nearly all the available space in the rooms and corridors was occupied by wounded men. Directly, a tall, matronly lady entered our apartment with a cup of coffee in her hand. She seemed to regard each one of her unfortunate guests as her special charge. . . . Toward midnight, General Ewell passed in through the hall. . . . He walked on crutches. . . .[10]

Today what is left of this old farm is surrounded by the northern most sprawl of Gettysburg, including a school, housing developments and a large (and expanding) shopping center.

THE JOSIAH BENNER FARM

The Benner farm is located along the west side of the old Harrisburg Road, and is the first place situated north of Rock Creek. The house, springhouse, and barn are all in excellent repair. However, the stone barn is no longer a part of the farm—as of this writing, it has been sold as a separate commercial site. Unfortunately, due to lack of protection or zoning in this county, *anything* could, and probably will, happen to this exceptional and rare old structure.

The Josiah Benner farm dates far back into the history of Adams County. In 1776, five hundred acres became the property of a man named John Reid. At that time, the farm boasted the beautiful name, "Spring Garden," and the springhouse was noted for its excellent quality of water, some of the purest and coldest in the Gettysburg area. This springhouse is reportedly where General R.S. Ewell rested for a short time on July 1, and as some say, bathed the stump of his eleven-month-old amputated leg. This small stone structure, which no longer has freeflowing water, may possibly date back prior to the American Revolution.

Mr. W.E. Jordan, who now owns the house, and is proud of his home and its history, will obviously do what he can in his lifetime to save it from development.

A federal officer, Lieutenant Theodore A. Dodge,

The Josiah Benner farmhouse as it appeared in 1863. (G.N.M.P.)

119th New York Infantry, wounded in the ankle-joint on July 1, said in his memoir in 1869 that at about 8 p.m.,

> . . . through the kindness of a rebel surgeon, I was carried into a neighboring house and given a much more comfortable place than I had a right to expect, a bed and mattress . . . one of our captured men, Francois by name, (was assigned) to me and my comrades as nurse. . . .
>
> One of our General officers, a division commander, (Barlow) lay in the next room to me (my bed was in a little room, [upstairs] where I was all by myself), severely shot through the body. . . . I only once caught a sight of the General, as they were bringing him into the house on his stretcher . . . (On July 2) . . . many shells . . . burst in the immediate vicinity of our hospital, and . . . three . . . went through it.
>
> [One is still embedded in the wall in 1988.]
>
> These last were missives from our friends (Union batteries), which could well have been spared. One of them set the house on fire, and only by considerable exertion were the flames extinguished. The other two contented themselves with scattering the plaster . . . and one of them brought the ceiling down upon my bed, much to my astonishment, discomfort and pain.

On July 4, Dodge was picked up by a Union ambulance team and carried to a more permanent hospital.[11]

In a letter written to his mother on July 7, General Francis C. Barlow told his story:

> . . . I was shot in the left side about halfway between the armpit and the head of the thighbone. I dismounted and tried to walk. . . . Soon I got too faint to go any further and lay down. . . . Major Pitzer, a staff officer of General Early, had me carried by some men into the woods and placed on a bed of leaves. . . . (Later, my own men who were prisoners) carried me in a blanket to a house further off (the brick farmhouse of Josiah Benner). I was in considerable pain and bleeding a good deal. . . . They put me on a bed and about dark on July 3 Confederate surgeons came. They gave me chloroform and probed my wound. When I woke up they told me . . . that there was very little chance for my life. . . . In the morning one of our captured surgeons and the same Confederate doctors came to see me . . . On Thursday morning I moved up into another house just inside of the town. . . .[12]

This was the John S. Crawford house. Later he was moved to a "small house . . . 3 miles out on the turnpike (to) Baltimore."* Obviously, from Barlow's writings, he never actually met Confederate General John Gordon.

*This house may have been Hoke's Toll House (site #90). A visitor there on July 9 said that two wounded general officers had stayed at the toll house—Zook, and another *whose* name was not known.

The Josiah Benner barn as it appeared in 1863. (G.N.M.P.)

General Francis C. Barlow. (MOLLUS-MASS)

124

The Josiah Benner farm in 1987. Mr. Jordan stands near the old springhouse.

Mr. Jordan possesses copies of two original photographs of the Benner house and barn, which have the following information on the back:

(Photo #1) "Former residence of Mrs. Hattie M. Diehl. During the fight the house . . . (was) struck by eight shells, one passing through, setting fire to the building, but for the continuing efforts of Mr. Benner the house would have been burnt . . . General Barlow . . . was brought to this house, also Colonel Morgan of Ohio."

(Photo #2) "Barn and other outbuildings of J. Benner—used as a hospital by the rebels during the Battle of Gettysburg. . . ."

There were fourteen Federal and ten Confederate identified burials on this farm.

THE WILLIAM ROSS FARM

122

This 114-acre farm was located on the old Newville Road (Route 34) and had at least fifteen acres in crops destroyed in 1863 by the Rebels. This site, then owned by forty-one-year-old Ross and his wife, Sarah, stood across the road from the Samuel Cobean farm.

Only one identified burial, a soldier in the 12th Alabama Infantry, was listed on the fringes of this farm.

In 1868, when Ross filed a damage claim, one of his witnesses was Isaac Deardorff who lived about a mile from the Ross place. Deardorff stated in his affadavit:

"(I) saw the Rebel armies upon the farm of said Ross during the three days of the battle of Gettysburg;

. . . . wounded men were brought to the house (and) (I) walked over part of the land of said Ross after the battle and found the grain and grass destroyed . . ."

The house that stands on the site may not be the original one—the barn is long gone. One small shed on the property, however, was used by the veterans in 1938 during the seventy-fifth anniversary of the battle. At one time, this shed was located near the Eternal Light Peace Memorial.

The William Ross farm in 1987. The house may not be the original Civil War structure.

THE SAMUEL A. COBEAN FARM

123

In 1863, Samuel Cobean lived on a 136-acre farm just north of Gettysburg along the Carlisle or old Newville Road. His house had been built in 1805 by a family named Sloan. Cobean's wife, Eliza Jane McCullough, had died years earlier, and he and a niece, who "kept house" for him, were alone on the farm during the battle. Both of Samuel's sons were in the military service in 1863.

Mrs. Hugh McIlhenny Sr., who was a granddaughter of Samuel Cobean, recalled several incidents he related to her:

Just before the battle, the Cobeans were warned to leave . . . but Grandfather refused. . . . The Rebels were encamped all around the . . . farm and finally took possession of the house. The family moved into the basement.

(On July 1) Grandfather stood at the window and watched the shells come across from near 'Barlows Knoll' until the house was struck several times. . . .

The Samuel A. Cobean farm in 1987.

The Jacob Kime farm today—the buildings may be post-Civil War.

.The Rebels stole everything eatable about the place, took all the cured meat and killed the cattle. . . . ˙

General Trimble's leg was amputated in the 'parlor.' We still have the old inlaid mahogany grandfather's clock that always stood in the corner and looked down with its moonface upon that amputation. General Trimble was taken to Gettysburg as soon as he was able to be moved . . . to the home of Robert Mc-Curdy. . . .[13]

Captain Duncan wrote in about 1915 that when Trimble was wounded he was first taken to the David Whisler house which is northwest of Gettysburg. General Marsena R. Patrick, who visited Trimble on July 6, said that he was, "out some 3 or 4 miles beyond Gettysburg." So it is possible that the general was either at one or both places before being taken to McCurdy's.

After leaving the McCurdy home, Trimble stayed at the Seminary hospital for awhile until he was transferred to a military prison in Baltimore.

124

THE JACOB KIME FARM

This farm is located about three miles north of Gettysburg on the east side of the Table Rock Road, just across the Cumberland Township line. It is situated inside the very northwest corner of Straban Township and south of the Mummasburg-Hunterstown Road.

Lovina Witmer lived on her father's rural farmstead just northeast of Kime's farm, and later married Jacob's son. She recalled several interesting incidents regarding both the Henry Witmer* and Jacob Kime properties. In 1937 when she was ninety years old, she

remembered that

eight of her father's fields were filled with the encampment of southern soldiers during the battle of Gettysburg. A Massachusetts soldier in the Confederate ranks sat on the porch and talked to the seven girls of the family. . . . Her father, sister Hanna, and (herself), stayed on the farm throughout the battle, but (her) father forced the rest of the family to move into safe quarters with friends. . . .

During the battle, Mrs. Kime's (future) husband's home (the Jacob Kime farm) was seized for use as a hospital. . . . Everyone but her grandfather, who stayed in the cellar, moved out of the house. When they returned to the house they found the floors piled high with arms and legs that had been amputated from the wounded soldiers. Her grandfather (in the cellar) plainly heard the mad cry of the soldiers for morphine when the operations were being performed.[17]

Today, the house is owned by Angela and Julian Nadeau, who kindly showed me their residence. Although very much altered since 1863, the old log house still exists, but only buried under many modern alterations. The original house was approximately 24' x 28' in size, with four rooms, two up and two down, with two front doors leading out to a porch from the downstairs rooms. Evidently, the log house dates to very early in the 19th century. A 46' x 84' barn was built on the place in 1876, probably replacing a similar structure which stood on the site in 1863. Mrs. Rosie (Kime) Welker, who is ninety-five-years-old this year (1988) moved out of the house in 1915, when she married. Mrs. Welker, who now lives nearby, recalled hearing stories when she was growing up about the Confederates who occupied her family's farm.

*Henry Witmer, sixty-two, and Catherine, sixty, had at least six children in 1863.

Three burials were listed on this property, all from the 38th and 61st Georgia Infantry regiments indicating that this hospital was used by Gordon's brigade of Early's division, the same organization which used the Josiah Benner farm.

In 1860, records indicate that Jacob Kime age thirty-three had four children. His spouse was Elizabeth, thirty-one.

THE JOHN HAMILTON FARM

The buildings of this old farm were, regrettably, burned down in 1971 to make room for the modern house shown in the photograph. The barn was quite large and would have made a good shelter for Confederate wounded. The farm was located north of Cobean's and just west of the junction of the Carlisle Road and Herr's Ridge Road. Fortunately, through the courtesy of Mrs. Donna McGlaughlin, I was able to locate a photograph of the old place that was taken the day it was burned. The original farm consisted of "more than 25 acres."

The Hamilton family evidently owned a blacksmith shop in the year of the battle. This building stood near the junction of the two roads mentioned above, but on the east side of the Carlisle or Newville Road. This area was a high elevation known as Keckler's Hill. William Hamilton Bayly, a youngster in 1863 who lived nearby on the Table Rock Road, recalled the scene near this farm on July 1:

The John Hamilton farmhouse in 1971, before it was destroyed.

The John Hamilton barn in 1971, prior to its destruction.

The Hamilton farm, circa 1900. The buildings were completed between 1780 to 1802 by William Sheakley. (D. Neville)

John Hamilton's butcher shop in 1971, before it was destroyed.

Arriving on the top of the ridge on the Newville Road, we stopped for breath and to survey the situation. Several farmers whom we knew were standing at a blacksmith's shop, by the roadside. . . .

. . . we (soon) noticed up the road, coming over the nearest hill, great masses of troops and clouds of dust . . . the first wave swelled into successive waves, gray masses with the glint of steel as the sun struck the gun barrels, filling the highway, spreading out into the fields, and still coming on and on, wave after wave, billow after billow.[14]

Bayly said in his memoir that John Hamilton was his cousin, and his uncle was William Hamilton. The 1858 and 1872 Adams County atlases show "J. Hamilton" as owner of the farm on this site. John Hamilton's fifty-year-old wife, Sarah Ann Eline, lived with him at this farm. They were married in 1838, and both died in 1894. The 1863 tax rolls identify *Sarah* as owner of the 150 acre farm. John was evidently a blacksmith only—not a farmer.

A Pennsylvania damage claim filed after the war by John Hamilton of Cumberland Township stated that, his "farm was 2 miles north of Gettysburg and was occupied by the rebel army and his Barn and grounds were used for a hospital during the battle. The rebels took or destroyed 2 horses, flour, shelled corn, hay, and 8 acres of wheat . . . (also) blacksmith tools and iron from his shop."

Dr. John O'Neal, mentioned several times in this narrative, was also at one point near this location. He reminisced about trying to get home from Cashtown on July 1:

. . . supposing I could ride around the advance (of the Confederate) army and get home I followed lanes and other roads until I got to Keckler's Hill at Hamilton's blacksmith shop. . . . There I stayed with a number of Confederates who seemed off duty. (While there) columns passed down the road and I could see other columns along the Harrisburg road.[15]

John's brother, Calvin Hamilton, was wounded in the Battle of Gettysburg while serving in the Pennsylvania Reserves. Their mother was the former Evaline Bayly.

Ruth Hamilton Keppel wrote the following in 1935 concerning this farm:

When the first day's fight was in progress my grandfather William Hamilton age then 53, his brother John Hamilton age 47 with 2 of William's sons and John's son—boys in their early teens . . . were sitting on a fence rail, atop Keckler's Hill near the present Oscar Shaw home—then John Hamilton's home—watching the fight. Two men on horseback riding by stopped and the one engaged the Hamiltons in conversation. He told them he was Gen'l. Early and seemed delighted with the prospects of victory. Then he asked why these five were not in the army. . . . (after an explanation) Early shook his head and said 'You'd all be in the service if you were in the South.'[16]

THE JOHN S. FORNEY FARM

John S. Forney, who was born in 1830, was reared in and attended school at Gettysburg. In 1849, he boldly journeyed to California where he engaged in gold mining. In 1859 he returned to Adams County and purchased this 150-acre farm. Three years later, Forney married Mary E. Schriver, and the following year his peaceful home site became a battlefield.

During the fighting on July 1 on Oak Ridge, the Forney place, which was very near the actual lines of battle, became a shelter to many Confederate wounded who attempted to reach safety in the rear of their army. In his damage claim application, Mr. Forney listed his buildings as "greatly damaged by shells." He also stated that his farm was "occupied as a field hospital."

Major Charles Blacknall, 23rd North Carolina Infantry, was one soldier who used the Forney farm. Blacknall was hit by a bullet which entered his mouth while he cheered his men on. After the bullet knocked out and loosened several teeth, it passed out through his neck. He was assisted to the rear, and stopped for a time at the Forney house before being carried to another hospital about a mile further to the rear. This is one of the only accounts I found which mentioned this farm as a hospital or aid station.

On a visit to this place in 1897, Blacknall's son, Oscar, related:

The John S. Forney site in 1987.

The John S. Forney farmhouse as it appeared in 1863. (G.N.M.P.)

The John S. Forney barn as it appeared in 1863. (G.N.M.P.)

Old Mr. Forney, who witnessed the battle, was then still alive. He was able to give me a very clear idea of all that part of it. He showed me the 'Iverson pits' the trenches in which held (that) brigade's dead till years afterwards when they were removed to Richmond. The luxuriant growth of the bitter or smart weed marked their course and some of the pits still yawned. In one of these I found a flattened and deformed bullet which, at the disinternment must have fallen from the skeleton of its victim.[18]

The site today is a slight rise in an open field just across from the Eternal Light Peace Memorial on the Mummasburg Road.

127

THE DAVID SCHRIVER FARM

The Schriver farm is situated two-and-one-half miles northwest of Gettysburg on the Mummasburg Road. The old stone house still sits along the road, but the barn which was just across the road, is no longer standing.

In 1863, this farm consisted of about 150 acres of land. David Schriver and his wife, Susannah or Susan (Hartzel), were both fifty-one years of age at the time of the battle. Their daughter, Mary, had married John S. Forney in 1862. Schriver's father, John, was among the early German settlers of Pennsylvania and had fought in the War of 1812.

Schriver's post-battle damage claim with the state of Pennsylvania testified:

(My) farm was occupied by the rebel army and was held by them until July 5 . . . they established a hospital in and about the house and barn and they had a large number of wounded men there; this hospital was continued after the rebel retreat for about (five) weeks by the Union authorities . . . the buildings and grounds were occupied as a hospital for about a month and were very much abused and damaged.

Schriver received $242.00 for hospital damages from the government.

Dr. J.W.C. O'Neal wrote in 1905 of what might have been one of the first deaths in the Gettysburg campaign:

. . . on June 30, 1863, I got word to go out to Schrivers on the Mummasburg road, that a sick man there

The David Shriver farmhouse in 1987. The barn was located where the photographer is standing.

129

needed attention. I discovered the man to be a dropped Rebel, he couldn't march along and was left behind and had taken quarters in the Shriver barn. . . .

I visited the man . . . , and prescribed for him. He was from New Orleans and was overmarched. He died later and was buried by the roadside.[19]

In his book, Captain Duncan said that Rodes' Confederate division hospital was at this farm. Federal records indicate that eight hundred wounded were found there. General Rodes himself, reported that he left one-half of his wounded, about 760 men with four surgeons, six assistants, ninety-seven attendants, and ten days' rations. From the identified burials listed there in 1866, it is possible that this was O'Neal's brigade hospital. Eleven remains were found there in the 1870s, but only five of the graves were still marked.

A Christian Commission agent remarked after a long visit to the Confederate hospitals around Gettysburg:

At Shrivers barn a lad 21 years of age was pointed out by the surgeon as one who could not live but a day or so. After conversing and praying with him, we wrote for him—'Remember me to all at home; I hope to see the little ones.' Such was the condition of filth that we had to stand on a rail.

THE JACOB HANKEY FARM

In 1863 this was a large farm, with over 230 acres. It was operated by the heirs of Jacob, very possibly his son, P.D.W. Hankey. Originally from Baltimore County, Maryland, Jacob was married to Elizabeth Schriver. He was not only a farmer, but also a cattle dealer and drover. The Hankeys had eight children, with P.D.W. being the eldest. Jacob died in March of 1860, the year that Elizabeth celebrated her fifty-third birthday.

The farm, which was located along both sides of the Mummasburg Road, stood just one-quarter mile northwest of the Schriver place. It, too, was an important field hospital of Rodes' division, which in 1866, showed a very high number of burials, among which were thirty-nine identified Confederate gravesites.

On July 1, Dr. Charles Krauth and his family were forced out of their house at the Lutheran Theological Seminary by the wounded who were brought in. The family left, and after spending the night nearby, "walked on to Mr. Hankey's farm on the Mummasburg road, where they got some breakfast, the first

The Jacob Hankey farm in 1987. The house is postwar.

The well which was once part of the original Hankey front porch, in 1988.

food they had eaten since Wednesday breakfast in their own home." Their story continued:

The Hankey's fed and housed thirty or more neighbors during those battle days and afterwards had on their farm a hospital of one thousand wounded Confederates for some weeks for whom they were compelled to supply milk and bake bread of their own flour and made full use of their own crops and all their farm produce. . . .[20]

Confederate Major Charles Blacknall, 23rd North Carolina Infantry, recalled an experience at this farm. Blacknall had been wounded in the mouth and was first taken to the Forney farm, but soon reached . . .

the house of Mr. P.W.B. Hankey (sic) which stood on . . . the Mummasburg road about a mile further

130

out. Col. Christie,* Lieut. Col. Johnston and other wounded officers of the 23rd reached this house about the same time.

Here they lay till the retreat begun. The place is well remembered from the fact that there was a well on the front porch. The demand for drinking water was so much greater than the supply. . . . The well in the Hankey porch was soon pumped dry by thirsty soldiers. But still they came working the pump, jarring the house and adding to the tortures of the suffering officers inside. . . .

Finally Blacknall placed a soldier named Coghill to guard the pump. Still, Coghill almost had to bayonet the eager and thirsty men to keep them away from the well until it filled up again.[21]

A unidentified black servantmaid who worked for a "Mrs. Hartsell" on the Chambersburg Pike, said that when the battle began,

> some one came and told us we must get out of there and go across the fields to another house. That house was Dave Hankey's (P.D.W.). His place was thronged with Rebels . . .
>
> We got down in the cellar. Up in the kitchen was a sick officer, and he wanted (us) to come up out of the cellar to take care of him and do some cooking, and he promised (we) should be well treated. Mr. Hankey says to him, 'Would you see a colored person protected if she was to help with the work here?' He said he would . . . The officer must have been pretty sick . . . I (didn't) know what was the matter with him, but he just lay on the broad of his back. I had to comb his head, wash his face, and take off his shoes and stockings. We stayed up all night doing nothing but cook and bake for the Rebels. . . .
>
> By morning we were pretty near dead. There was no chance to sleep, and I couldn't have slept anyway for hearing the miserable wounded men hollering and going on out in the yard and in the barn and other buildings. They moaned and cried and went on terribly. 'Oh! take me home to my parents,' they'd say.[22]

Dr. Hayes was in charge of Rodes' division hospitals, with eight hundred patients reported in late July of 1863.

The original Hankey farmhouse is long gone, the barn, however, is in excellent condition. The pump, which was part of the porch of the house, is still visible along the road in front of the new house.

*Colonel Daniel H. Christie died July 17.

THE "GROVE"

Just north of Hankey's farm was a site marked on the July, 1863, Sanitary Commission hospital map as "GROVE." It was not the name of a farm, and evidently meant that a Confederate hospital was situated there in a grove of trees. I have no doubt that this particular hospital existed—in fact it is so typical of Southern descriptions of their field hospitals in the Gettysburg area, and, the map has been accurate in all other locations for Union and Confederate medical facilities. Therefore, I have attempted to find the corresponding place on the actual terrain, and came up with the tree copse seen in the photograph from studying a U.S. Geological Survey topographical map and from actually visiting the area. It is very possible that the Rebels had a hospital somewhere within this view taken along Russell Tavern Road.

The "grove," a possible Confederate hospital, north of the Hankey farm. The trees in the distance stand on the original site.

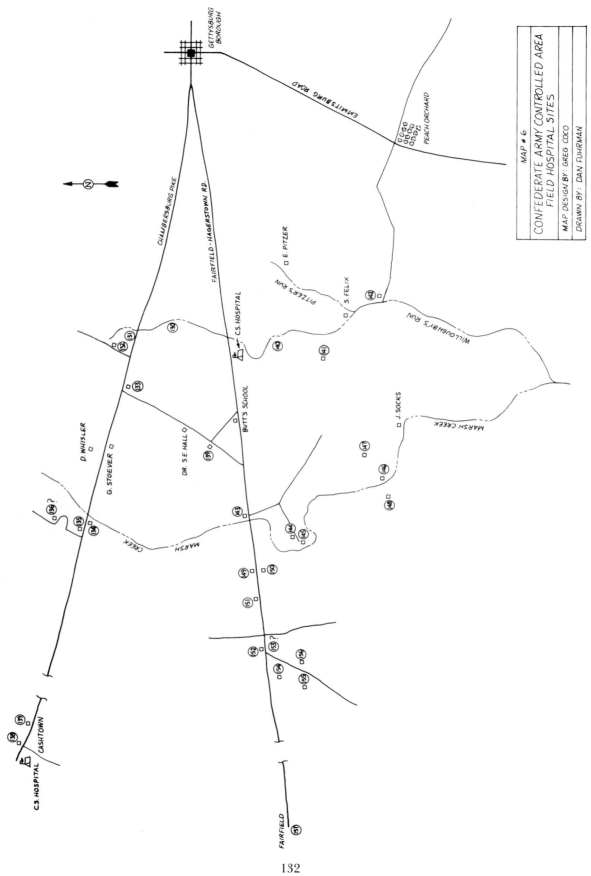

MAP # 6

CONFEDERATE ARMY CONTROLLED AREA
FIELD HOSPITAL SITES

MAP DESIGN BY: GREG COCO

DRAWN BY: DAN FUHRMAN

GETTYSBURG BOROUGH

EMMITSBURG ROAD

PEACH ORCHARD

CHAMBERSBURG PIKE

FAIRFIELD - HAGERSTOWN RD.

E. PITZER

PITZER'S RUN

S. FELIX

C.S. HOSPITAL

WILLOUGHBY'S RUN

D. WHISLER

G. STOEVER

DR. S.E. HALL

BUTT'S SCHOOL

J. SOCKS

MARSH CREEK

MARSH CREEK

FAIRFIELD

C.S. HOSPITAL

CASHTOWN

132

CONFEDERATE "HOSPITAL WOODS" ON WILLOUGHBY'S RUN

This site, located south of the Chambersburg Pike along Willoughby's Run, originated out of the natural medical tendency to establish a depot or collecting point for the wounded in the immediate rear of an army's battle lines. Due to the surprise of the July 1 combat, and the lack of preparation, injured soldiers were simply carried or walked to this convenient spot in the rear of Confederate-held territory. It had shade, was somewhat sheltered, and had water from the small stream and a natural spring nearby. Although little in the way of first-hand accounts exist, the place must have been filled for awhile, with wounded waiting for their chance at transportation to a division hospital.

Surgeon LeGrand J. Wilson, 42nd Mississippi Infantry, was one of the first medical people to record the use of this place or at least a similar site. In his memoirs, he stated that as the Confederate skirmishers advanced over Willoughby's Run, he found cool, fresh water in this brook and, "established my field hospital under some trees, and ordered my litter corps to bring the wounded to that place." Wilson added:

"Up to this time, only three men had been wounded, but they rapidly increased to more than forty." Later, he mentioned that some Federal wounded were also carried to this station.[23]

Amanda E. Reinecker, a twenty-two-year-old Gettysburg resident, went along with her aunt "to this field hospital in the woods at the natural springs park where both worked (July 2 and 3) until exhausted to

The spring area along Willoughby's Run in 1987.

alleviate pain and dress the wounds of the injured."[24]

This wooded spot was probably used for only a few days until the wounded could be moved to permanent field hospitals.

131

THE JOHN CRIST FARM

John Crist's farm was probably situated along the Chambersburg Pike, because in his claim, Crist stated that he lived adjacent to Abraham Spangler's farm, which was on the pike, four hundred yards southeast of Herr's Tavern in 1863. That would place John's farm just south or at least in the vicinity of Michael's, which is listed next. It was 125 acres in size and had been purchased early in the year 1863.

John Crist went on to say that his farm in Cumberland Township was used as a Rebel hospital, and there was damage done to the barn and the area around it.

Five identified Confederate burials were noted on this farm in 1866.

The "mineral springs" along Willoughby's Run, which was a temporary Confederate field hospital. (A.C.H.S.)

THE MICHAEL CRIST FARM

132

Michael and John Christ were probably relatives. Michael's farm was located north of the Chambersburg Pike along Willoughby's Run and about 250 yards northeast of the old Herr Tavern and on the present Herr's Ridge Road. The stone house and large barn were in excellent condition when photographed in 1987. The original estate was 141 acres, and like John's, had been bought a few months prior to the battle.

Duncan, in his 1915(?) book on the Medical Department, said that one of Early's brigade hospitals was at "a stone house 200 yards north of the Chambersburg Pike. (Colonel) Roy Stone of the Bucktail Brigade was taken there when wounded and captured." This *seems* unlikely since Early did most of his fighting *east* of Gettysburg. However, the burials of John Crist's farm were all from Early's division. So it is obvious that the John and Michael Christ farms were confused by either Duncan or on the burial roster.

Crist's damage claim stated that his house and barn were used as a Rebel hospital. He said that John Q. Allewelt lived with him and when the Rebels came, Allewelt left with the farm's horses for a safer place. Crist also noted that his farm was on the battlefield of July 1, and within Rebel lines. He reported that his family left, but he remained behind.

The farm suffered the loss of fencing and crops, and the buildings were damaged.

Two burials were listed, one Georgia soldier, and one 13th North Carolina enlisted man. This burial indicates a possible hospital of Scale's brigade of Pender's division.

The Michael Crist farmhouse in 1987.

The Michael Crist barn in 1987.

FREDERICK HERR'S TAVERN AND FARM

133

Prior to 1857, this tavern may have been known as the "Redding House." In 1863, Frederick Herr owned a ninety-five-acre farm at this site. There is little or no evidence that this place was a field hospital, however, six Confederate burials were noted here from the 11th and 26th North Carolina and the 33rd Virginia Infantry regiments. Also, bloodstains could be seen on the upstairs floor as late as 1986.

One visitor to the tavern in early July of 1863 did not notice a hospital, but said:

> Near us was a brick tavern, and in this tavern a company of soldiers put up after the battle. We used water from the tavern well, but it got so ugly and smelt so bad we could hardly drink it. The soldiers were sick, and we were sick. They thought there were dead frogs down in the well, and so one day they pumped and pumped to clear it out, and by and by here comes up a little piece of a wrist and thumb . . . now that they knew what was the matter there was a lot of gagging done among them. . . .[25]

Tax records for 1863 show that Frederick Herr also owned a house on West Middle Street in Gettysburg.

Also in this site analysis, I shall take the opportunity to deal with several other possible hospital locations.

While searching through some old files at the Adams County Historical Society, notations were discovered that the G. Stoever house on the south side of the Chambersburg Pike, which was just to the northwest of Herr's, was used as a hospital for Heth's divi-

Frederick Herr's tavern in 1987.

The David Whisler farm site in 1988.

sion from July 1 to July 4. This file mentioned that the Daniel Polly, C. Schultz and David Whisler houses were "used by the Confederates." It did not say used as hospitals. In fact, the Polly damage claim filed in 1868 by his son, Charles B. Polly, does not mention a hospital on the premises.

The three homesteads mentioned above were just northwest of Herr's but on the north side of the Pike. Captain Duncan did record in his book that, "General Trimble, when wounded, was taken to the house of David Whistler, north of the pike, which makes it appear that this place was the headquarters of (Pender's Division) hospitals." No burials were noted on any of these last four properties.

Although the David Whisler farmhouse and barn no longer stand, in 1880 the place was described as having a two-story weatherboarded dwelling and a large log weatherboarded barn. There were also other outbuildings and an orchard on the property.

One other house used as an aid station in this lo-

cality, was that of a widow, Mary Jane Buser, who lived two miles west of Gettysburg on the Chambersburg Pike. She had two children, and stated in her claim that on July 1, "was obliged to leave because of the battle raging around the place." A witness for her, Mr. George W. Erb, said that her house was used for the wounded. Unfortunately, neither the 1858 or 1872 Adams County maps, or any of the battlefield maps indicate where she lived. It is possible she was a tenant on one of the small farms along this part of the Pike.

THE SAMUEL LOHR FARM

134

A history of Adams County published in 1886 noted that, "Samuel Loahr (the older spelling) was born in Gettysburg, the son of Jacob and Catherine (Ziegler) Loahr, (and) afterwards lived on a farm from which the first cannon was fired, in front of (his) house, at the beginning of the battle of Gettysburg."

The site of this historic shot, and the farm of "Major" Samuel Lohr is along the Chambersburg Pike about one-quarter mile northwest of the crossing over Marsh Creek. The house sits on the south side of the Pike. Unfortunately, this large and beautiful solid log structure was partially burned down some time around 1982. Prior to that disastrous fire, the logs, encased in wide original clapboards, were in excellent condition, as was the whole building. Just in rear of the main house stands a dilapidated stone outbuilding which was probably the springhouse. The barn on the site today, however, is a more modern replacement.

In 1863, Lohr, who had a son, Aaron, in the 21st Pennsylvania Cavalry, farmed 126 acres in Franklin Township. His property became a large hospital of General Henry Heth's division of Hill's Third Corps. The twenty-nine identified burials on the land around his place indicated that all four of Heth's brigades transported at least some of their wounded to Lohr's farm. Three accounts, one from the 26th North Carolina and two from the 42nd Mississippi, do describe, in part, the activity around this important site.

Chaplain T.D. Witherspoon of the 42nd, wrote on January 5, 1864, to J.W. Phillips, that he spent time in a hospital on the Chambersburg Pike in which Dr. Ward, Surgeon, 11th Mississippi, and Dr. Green, Surgeon, 55th North Carolina, performed amputations. Witherspoon, writing about the death of Phillips' brother (R.S. Phillips) said:

The Samuel Lohr farmhouse in 1987. The spring-house still stands in rear of the house.

The Samuel Lohr farm, looking west on the Chambersburg Pike in 1987.

I was absent from the hospital at the time and as soon as I came back hastened to see him. When I arrived he was speechless and in a short time afterwards sank gently and quietly into the arms of death. We buried him near our hospital by the side of Lieutenant George H. Howze and many others of our brave comrades . . .

In a memoir written in 1880, Witherspoon recalled:

On the evening of the 4th of July, 1863 . . . I found myself in the midst of three or four hundred men of the brigade (Davis') . . . who were too severely wounded to be transported to (Virginia). (I) then turned to the tenderest and saddest ministry of my life, as under open skies, on the bare ground, or a mere pile of straw, these gallant men lay heroically suffering or unconsciously moaning their lives away. For a few . . . days this ministry was permitted me, and then our field-hospital was broken up, the few surviving wounded were removed to the field hospitals of the Federal army, and the Confederate surgeons and chaplains transported to Northern prisons.[26]

Howze's grave was mentioned as being interred on the Lohr farm. Evidently, Phillips' grave lost its identification and was one of the unknown on that site in 1866.

After seeing to the burial of the dead soldiers of his unit on July 1, Surgeon L.J. Wilson, 42nd Mississippi Infantry, wrote that,

It was midnight before we finished our sad task, and turned our weary steps toward the division hospital. Among the dead of the 42nd Miss regiment was my own nephew, Lieut. George Advin Howze, who was shot in the advance upon the enemy in the morning, or about noon. His faithful servant . . . found his body, and carried it back to the hospital for burial.

July 2d . . . Drs. Hubbard and Ward both kindly

proffered all the assistance they could render, and by dark I had all the wounded in pretty good condition. . . . Longstreets corps passed our hospital about noon . . .

(On July 4) Early morning found me back at the hospital, where we were busy all day, performing necessary operations, and re-dressing the wounds of the first day's fight.[27]

Julius A. Leinbach, 26th North Carolina Infantry, was a member of the band of that regiment and performed his duty at a hospital in rear of the battle lines of July 1 and along the Chambersburg Pike. Around the turn of the century he wrote:

It was with heavy hearts that we went about caring for the wounded. We worked until 11 o'clock that night, when I was so thoroughly worn out that I could do no more and lay down for some rest. At 3 o'clock I was up again and at work. The second day our regiment was not engaged, but were busily occupied all day in our sad tasks . . . Dr. Warren sent . . . a note to the commanding officer of the brigade, that we could not be spared from attending to the wounded men.

Later, Leinbach and the regimental band were ordered to play for a while near the front lines. He described his return from that duty:

We got back to camp after dark (July 2) and found many men in need of our attention. Some of those whom we had tried to care for during the day had died during our absence.

. . . we got plenty of cool water, which the poor wounded men wanted constantly. We continued our administrations until late at night and early next morning.[28]

In 1868, Samuel Lohr filed a damage claim with

136

Surgeon LeGrand J. Wilson.

the state of Pennsylvania in which he stated:

(My) farm and buildings . . . were occupied by the rebel army . . . for a hospital—a large number of wounded men and other portions of their army were there, and after the rebels retreated the hospital was continued several weeks . . . the House and Barn and out-buildings were all occupied and much damaged and the family had to leave and did not get possession of these buildings until the first of September.

Lohr also said that $400 would repair the barn, and that the house had to be repainted and wallpapered.

Dr. Spencer G. Welch, a surgeon in the 13th South Carolina Infantry, (Pender's division) was working near the Lohr farm. He wrote the following to his wife on August 2:

When I arrived at the hospital* (the evening of July 1) my ears were greeted as usual at such time with the moans and cries of the wounded. I went to work and did not pretend to rest until next morning after daylight. I found that Longstreet had come and that McLaw's Division of his corps was encamped near the hospital. Kershaw's Brigade was almost in the hospital grounds.[29]

A good description of the hospital near Lohr's was penned in 1899 by D.A. Dickert, who had been a member of Kershaw's brigade during the battle. Marching from Chambersburg toward Gettysburg, his brigade arrived near the farm very early in the morning of July 2.

*The division hospitals of Pender and Heth were in the same area.

About three o'clock at night, when we had reached the summit of an eminence, we saw in the plain before us a great sea of white tents, silent and still, with here and there a groan, or a surgeon passing from one tent to another relieving the pain of some poor mortal who had fallen in battle on the morning of the day before. We had come upon the field hospital of Hill where he had his wounded. . . . I heard here of the desperate wounding of an old friend and school mate, Lieutenant W.L. Leitsey,** and left the ranks long enough to hunt him up in one of the many tents to the left.[30]

**Records show a Lt. D.M. Leitzey, 13th S.C. Infantry was wounded on July 1. He died soon afterwards.

135

THE ANDREW HEINTZELMAN FARM AND TAVERN

Just about one-quarter mile northwest of the Lohr farm and on the north side of the Pike, in the village of Seven Stars, there was a tavern and an eighty-two-acre farm operated by the Heintzelman family, which consisted of Andrew, his wife, Elizabeth (Arnold), and his son, William. In 1856, the tavern was said to cater to railroad construction men who were building the bed for the continuation of the Hanover Junction, Hanover and Gettysburg Railroad. The tavern had been in operation there since about 1826, and went under, "the Sign of Seven Stars."

In 1846, Mr. Heintzelman was elected a county commissioner and in 1861, he was the postmaster at Seven Stars.

An 1863 Sanitary Commission map, mentioned sev-

The Andrew Heintzelman tavern on the Cashtown Road at Seven Stars—where the gas pump is located.

eral times in this book, listed this tavern on the Pike as the hospital of "Porcher's" division. This may have been Pickett's or Pender's division. Heintzelman's damage claim stated:

". . . the house and barn occupied about 10 days after the battle as a rebel hospital. The farm was four miles west of Gettysburg on the Cashtown Pike, my neighbors were Israel Little and C. Dougherty."

(On the 1858 Adams County map, the farm is shown just northeast of the tavern establishment, which was on the pike.)

THE CHRISTIAN SHANK FARM
136

The Shank farmhouse was located on the crossroad which runs between Seven Stars and Mummasburg, now called the Crooked Creek Road. A "C. Shank" was shown on the north side of the Pike, as the first building you approached as you entered the village. This was possibly Christian Shank. Another Shank, John, lived nearby on ninety-four acres and ran a sawmill on an adjacent creek. In 1863, the farm consisted of at least three hundred acres. Mr. Shank's claim recalled:

The rebels overran and ravaged the neighborhood from June 19 to July 6. The Confederates camped in (my) fields and the buildings . . . were used by the Rebels for Hospital purposes for about two weeks and the damage done to said buildings amounted to two hundred dollars. They took weatherboarding off when (the barn and outbuildings) were used as hospitals

This stone house is possibly the Christian Shank farm. (1987)

and so damaged buildings. (Also) granaries were torn down.

As with so many of these places, no other eyewitness accounts are available at this time.

A neighbor, Daniel Shank, who lived south of Christian Shank, and west of Heintzelman, said in his claim:

". . . (my) residence was within 4 1/2 miles from Gettysburg (in Franklin Township). The rebels camped on an adjoining farm and established a hospital there." The "adjoining farm" could have been either of these sites which were definitely field hospitals.

THE ELIZABETH MICKLEY FARM
137

The Mickley farm was the second *farm* on the right as you entered Cashtown on the old pike from Gettysburg. It was two buildings past Isaac Rife's property, which was the first farm on the right as you enter the town from the east.

Mrs. Elizabeth Mickley, the widow of Israel Mickley, filed a damage claim stating that she lost "wheat, fencing, wood, hay, and corn fodder. There was damage done to the barn by being used for hospital purposes by the rebels for two weeks." One other source mentioned that her barn was used by the Confederates as a hospital.

Two burials were noted nearby, a Lieutenant of the 7th South Carolina Infantry and a soldier of the 47th

The Mickley and Rife farms were located north of the Cashtown road along here.

North Carolina Infantry. These burials were listed on the Isaac Rife farm in Cashtown, which may indicate that the Rife farm, as well as the Mickley place, was a small Confederate hospital. However, neither Isaac Rife Sr., nor his son, made note of hospital damages in their post-battle claims.

THE DR. WILLIAM C. STEM HOUSE AND OTHER CASH-TOWN AREA HOSPITALS

138

It stands to reason, that Cashtown, Pennsylvania, like Fairfield, should have become an important hospital area and collecting point for many of the Confederate wounded. Lee's army marched through there going to and from Gettysburg, and camped in both places. However, that does not seem to be the case. Most wounded were taken care of much closer to the battlefield in the various division field hospitals. In fact, I have had difficulty locating more than a few hospitals in the Cashtown or Fairfield areas.

One of the best documented accounts is of Dr. Stem's one-acre property in Cashtown. Both the 1858 and 1872 maps of that borough show Dr. Stem's stone house and lot situated on the old pike in the town, at the junction of what is today the Orrtanna Road. The house was built about 1826. Dr. Stem, thirty-nine, was married to Eliza Watson and they had two children.

His damage claim stated:

> The Rebel General Heath (sic) and staff, a division officer of the advance of Lee's army took possession of the premises of Dr. William C. Stem and pitched their tents in his lot upon the 29th day of June 1863

and remained in full possession. They were also in possession of the said Dr. . . . Stems office (as they had their sick and wounded in it) until the night of the 4th of July when the Army was in full retreat. . . .

Stem claimed many stolen and damaged items, including medicines, such as chloroform, ether, morphine, alcohol, and sulfur.

An Adams County history published in 1886 gives additional information on the Stem property. It reads:

> During the Rebellion, the quartermaster and clerks of Hill's division, with Gen. Heathe (sic) in command, were encamped on the Doctor's lot, while the headquarters of Gen. R.E. Lee were in the adjoining field. On Thursday, while the battle of Gettysburg was in progress, Gen. Lee came with his staff, and they pitched their tents in the field adjoining our subject's place, at about 11 o'clock, and then Gen. Longstreet with his staff came about a quarter to twelve, visiting Gen. Lee, and all moved away toward Gettysburg about half an hour after. . . . The Doctor's office was full of wounded Confederates after the battle, and both he and his wife did all in their power to make them comfortable, being charitable alike to both friend and foe.[31]

Dr. J.W.C. O'Neal, the physician who had recently moved to Gettysburg from Baltimore, was at Marsh Creek on June 30. He wrote about his experiences with the Confederates:

> There I met a Dr. Montgomery, (Archer's brigade), who had known me in Baltimore. He was in . . . the rebel army . . . and I was very glad to see him. He took charge of me and we fell back to Cashtown. This was between 10 and 12 o'clock and on the way we met . . . (more) confederates.
>
> At Cashtown I proposed to Dr. Spence. Div. Surgeon and Dr. Montgomery his assistance to go back

Dr. Stem's house about 1880. General Lee made his headquarters nearby. (Mildred Bucher)

Henry Mickley's house across from Flohr's Church in 1988.

with me to Mrs. Bough's for dinner. We went there and got dinner. They brought me back to Cashtown toward evening and we stopped at the home of Dr. Stem.

In the yard of Dr. Stem the General in Command had encamped. . . .

(The next morning) I went and sat on Dr. Stem's porch and watched the different detachments of the Rebel army pass. I remained at the Stem house July 1 until the first cannon sounded in the advance. . . .

(Later that day) On the road I encountered a Gen. Stuart (sic) (Gen. Geo. H. Steuart's father), a hanger-on to the . . . Confederate commands, who was making his way to Baltimore, where he had been in command of Maryland militia previous to the war. . . .

(We) rode down the pike until we came to the church right above McKnightstown. There Gen. Stuart—an old man—said he was tired and required rest. I called old Mr. (Henry) Mickley who then resided in a brick house opposite the church, and stated that the General would like to rest. Mickley was glad to entertain him for the reason that Stuart would be some protection to his property.[32]

It is an interesting fact that on the second floor of the Henry Mickley house is an old cypress-wood door which was damaged by shell fire during the Red River Campaign in 1864. Coincidentally, a second door, also from the same Louisiana house and damaged likewise, is in the "N.G. Wilson House" (c. 1869) in Bendersville, Pennsylvania.

Several sources name Cashtown as a place where several hospitals were established. For instance, the 1863 Sanitary Commission map placed a hospital near the hotel which was owned by Jacob Mickley in 1863. Mickley said later that "the entire force under Lee . . . passed within 20 feet of my barroom." The hotel had been in operation since about 1815 when it was owned by Peter Mark, son of Nicholas Mark, who built the house which is in this book, as the Daniel Sheaffer farm (Site #92).

Surgeon R.P. Myers, 16th Georgia Infantry, wrote simply in his diary on July 5: "The wounded left at Cashtown." And a soldier, C.C. Cummings, 17th Mississippi Infantry, stated in 1916: ". . . Chester Hospital . . . seemed like a fairy scene compared to the rough barn where I lay (wounded) at Cashtown, eight miles from the Gettysburg battlefield, awaiting my turn to be cared for." Evidently, according to these two accounts, Cashtown was the site of one of McLaws' division hospitals.[33]

The Sanitary Commission Report on the Campaign, written in August of 1863, stated that Dr. Wilson was in charge of the Cashtown hospitals, and he cared for 171 Confederate wounded.

THE ADAM BUTT FARM AND SCHOOLHOUSE

On the 1858 Adams County map, this farm is shown as belonging to Samuel Herbst, who, in 1863 farmed 180 acres in Cumberland Township. Also, the 1863 Sanitary Commission Gettysburg Hospitals map listed Herbst on this location as a Confederate hospital site. However, several other references to this site, including 1863–1866 burial lists, indicate the farm's owner was Adam Butt. There is a possibility that Herbst occupied the farm until some time around July of 1863 when Butt purchased it. Butt's acreage in 1863 totaled 124. He was fifty-three-years-old and lived with his wife, Nancy, and their four children. He listed his occupation in 1860 as "carpenter."

Today, the farm sits along Herr's Ridge Road between Marsh Creek and Willoughby's Run, just northwest of the Fairfield Road. The old "Butt Schoolhouse"* stands just about five hundred yards southeast of the farm and also along this road. Both of these locations were hospitals of Anderson's division, which included Wilcox and Wright's brigades. Burials for the Herbst/Butt property show six identified Union and thirty-eight Confederates. (Seven of the latter were buried near the school.)

In his 1868 damage claim, Adam Butt stated that his farm "was used by the rebels for hospital purposes for five to six weeks," and he mentioned that because he was ill during the battle, he stayed at another house nearby.

Captain Duncan said that, "The hospitals of (Anderson's) division were near the house of Adam

*As with many Adams County "one-room" schools, this building may not date back to the Civil War years.

The Adam Butt farm in 1987.

Butt's Schoolhouse or site in 1987, along the Fairfield Road.

Butt. . . . This division reported 1,128 wounded and 840 missing, many of whom were probably killed or wounded. The wounded from this division seem to have been taken to Fairfield, as but 111 were left in the hospitals on the field. Dr. Miner was in charge."

Dr. J.W.C. O'Neal, in one of his medical notebooks has a notation that, "Wilcox and Wright's Brigade Hospital at Butt's Schoolhouse, Minor Surgeon."

Dr. H.A. Minor was a surgeon in the 8th Alabama Infantry.

Just one-half mile northeast of Butt's house was the 138-acre farm of Dr. Samuel E. Hall. He had set up practice here in about 1837 after moving from East Berlin, Pennsylvania. Hall's claim does not list his home as a hospital, but it is possible he cared for some wounded there, as two burials were listed on his farm, both from the 52nd North Carolina Infantry (Pettigrew's brigade). He did mention, however, that the, "trains of the C.S. Army" camped on his place. After the war, Hall, sixty-seven, and his wife, Ellen, moved out west.

A stone house, somewhat larger than Hall's 1863 residence, now occupies the site, which is owned today by the Barnes family.

THE GEORGE CULP FARM

140

In 1863, George Culp lived about three-and-one-half miles southwest of Gettysburg and just about one mile south of the Fairfield Road, along the west side of Willoughby's Run. He had a son, George R. Culp,

who filed a damage claim in 1868, remarking that, "the farm was in possession of the rebels during the battle, July 1–5, and they used the house and farm as a field hospital."

Today the entire farm, buildings and all, is only a memory, with just a temporary hospital marker to indicate the site. Since a very large division hospital was set up nearby at the Plank estate, Culp's was very likely used in conjunction with that farm. Incidentally, the only hospital actually indicated on a map in the U.S. Government's Gettysburg Volumes of the Official Records of the War of the Rebellion is in this particular area. On page 486 of Volume XXVII, Part 1, the map marks a group of Confederate hospitals along Willoughby's Run, south of the Fairfield Road. This would be very near George Culp's.

The George Culp farm site in 1987.

THE JOHN EDWARD PLANK FARM

141

When Hood's and McLaws' divisions advanced against the Union's Third and Fifth Corps on July 2, they suffered terrible casualties—most of which ended up on several farms a few miles southwest of Gettysburg. One of those sites, and one of the major Confederate hospitals, was located on the estate of J. Edward Plank.

The Plank farm, 220 acres large in 1863, was evidently owned prior to the Civil War by a "M.E. Plank," as on some maps it is shown as the farm of Mrs. M.E. Plank. This Mrs. Plank may have been J. Edward's mother. In 1859, J. Edward married Sarah Rinehart and probably took over the operation of this

The John Edward Plank farmhouse in 1978. (Kathy G. Harrison)

The John Edward Plank farm in 1987.

large farm. J. Edward Plank must have had a long and interesting life. He and Sarah celebrated their fiftieth wedding anniversary in 1909. And in 1917, he died at the age of eighty-one. During the battle, John Edward was twenty-four years old. Sarah was twenty-three and they had two children, Mary and James.

In his physician's notebook, Dr. J.W.C. O'Neal mentioned briefly that, "Hoods Div'n Hospital at Edward Plank's—(Dr.) Means Surgeon." In the Adams County Historical Society there is a surgeon's medical kit with this label:

Presented to Dr. J.W.C. O'Neal by J. Edward Plank Marsh Creek May 1892. After the Battle of Gettysburg the Confederate right opened a hospital at the Plank Farm on Willoughby Run and occupied the farm for a number of weeks. Dr. J.A. (F.A.) Means (11th Georgia Infantry) who was left in charge of Longstreet's wounded, gave this case to Mr. Plank—it was then in fair order . . . this interesting relic was used by Dr. Means and other surgeons quite a number of times at the Battle of Gettysburg!!

Captain Duncan stated in his book:

The hospitals (of Hood's division) were on the W. Plank (sic) farm, about two thirds of a mile southeast of Blackhorse Tavern, and on the road leading from the Fairfield Road to the peach orchard. They were directly behind the division, as were all those of Longstreet's Corps. There were 1,542 wounded in the division and 515 were left behind. Dr. Means was left in charge.

Private W.C. Ward, 4th Alabama Infantry, wrote in 1900:

. . . John Mosely, going forward to his company . . . (fell) mortally wounded. . . . Soon they came to him,

placed him on a stretcher, and carried him to the rear. . . . In the meantime the field surgeon had administered a stimulant and morphine. All night in agony he lay, until about 3 o'clock in the morning, when he, with two others, was placed in an ambulance and carried to the Plant (sic) Farm Hospital, just in rear of the line of battle. The wounded of the division were gathered there, those most severely wounded receiving surgical aid first. . . . (Later) When all had been removed but the helpless, three grand, Christian women from Baltimore came out to the field hospital where the badly wounded of Hood's Division had been gathered.

Ward mentioned that two Gettysburg women also went out to aid these Confederates. They were Mary and Sally Witherow. He said that a wounded comrade was saved by a bottle of "Medeira Wine" brought by these kind ladies.[34]

Elizabeth Plank, who lived at this farm in 1863, recalled:

(This) is a true story of the happenings on a farm about three miles west of Gettysburg, situated on the west bank of Willoughby's Run. The house is a large brick with two large halls, one on the first floor and one on the second, each opening into four large rooms with kitchen off. The family consisted of three small children, parents and an uncle.

(On July 2) . . . an ambulance arrived at the farm house and without any ceremony forced open the front door and carried in a wounded officer and placed him in the guest's room and the best bed in the house. Now, the family hearing the racket and thinking of the baby asleep up-stairs, rushed up, where they were met by several orderlies and doctors who said, 'Now don't be frightened this house will be a hospital and you can expect many wounded men here!' While other men were driving a staple in the ceiling and with a rope and pulleys made a swing for the officer's wounded foot, tearing the sheets and linens into bandages for the emergency. Now it was not long before all the beds were filled with wounded, and the floor covered with straw carried from the barn, all over the floors in the halls on the porches in the out buildings, on the barn floor and every place were wounded men—hauled there in the ambulances, on wagons, gun (carriages) and every way possible, and using the Garner Organ room for a surgical or operating room. Many limbs and arms were amputated and their wounds dressed, while the battle raged. As the horses tired out in the ambulance, they were turned into the wheat and oats field near the house to rest and feed on the growing grain, unfortunately two wounded horses died in the yard back of the house . . . the family . . . were advised to leave their home for awhile. . . .

These wounded soldiers were left at this hospital five or six weeks after the fight. Every morning they buried their dead in shallow graves in the orchard. . . . (When the wounded left) The yard and garden fences were gone, the flower and garden beds were as the mud roads, the poultry, hogs and cattle were consumed for food . . . part of the buildings were burned for camp fires, the floors of the house were strewn with blood caked straw, also the flies and vermin of the dog days. Most of the furniture was out in the fields.[35]

Captain O.H. Miller, 59th Georgia Infantry, wounded on July 2, remembered his stay on this farm:

The wound was a compound fracture of the upper third of my right thigh. I was taken to Hood's division hospital, on John Plank's farm, where there was a surgeon of the Eleventh Georgia. They carried me to a tent, but said it was no use, I would certainly die. *They ordered me to the dead-house where I remained fifteen days.* A young man of my company got a piece of rail and with a shirt tied my leg. When they took me into Plank's house, they said, I would certainly die, and to give me whatever stimulants I would have. After this a surgeon from Gettysburg came and suggested Smith's Anterior and Post-splint, which they applied with success. But in that time my leg had shortened four and a half inches . . . On (the) twelfth of August was taken to the Field General Hospital. . . .[36]

There were sixty-four identified Confederate graves listed at the J. Edward Plank farm in 1866. Almost all of the burials were members of Hood's division.

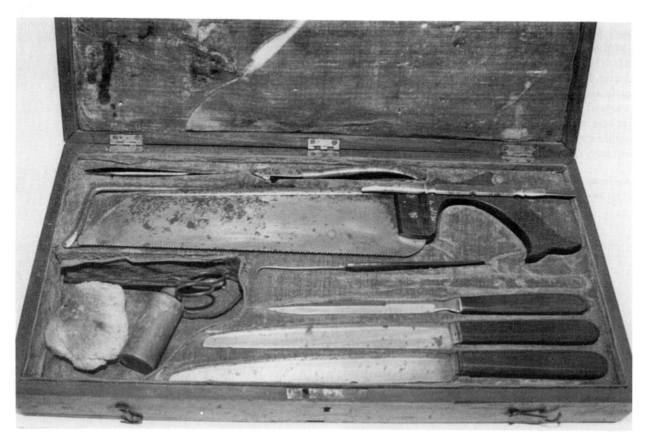

The medical kit used at the John Edward Plank farm by C.S. Surgeon F.A. Means, 11th Georgia Infantry. (Cindy L. Small)

THE PITZER'S SCHOOLHOUSE
AREA

This particular region includes the school as well as several farms nearby, namely John Socks (Sachs), Samuel Pitzer, and S.A. Felix. My reason for this particular combination is due to the lack of any definite sources which mention these sites as hospitals. However, at least twenty-one identified Confederate graves are noted in the area surrounding Samuel Pitzer's, the school, the Socks place, and the Felix farm. So it is more than possible that one or more of these buildings was used, at least temporarily, by some of the many wounded men making their way westward, out of danger, from the fighting on July 2 which took place along the Emmitsburg Road and beyond.

All of these burials commonly mention "near the Felix house" or "in woods near Pitzer Schoolhouse" or "along country road between Pitzer's and Socks," etc. Socks operated a farm and mill nearby and Pitzer farmed about two hundred acres near and including the school.

General John Hood, wounded in the arm by a shrapnel ball on July 2, was taken past this same area, probably to the J.E. Plank farm. John Haskell, a Confederate artilleryman, said of Hood: ". . . (he) reeled and fell from his horse, utterly prostrated and almost fainting. The wound, which was not very severe, seemed to shock him much more than a far more serious one would ordinarily have done. He was not a sensitive or nervous man. . . ."

And later, Captain F.M. Colston said,

As we were waiting there an ambulance came along, and we saw Gen. Hood sitting in front with the driver,

John Sock's farmhouse/mill area in 1987.

his arm in a bloody bandage. . . . Just as he arrived by the schoolhouse, a shell struck the roof almost in his face, but the General merely looked up.

On July 6, during the Confederate retreat, Colonel James Fremantle, a British visitor with the Army of Northern Virginia, noted in his diary:
"I saw General Hood in his carriage. He looked rather bad, and has been suffering a good deal. The doctors seem to doubt whether they will be able to save his arm."[37]

The Socks and Pitzer farms are still standing, whereas the school and Felix buildings have vanished forever.

FRANCIS BREAM'S "BLACK
HORSE" TAVERN AND FARM

Francis Bream was born in 1806 as the second son of Henry Bream. For a few years around 1840, he kept a hotel in Whitestown, the present-day Idaville, Pennsylvania. He was later elected the first sheriff of Adams County. In 1842, Bream married Elizabeth Slaybaugh and during the following fall, purchased the old and well-known Marsh Creek farm and stone "Black Horse" Tavern. It was then the property and home of the William McClellan family, who in 1809, had built a stone bridge over Marsh Creek for $2,500. The farm contained over four hundred acres. The Breams raised eight children, and, the youngest, Robert, took over the homestead when Francis Bream died in 1884.

The Battle of Gettysburg seriously hurt the Bream family's holdings. All of their growing and stored crops were destroyed, along with most of the fencing.

Pitzer's schoolhouse stood on this site in 1863, near where the tree is seen in this 1987 photograph.

Francis Bream's farm and "Black Horse Tavern" is seen across the Marsh Creek bridge as it probably appeared in 1863. (G.N.M.P.)

Every building on the property was a hospital for several weeks during and after the battle. Damages amounted to over $7,000, none of which was ever compensated.

Captain Duncan reported that Pickett's division hospital was "about the Bream House and Blackhorse Tavern, on Marsh Creek. . . . There were more than 1,200 wounded in this division, the majority of whom were taken prisoner. . . . Dr. Reeves was in charge of this hospital, which contained 279 wounded."

Dr. J.W.C. O'Neal, however, recalled a slightly different arrangement: "Pickets div'n Hospital at Curran's house and Bream's Mill—McLaws div'n Hospital at Crawfords, Cunninghams, and Bream's (Tavern)."

The identified graves located around the tavern and farm amounted to about seventy, most of which were from McLaws' division, and a few from Hood's division. Almost all of the graves at the mill or nearby belonged to Pickett's men.

Dr. Simon Baruch, a surgeon of Kershaw's brigade, McLaws' division, left one of the best descriptions of the medical activities around Bream's tavern. On July 2, he said:

All day and all night the work continued at the field hospital, and throughout the following day also the wounded came pouring in, many on foot, among them several captured Union soldiers, on two of whom I operated. . . . At sundown I threw myself on the hay and slept until aroused by an orderly who brought a command from General Lee for Drs. Pearce, Nott, and Baruch to remain at the Black Horse Tavern field hospital 'until further orders.' The morning found us. . . . The slightly wounded had been removed, most of them being able to march. The field hospital contained now two hundred and twenty-two seriously wounded men, ten orderlies, and three surgeons.

Baruch recounted how later on in the afternoon of

July 3, they were sitting down to their first meal, which they took in the orchard. It had been abandoned in the tavern by the fleeing family; suddenly, shells began to fall all around the peaceful scene:

> (Here) were an astonished and disappointed trio of doctors. The wounded began to moan, calling us to come to them. A yellow cloth was hastily fastened to the lightning rod of the barn, and we passed among the wounded to reassure them. . . .

On July 4, Surgeon Baruch and the entire hospital became prisoners of war. He continued:

"Six weeks were spent at this field hospital—weeks replete with interesting ethical and surgical experiences. On the morning of the second day of our captivity I was . . . greeted by . . . Dr. Winslow, of the Christian Commission." Winslow offered food and medical supplies to the Confederates, which were much needed, and were personally picked up in Gettysburg by Baruch himself.

Dr. Baruch also recalled,

> Two young women belonging to a historic Maryland family came to the hospital . . . and remained with us, occupying garret rooms, until the hospital closed. They administered to the wounded, prepared the food and dressings, and read the burial service over those who succumbed. Their services were inestimable. . . .
> When the wounded had been disposed of we were ordered to report to the provost marshal.

Baruch spent several months in the military prison at Fort McHenry until he was exchanged in October of 1863.[38]

Another surgeon who spent time at McLaws' hospital was Dr. Aristides Monteiro who was attached to Alexander's Artillery Battalion of Longstreet's Corps. In his memoirs, Monteiro said that on July 2, he and

Doctor H. Gray, an assistant surgeon of that corps, "rode over to Black Horse Tavern, a two-story building of field stone (which was) once a busy stop off for stagecoaches, located at the crossing of Marsh Creek and Fairfield Road."

At the tavern they found the medical director of Longstreet's Corps, Surgeon J.S. Dorsey Cullen, who was directing cooks, hospital stewards, and nurses in their various duties. Later that afternoon, Monteiro and Gray went forward and set up an aid station close to the fighting where they worked for several hours. At dusk, he and Gray returned to the tavern now easily identified,

> by the yellow flag waving over it. The wounded appeared to be everywhere. They lay on blankets or on the bare ground; some were waiting their turn at the operating tables. A few screamed in their delirium, calling for their wives, sweethearts, or mothers. Others in shock were quiet and pale. The critically wounded . . . had been placed to one side. . . .
> At the operating section makeshift tables had been hastily set up. Some were made of doors laid across barrels. The surgeons (looked like) butchers, with their blood-spattered white shirts and navy trousers. At their feet were dark clots of blood mingled with the dirt. To one side lay a pile of amputated, mangled limbs, stacked like cordwood.[39]

Monteiro noticed many surgeons, "cutting and sawing through skin, muscle, and bone, then cauterizing the stump with a searing hot iron, not ligating or tying the arteries. . . . Swarms of big green horseflies were everywhere, biting into the open wounds, and the air was filled with the sickening odor of burning flesh."

Monteiro operated all during the nights of July 2 and 3. On July 4, he began the march to Virginia with the retreating army.[40]

Francis Bream's tavern in the 1880s. (G.N.M.P.)

Francis Bream's farmhouse and tavern in 1987.

Rev. Gordon Winslow, courtesy of Henry Deeks.

Francis Bream's barn in 1987.

An Austrian captain, Fitzgerald Ross, visiting with the Confederate Army in 1863, wrote in 1865 of his experiences:

> (On July 4) I . . . rode off to see General Lee, and when he returned, told us that a retreat had been decided on. We were kept a long time at the cottage of a silly old Dutchman, by a heavy downfall of rain, and then went to Bream's tavern on the road to Fairfield. . . .
>
> Bream's tavern, house, stables, barn and every outbuilding were full of wounded men, some of whom were being moved into the ambulances, and others more badly wounded were being removed to the better accommodation left thereby vacant.
>
> It was a grievous sight to see these fine young fellows, many of them probably crippled for life. . . . Many were to be left behind, too severely wounded to bear removal. . . .
>
> For a time the yard in front of Bream's tavern seemed a regular rendezvous for generals and their staff-officers, and all who passed stopped on their way and entered into conversation. Here I met General J.E.B. Stuart for the first time, and was introduced to him, and to many others too numerous to name.[41]

As this is written, the old Bream farm/tavern is in excellent preservation. The huge barn, which may partially be a replacement, was once known as the largest barn in Adams County. Farmland still mostly surrounds the site—however, the "historical" era of this farm is about over. Across the Fairfield Road toward Marsh Creek, housing developments are beginning to appear. And sadly, the family who until recently farmed much of the old Bream property, now has 198 acres up for sale. The advertisement, in part, reads: "Out buildings on property. Potential development land."

The banks of Marsh Creek in 1987, looking south, which was part of this large Confederate hospital.

144

THE JOHN F. CURRENS FARM

As was noted in the last site, Dr. O'Neal mentioned that a portion of Pickett's division's hospital was located at the Currens farm. The farm consisted of 105 acres in 1863; the house sat about four hundred feet northeast of Bream's Mill, and was described, in 1853, as a two-story log structure. John Currens was thirty-six years of age that year. His family consisted of Elizabeth, thirty-three, and two young children.

In 1868, when Mr. Currens drew up a claim for damages suffered during the Gettysburg campaign, he noted that he was a "neighbor of John Cunningham; and William E. Meyer (sic) with mill on Marsh Creek lived near by." Currens also reported that there were five hundred panels of snake fence destroyed, and damage was done to his orchard, grain crops, house and barn. He repeated that, "a hospital was on the grounds."

In 1988 both house and barn, if they are the originals, are in fine condition.

John F. Curren's farmhouse and barn in 1987.

BREAM'S MILL AND THE WILLIAM E. MYERS HOUSE

145

About 1845, Francis Bream bought this mill, called "Mineral Mills," which adjoined his land on the southwest. On the site was a large three-story flouring-mill, a sawmill and two sets of buildings, all situated on seventy acres of land. Contrarily, the mill was reported to have been built about 1850 by Robert Cobean; this according to a Gettysburg newspaper article written in 1896, the same year the mill was destroyed by fire.

During the Civil War, twenty-seven-year-old William E. Myers occupied the property as the Master Miller. He lived in a two-story log dwelling with a stone building attached in the rear. There was also a cooper shop and blacksmith shop on the premises, as well as an orchard and a mineral springs.

Captain Duncan reported that a hospital was at the Myer's house, however, he said it was Early's division, which is probably incorrect. He also stated that, "General Kemper, shot through the breast, was left at Bream's Mill." This is correct. Another source, Sergeant D.E. Johnston, 7th Virginia Infantry, who was wounded in "Pickett's Charge," later recalled:

General James L. Kemper. (MOLLUS-MASS)

About dark I was removed by ambulance to the shed of a farmer's barn, a mile or more away . . . to the place where General Kemper had been removed, the farmer placing him in his dwelling house. I visited the same house 22 years later, where I saw distinctly the stains of Gen. Kemper's blood on the floor. The shed in which I was placed was filled with the wounded and dying. Throughout that long night and until a little before dawn, I spoke to no one, and no one to me, never closed my eyes in sleep; the surgeons close by being engaged in removing the limbs of those that needed to be amputated, and all night long I heard nothing but the cries of the wounded and the groans of the dying, the agonies of General Kemper, who lay near by, being frequently heard . . . Comrade Grubb was very kind to me preparing for me a day or two later a bed and shelter in the orchard, to which I was removed. . . . During the morning of Sunday (July 5) many of our wounded men were brought in, among them Capt. John H. Parr, adj. of the 7th regt., and Lt. Lewis Bane of the 24th regt. Some of these wounded men died during the day. During Sunday night and the following day the Confederate army was withdrawing from the field. Our brigade surgeon, Dr. Morton, and General Early made visits to the field hospital, urging all the men able to ride in wagons to go. . . . Shortly after the Confederate rear guard had passed the field hospital where I was, the Federal advance guard appeared, the Federal surgeons taking charge of us.[42]

On July 27, 1863, the *Gettysburg Compiler* conveyed the following:

Not Killed.—Gen. Kemper, of the Confederate army,

Francis Bream's mill about 1890. (G.N.M.P.)

reported killed at Gettysburg, it is now stated, was only wounded, and is in a fair way to recover. He is now lying at Bream's Mill, three miles from Gettysburg, and was shot through the breast the ball lodging in his back. Col. Patton, of the 7th Virginia Infantry, . . . was also left upon the field as dead; but he too is in a Federal hospital, and with a prospect of recovery.

Dr. J.W.C. O'Neal also placed Pickett's division at Bream's Mill and at John Currens' farm. The identified Confederate graves here bear this out. Of the twenty-four or so in the area of the mill and Currens', nearly all belonged to that division.

A few of these burials were marked, "at Bream's Mill above Myer's house at the side of a fence," "at Bream's Mill on the hill," or "in the woods across the creek from Bream's Mill," etc.

Today the mill is totally destroyed. Even the stone foundation was filled in a few years ago. A house nearby may be where the Myers' place stood. A portion of this building is quite old.

Francis Bream's mill site in 1987, along Marsh Creek.

This may be the site of miller William E. Myers' house. A rear portion of this house is very old. It stands just to the right of the mill location.

THE JOHN S. CRAWFORD FARM

146

A little over a mile south of the mill and the Currens farm, and along the east bank of Marsh Creek, was a farm which belonged to the Gettysburg attorney and farmer, John Crawford.

During the battle, a thirty-seven-year-old black tenant farmer, Basil Biggs, lived on and worked the 289-acre farm. Biggs was known as a veterinarian of sorts, but in the 1860 census he is listed as a farmer with a thirty-four-year-old wife, Mary, and five children. It is interesting too, that after the battle, Biggs was involved in reinterring the Union dead. Leander H. Warren, a Gettysburg civilian, said:

Joseph S. Townsend was the surveyor and managed the burying of the bodies. . . . John Hoke and Frank Biesecker had the contract to dig and bury the dead. . . . Basil Biggs had the contract to raise the dead and put them into coffins. He had a two-horse team and hauled nine at a time, and I had a one-horse team and hauled six at a time. I hauled about as many as he did, because I could go a little faster and not have as many coffins to handle.[43]

Biggs must have been fairly accustomed to dealing with dead soldiers because in 1866, over forty-three identified Confederate graves were listed as being on Crawford's land. Almost all were from Barksdale's and Semmes' brigades of McLaws' division, of which this farm was most certainly a major hospital.

Dr. O'Neal noted in his 1863 ledger that "McLaws' div'n Hospital at Crawford's, Cunningham & Breams."

The post-war claim on this place suggested a very extensive medical facility. In it, Crawford stated:

(My) farm on Marsh Creek, Rebels occupied and encamped thereon, establishing a large hospital occupying the house, barn, sheds, and outbuildings and the adjacent grounds. The hospital had tents and buildings, and used the dining room as an amputation room. There were hundreds of wounded, and it was in use for five to six weeks. There were 9 1/2 acres of corn, 9 1/2 acres of oats, and 22 acres of wheat destroyed, plus all fencing. A part of the U.S. 6th Corps marched over the farm after the battle in pursuit of the enemy. John Cunningham lived within 1/4 mile. . . .

The stonehouse and barn in 1988 are in a well-preserved state—both are near an old ford which crosses Marsh Creek leading to the Cunningham farm.

The John S. Crawford farmhouse in 1987, with Marsh Creek in the foreground.

The John S. Crawford barn in 1988.

150

This small house was owned by John Crawford, and was located about one-half mile southwest of J. Edward Plank's and about three-quarters of a mile northeast of John S. Crawford's farm. Samuel Johns was a tenant; the tax records of 1863 listed Mr. Johns as taxable for one acre. In 1860, forty-seven-year-old Johns was carried on the tax roles as a "day laborer." He had two children at home, and because he was a widower, Johns had a twenty-six-year-old house-keeper, Catharine Shulz, living with him.

There were three wooden buildings at this location during the battle: a house, small barn and one outbuilding, all situated along a small brook which emptied into Marsh Creek. There is nothing remaining there now, but in July of 1863, it was very likely the field hospital for the artillery reserve of the Army of Northern Virginia. There were ten Confederate artillerymen buried on this property, several who died as late as July 18 and 28, which may show the duration of this hospital. It was reported also, that Captain John C. Fraser, of the Pulaski (Georgia) Battery, mortally wounded on July 2, might have been brought here for a while before his death. All were interred behind the barn.[44]

Samuel John's tenant house site in 1987 is up this brook about 200 yards and to the left.

John Cunningham was a native of Freedom Township in Adams County and was married to Margaret R. Scott. He farmed about two hundred acres just across Marsh Creek from Crawford's, until 1884, when he began the operation of his son's, James', mercantile store in Fairfield, Pennsylvania.

The reader may remember that Dr. J.W.C. O'Neal mentioned the Cunningham farm as part of the hospitals set up by the medical staff of General Lafayette McLaws' division, more specifically, by General W.T. Wofford's brigade. A notation placed "Drs. Eldridge and Ransom" at this site. There were also seventeen graves on the place, seven of them unmarked and unknown, except for the fact that they were all Georgians.

The 1868 damage claim mentioned that Cunningham's buildings were used as hospitals and suffered $20 damage. Mr. Cunningham further testified that the hospital was at his barn, with "some wounded in the house" itself. Among the items claimed were twelve barrels of flour, five cords of wood, and a sharp spring wagon, all used or damaged in connection with the Confederate hospital at his farm.

A Michigan newspaper article dated August 7, 1863, reported:

> (Two nurses, Mrs. Brain and Mrs. Barnard) accidently learned the revolting fact, that two or three Union soldiers were lying in a barn, about three miles from town. The barn belongs to a Mr. Cunningham, a true Union man, and is used as a rebel hospital. They immediately set out, after ascertaining the facts in the case, determined to remedy the thing, by having them brought to town. They visited the barn, . . . and found them; but in a sad and neglected condition, having laid on a bundle of straw for four weeks with broken thigh bones, and that, too, without being set or cared for properly. The rebel surgeon in charge of the hospital seemed to be a humane man, and rendered an excuse for their condition, that he had nothing to do with it; but this was really no excuse, for everything that was needed could have been had by simply asking for it. . . . One of them belonged to the 4th Michigan. . . .[45]

One of the finest accounts concerning the use of a farm as a Confederate hospital was written by Mrs. J. Paxton Bigham in 1941.* She was a young child in 1863 and recalled the family's experiences:

*I was unable to determine the actual or true name of Mrs. Bigham.

When the cannonading began that first day of July . . . mother gathered her children . . . into the carriage and drove to Grandfather Cunningham's two miles farther south. . . .

Towards evening of July 2nd a Confederate officer rode to the door and told father that the buildings would be required for hospital use. It being July, the big barn was almost empty and that was preferred rather than the house. All night long the wounded were carried in on stretchers. It was fully two miles from the wheatfield, where they had fallen and they were carried through pouring rain.

Father . . . went out with a notebook, and took the names and addresses of all who were alive. Many had died before morning. . . . Union wounded within the Confederate lines were brought in, too. The Union wounded were laid down in the orchard, and Father found many of them lying in pools of water. Later, tents were put over these men, and on the whole, they recovered better than those housed in the barn.

Adams county barns were built with a ramp at the back leading to the big threshing floor above the stables. This floor has two great doors. . . . There is . . . a small door in one of the large ones for everyday use. This small door was taken from its hinges and laid on trestles for an operating table.

Father had no means of knowing how the battle was going until an order came to 'use no more chloroform on Union soldiers.' . . . on July 3rd, Mother and the children came home . . . for six weeks Cassie (a hired lady) baked all the bread the big brick oven would hold every day. Every wounded man who could walk found his way to the house when the odor of baking bread floated out from the oven . . . twenty five barrels of Father's flour were in the store room in the barn. When Cassie would bake up one barrel, a hospital attendant would roll out a fresh one, until all were used. . . .

Mother was unable to keep the children away from the homesick soldiers. They would carve them toys . . . and play with them endlessly. The children would trot to the well with canteens strung around their necks, carrying cold water to the men. When Mother would go to the barn to take milk to the wounded, she would sometimes find a soldier asleep on the hay with a sleeping child on each arm.

Mrs. Bigham wrote that one Union man who had a leg amputated was Frank Clark of the 4th Michigan Infantry. Clark stayed at the farm for several weeks, and after the war, returned several times to visit the family. She also sadly reminisced about two of the little children who died during those days, one, Lizzie, from a heart ailment; and another, Willie, who contracted blood poison "from being about the wounded men."[46]

One hundred and twenty-five years after these events finds this farm as good as ever; the buildings in fine condition, and the land still used for farming and not yet developed.

The John Cunningham farm in 1987.

 THE CHRISTIAN BYERS FARM

149

Christian Byers, sixty-six, and his wife, Elizabeth Reinecker, forty-six, were both natives of Adams County, and were two of the first German settlers in the western part of the county. The Byers farm was located just north of the Fairfield Road, about a mile west of Bream's Tavern. The deed to the farm was recorded in 1769, with the land costing one-half penny per acre. At the time of the battle, the farm consisted of about 120 acres and had been in the Byers' name for nearly ninety-four years. It was one of the oldest farms in Highland Township. The house Christian and his family lived in was almost a hundred years old in 1863, and was built by Mr. Byers' grandfather,

The Christian Byers farm in 1987.

Adam. Christian and Elizabeth had a son, Christian, Jr., who was born in 1840 and served during the Civil War with Company B, 138th Pennsylvania Infantry. The damage claim for this farm recalled that the site was, "about four miles west of Gettysburg adjoining Andrew Weikert. The rebels had possession for three days, during the battle, they pastured all the fields with cattle, and used the house and barn for hospital purposes for about five weeks. The hospital for three weeks had 100 patients, two weeks for 50 men, then all were removed."

Although the barn has long since disappeared, the house and one old outbuilding remain. Under a modern exterior, the house could be a jewel awaiting discovery.

The Jacob Plank barn in 1987.

150   THE JACOB PLANK FARM

Jacob and Sarah (Forney) Plank were born in 1804 and 1806, respectively. They raised several children on their 184-acre farm along the south side of the Fairfield Road. The sturdy and handsome main buildings were made of field stone, and are still standing after all these many years. Both of these structcures are as nice as any stone edifice in Adams County.

Located in Highland Township, this farm was obviously a hospital of Confederate General Junius Daniel's brigade, of Rodes' division. The nine identified burials all seem to indicate this, however, there were eight "unknown" graves reported there also.

Plank's 1868 damage claim noted a great deal of damage done, and, "rebels encamped on the farm in

large numbers, with use of the entire premises for Hospital purposes, the house and barn were occupied for several weeks, and used the house for 17 days. There were 500 wounded in and on the premises, they took possession of the wheatfield, oatsfield, other fields, and part of orchard for hospital purposes."

151   THE ANDREW WEIKERT FARM

Andrew Weikert, sixty-three, was one of ten children born to George Weikert and his first wife, a "Miss Spitler." By the year 1863, Andrew was living with his wife, Susan, fifty-nine, and two children in a stone house west of the Byers farm on ninety-seven acres in

The Jacob Plank farmhouse in 1987.

The Andrew Weikert farm in 1987.

Highland Township. The farm was occupied by the Confederate Army on July 2 and 3 as a camp ground. Weikert said he left the farm on July 1 and returned on July 7. At that time, according to his Pennsylvania damage claim, he found the barn damaged "in consequence of its being occupied as a hospital." The claim continued, ". . . they brought their wounded on Friday (July 3) to the said premises about three hundred in number and used the Barn and orchard as Hospital for about six weeks."

The farm today is still occupied by the Weikert family, and is as neat and well-tended as any farm you will find in Pennsylvania. In fact it is almost a showplace. The house boasts some of the most beautiful stone work you will find anywhere—sadly, in viewing the hospital sites as a whole, this farm is by far (condition wise) an exception to the rule.

THE LOWER MARSH CREEK PRESBYTERIAN CHURCH

152

This graceful and well-proportioned stone building was constructed about 1790. The church organization, however, was much older, probably as early as 1745. Both in 1851 and 1890, the church was remodeled to its present appearance. During the battle, the church was under the charge of Reverend John R. Warner, who it was said, "exposed himself to great danger to witness the battle of Gettysburg." He later became a well-known guide of the famous battlefield.

In 1857, a union between the Lower Marsh Creek and the Great Conewago Presbyterian Churches (near Hunterstown) was formed. This was about the time Warner took over as pastor.

The only direct evidence I have been able to find that this church was a hospital, was in the 1886 edition of a history of Cumberland and Adams Counties. The history chronicled this information:

> During (Warner's) connection with these churches the battle of Gettysburg was fought and both of the church edifices were used for a short time as hospitals for the enemy. Mr. Warner sent his sermons, and many papers valuable to the congregation, to Chambersburg for safe keeping.

It is not surprising that this church was used as a field hospital, in fact, several eyewitnesses enumerated what the following soldiers noticed:

On July 4, Lieutenant Wilson Paxton, 140th Pennsylvania Infantry, who was near this area, wrote in his diary, ". . . the rebs skedadling. What a sight

of wounded men. Every house, barn fence corner and shade (tree) a hospital. Rained terribly. Glorious news. Rebs driven back."

And Surgeon George T. Stevens, 77th New York Infantry, recalled:

"Every house and barn from Gettysburgh to Fairfield was a hospital, and about most of the large barns . . . tents served to increase the accommodations for the wounded."

A final and excellent source comes from Lieutenant Thomas H. Tolson, 2nd Maryland Infantry Battalion, C.S.A., who wrote in his diary on July 4:

> *Saturday.* Aroused at 2:30 P.M. with the report that our army is retreating, and (I) did not know what to do, not being able to walk. Fortunately I was offered the use of a horse, which I mounted and made to the west side of town, where the wagons were parked.* All of our wounded are moved to this place, where there is a stone church.[47]

*This was the Fairfield Road.

The Lower Marsh Creek Presbyterian Church in 1988. The William Harner farm may have stood just back of where the telephone pole can be seen in the distance.

THE WILLIAM HARNER FARM

153

As of the publication of this book, the location of the Harner farm has not been positively identified. Kathy Georg Harrison, historian at Gettysburg National Military Park, believes it was somewhere along the Fairfield Road, possibly across from the Lower Marsh Creek Presbyterian Church (southside).

This must be essentially correct, because Harner's neighbors were Wintrode, Mickley, and others all of whom lived south of the church. In 1863 Harner was forty-seven years old and married to Elizabeth, thirty-three. They had six children.

Mr. Harner, who lived in Highland Township, filed a damage claim charging that, "the rebels encamped on (my) farm and damaged the land and the growing crops. The barn was used as a Hospital and was damaged in that use."

Several soldiers' accounts testify that there were many Confederate hospitals along the Fairfield Road. One excellent source told of scenes along this road and in one barn which could have been Harner's. This account was written by Surgeon Stevens, who was quoted above:

> Every . . . barn from Gettysburgh to Fairfield was a hospital; and about most of the large barns, numbers of dilapidated hospital tents served to increase the accommodations for the wounded. . . .
>
> At one of these barns some of our officers stopped, and as they passed among the gray-clad sufferers who were lying in rows upon the barn floors, one, a boy apparently not more than sixteen years of age. . . . The lad looked more like a delicate girl than a soldier; his hair fell from his fair forehead in long flaxen curls upon his pillow of straw, some of them matted with blood; his cheek was rosy, and his soft white hand told of a youth spent amid more tender scenes than those of the camp. A piece of linen laid across his face covered a ghastly wound where a ball had passed through his face, and had torn both his eyes from their sockets . . . (I) was far from being a rebel sympathizer, yet . . . turned away from the poor boy, with a sad face and a deep drawn sigh, to join the moving column.[48]

The David Stewart farm in 1987.

house, sat on the north side of the road, east of the Lower Marsh Creek Church. Even in 1860, Stewart must have been in good financial shape, as the census showed he had both a farmhand and "domestic" living on the farm. Stewart died at age fifty-five in 1882.

After the Civil War, Stewart claimed that his "barn and OutHouses were used for a Hospital from July 4th, 1863 until July 30, 1863. The Joseph Mickley farm adjoins (my property)." Only one identified burial was found here, a soldier of the 1st Maryland Battalion, who died on August 1, 1863.

Although the buildings still stand in excellent condition, the entire farm is now a trailer campground which has completely obliterated the beauty and historical integrity of the original estate.

 THE DAVID STEWART FARM

154

In July of 1863, about forty of Stewart's cultivated acres were devastated by Confederate troops, along with over four thousand rails, while many other items were stolen or destroyed. His farm was in Highland Township, about three-quarters of a mile west of the Lower Marsh Creek Church and just south of the Fairfield Road. David Stewart who was thirty-seven years old in 1863, moved to Kansas prior to 1874 with his wife, Margaret, and two children. In September, 1874, an advertisement in the local paper indicated that he was selling two farms. One, with a brick house had 197 acres (the hospital site south of the Fairfield Road), and the second with 160 acres and a stone

 THE JOSEPH MICKLEY FARM

155

During the war years, the Mickley family consisted of Joseph, age forty-nine, Rebecca ten years younger, and six children.

Joseph Mickley's place of residence was just south of the Stewart farm, along a road leading south from the Lower Marsh Creek Church, and about three-quarters of a mile south of the Fairfield Road. His claim, entered in 1868, simply stated that "damage was done to the House and Barn (which were) used as a Hospital. (My) farm was about six miles southwest of Gettysburg, adjoining the farm of David Stewart."

There were no burials listed at this site. The farm is in an excellent state of preservation as this is being written. A stone house stands on the property, just south of the large barn.

The Joseph Mickley farm in 1987.

THE HENRY H. WINTRODE FARM

156

A short distance northeast of Joseph Mickley's and on the east side of the road, stands the Wintrode farm, also in Highland Township. The claim for this property transcribed that the farm was "encamped on by a large rebel wagon train . . . on the evening of July 2. On July 4 (the Confederates) occupied his buildings as a Hospital (the house and barn) and continued there until Sunday evening the 5th when the premises were taken possession of by the union troops who continued there until monday evening following."

Wintrode also reported damage done to hay, clover, and wheat, as well as many items stolen or destroyed.

The Henry Wintrode farm in 1987.

He was not yet thirty years old in those times; his wife, Rebecca, and one child, made up the household.

No known burials were recorded on this location.

Again, here is another example of a Pennsylvania farm still in its original state, quite unlike what has happened to places such as the Stewart holdings. It would be wise to remember that once we change these rural settings, it is almost impossible to go back—no, it *is* impossible to go back.

THE FAIRFIELD HOSPITALS

157

The Fairfield, Pennsylvania area (population 218, in 1860) came into use as a hospital location during the battle of Gettysburg when it was occupied by Confederate forces. Furthermore, on the afternoon of July 3, it provided additional field hospitals when a skirmish took place there between the Rebels under General William E. Jones and the 6th U.S. Cavalry which attempted to seize the town to prevent use of that road by the Southern army.

In his book on the medical department, Captain Duncan stated that on the 5th of July, Union troops found 871 wounded in Fairfield under the charge of Dr. Ward and Dr. Wilson. He conjected that these remaining wounded were from the July 1 fight. However, it is more likely that they were left behind by the retreating Confederate army due to the condition of these injured men or for lack of transportation. It is known that prior to the Southern withdrawal, a great many wounded from C.S. field hospitals near Gettysburg were collected in and east of Fairfield for transportation south.

The map drawn up by the Sanitary Commission just after the battle shows a hospital at Fairfield in the northeast section of the village, and listed it as a portion of Johnson's division. This is odd though, because most of Johnson's men were cared for *northwest* of Gettysburg.

On July 4, Corporal George Neese, Chew's Battery, noted:

> Just yesterday, after the little fight with the Yankee cavalry near Fairfield, a young lady came to me and asked whether our men would allow her to take care of a wounded man that was lying in the road near her father's barn.
>
> I told her to go and take care of as many wounded as she would find. . . .[49]

A member of the 15th New Jersey Infantry, Edmund

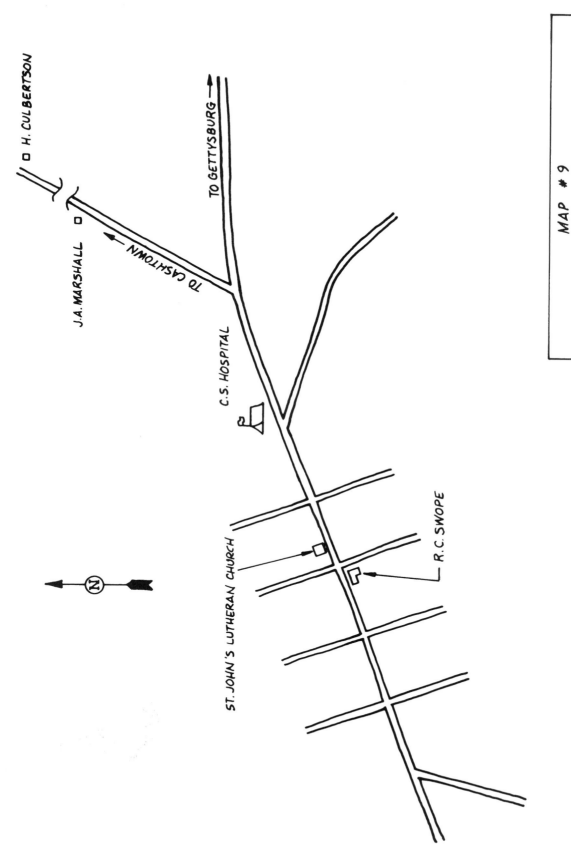

H. CULBERTSON

J.A. MARSHALL

TO GETTYSBURG →

TO CASHTOWN

C.S. HOSPITAL

ST. JOHN'S LUTHERAN CHURCH

R.C. SWOPE

N

MAP # 9

FAIRFIELD, PA AREA
FIELD HOSPITALS

MAP DESIGN BY: GREG COCO, FROM 1858 MAP

DRAWN BY: DAN FUHRMAN

D. Halsey, wrote simply in his diary:

"Almost 4 miles out overtook rear guard of the enemy near Fairfield—passing thousands of their wounded in tents, barns, etc. . . ."

Just southwest of Fairfield, a British visitor who travelled with the Confederate army, Lieutenant Colonel James Fremantle, came across this scene:

At 4 P.M. we stopped at a place where the roads fork, one leading to Emmetsburg (sic), and the other to Hagerstown. Major (R.J.) Moses and I entered a farmhouse, in which we found several women, two wounded Yankees, and one dead one, the result of this morning's skirmish. One of the sufferers was frightfully wounded in the head; the other was cut in the knee . . . he . . . belonged to a Michigan cavalry regiment. . . .[50]

There is no way to tell just how many more wounded were left along the roadsides during the retreat. The aforementioned account is one typical example.

Today, four markers in Fairfield and north of the town give information on the care of wounded in and around this village. One plaque stands in front of the St. John's Lutheran Church in the town, and another across the street on the "McKesson House," which was known as the R.C. Swope building in 1858 and 1872. Two more mark the J.A. Marshall and H. Culberson farms northward on the Cashtown Road. The "McKesson" marker reads: "Major Samuel Starr and other wounded officers of the 6th United States Cavalry were cared for here, July 3rd, 1863."

The plaque for the Marshall and Culbertson houses.

The J.A. Marshall farmhouse in 1987.

The St. Johns Church in Fairfield in 1987.

The H. Culbertson farmhouse in 1987.

PART IV
Other Important Sites Associated with the Treatment of the Wounded During the Battle of Gettysburg

THE WHITE RUN SCHOOL-HOUSE

The United States Sanitary Commission was "established" in April of 1861 as an outgrowth of various women's relief organizations in the New York City area. Its object was to do for the soldiers what the government was not doing adequately, such as caring for the wounded, supplying food and medical supplies, cleaning up military camps, and so forth. On July 4, portions of this group arrived in Gettysburg, first setting up a supply depot at White Run School. In a report issued in August of 1863, the Commission said:

"A school-house was taken on the Baltimore pike, near the different Corps Hospitals, and about three miles out from Gettysburg, and from it our stores were thereafter issued, until the opening of the railroad permitted our reaching the field by that route, when, on Tuesday morning, July 7, a storehouse was taken in town, and the school-house closed." The next day this same school was taken over by the Provost Marshal of the Army of the Potomac.

The Sanitary agents also set up a relief lodge about a mile east of town on the York Pike. Since the railroad terminated there because the rebels had burned the bridge over Rock Creek, the lodge catered to wounded men who were being transported to hospitals in several major cities along the eastern coast. The workers at the lodge provided rest areas and cooked for the soldiers while they waited for the trains.

Later, when the railroad was repaired, the lodge was moved near the depot in Gettysburg where it continued for several weeks after the battle. A worker at this lodge recalled:

The White Run School, or a successor, located a short distance northeast of the pike.

On the day (July 10) that the railroad bridge was repaired we moved up to the depot, close by the town, and (set up) a first rate camping ground, in a large field directly by the track, with unlimited supply of delicious cool water. Here we set up two stoves, with four large boilers, always kept full of soup and coffee, watched by four or five black men, who did the cooking . . . and sang at the tops of their voices all day.[1]

THE SAMUEL AND EDWARD FAHNESTOCK STORE

When the Sanitary Commission supply depot left the White Run Schoolhouse, it moved to this large building at the northwest corner of Baltimore Street and Middle Street. An eyewitness said:

> (It) became the centre of the busiest scene which I have ever witnessed in connection with the Commission. Car-load after car-load of supplies were brought to this place, till shelves and counter and floor up to the ceiling were filled, till there was barely a passage-way between the piles of boxes and barrels, till the side-walk was monopolized and even the street encroached upon. . . . Each morning the supply wagons of the division and corps hospitals were before the door, and each day they went away laden with such articles as were desired to meet their wants. . . . Thus, tons of ice, mutton, poultry, fish, vegetables, soft bread, eggs, butter, and a variety of other articles . . . were provided for the wounded. . . .[2]

This old store warehouse, although altered significantly since the battle, has at least been remodeled and is in use today as an apartment house.

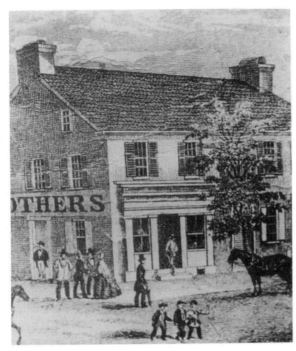

The Samuel and Edward Fahnestock store in 1863. (G.N.M.P.)

Some members of the Sanitary Commission and Camp Letterman medical staff at Gettysburg in 1863. Left to right: Mrs. Winslow, Surgeon Janes, Surgeon Chamberlain, Surgeon Breakey, Mrs. Sampson, Rev. Winslow, Surgeon Gauntt. (MOLLUS-MASS)

The Samuel and Edward Fahnestock building in 1987.

30 (161)

THE JOHN L. SCHICK STORE

The store of John Schick was mentioned in another part of this book in connection with its possible use as a hospital. His store was also used by the United States Christian Commission. Supplies were stored here and distributed to the hospitals in the same manner as was done by the Sanitary Commission.

However, in 1861, this particular commission had been primarily an offshoot of the religious community in the North; its main purpose was to bring spiritual and moral relief to the soldiers, both wounded and not. Early in the war, though, under pressure from the army, this commission was forced to do more in the temporal area; frankly, because the soldiers were primarily interested in these physical wants and were in greater need of food, clothes and medical supplies than religion. Schick's store was on the southeast corner of the "Diamond" or town square in Gettysburg.

The Christian Commission personnel made their headquarters at George Little's house on East Middle Street. Interestingly enough, on July 2, in a room vacated seconds earlier by the Little family, an artillery shell exploded, causing great damage.

Mr. John L. Schick in 1886.

 THE AARON SHEELY FARM

162

The provost marshal of the army was responsible for many duties, such as the care and transportation of prisoners, wagon train and hospital guards, law and order in the regiments, and so on. Since all of the wounded Confederates left in Union hands became prisoners of war, the provost marshal was active in many hospitals, even prior to the establishment of the general hospital (Camp Letterman) east of Gettysburg. Also, supplies had to be guarded, and other police-like duties were required, thus General M.R. Patrick, Provost Marshal General of the Army of the Potomac, was a very busy man indeed. In fact, on July 2, Patrick said in his diary, "I had my hands full, with the Prov. Guards to keep the Troops from breaking—It was hot work and I had several lines formed, so very few (of these temporary deserters) suc-

General Marsena R. Patrick, center. (MOLLUS-MASS)

ceeded in getting entirely through—."

On July 3, he repeated:

"It was terrific (the artillery fire) and I had my hands full with those who broke to the rear, but we succeeded in checking the disorder and organized a guard of Stragglers to keep nearly 2000 Prisoners all safe—."[3]

General Patrick continued: "Saturday night, July 4, Barn Near White Church Baltimore Road, Gettysburg, Pa.

"At night, as we had been drenched in a most terrific rain, we concluded to take shelter in a large barn, the only one in the whole country not occupied for a Hospital. . . ."

This barn was on the Sheely farm. Aaron Sheely, himself, said:

"(General Patrick) came up to the barn with his retinue. I invited him to the house. He refused, saying he preferred to stay in the barn."[4]

On July 6, Andrew Cross, a Christian Commission delegate, attempting to locate the Provost Marshal, received directions from an officer near Meade's Headquarters. He wrote:

Col. Sharp said we would have to go to Gen. Patrick's headquarters, which were nearby two miles further. (He was just south of the Cemetery gatehouse on the Baltimore Pike.) It was now after 9 o'clock, damp and dark at that. To comfort us, he said he would go along, and let us share his bed, which was on the barn floor, near the 3d Corps hospital. . . . (after arriving) Col. Sharp having ordered some one to tie up our horses, we laid down on the barn floor, where we slept more soundly than we have often done in the most comfortable bed.

I am sad to say that at this writing (July, 1988) the Sheely barn is in almost total disrepair, and nothing remains of the house but a small portion of the northwest wall.

A new sewer system runs right through the farm property carrying off the waste from an ill-planned "resort community" known as Lake Heritage. This over-grown housing development has already destroyed White Run, and now the sewer plant will bring in a new influx of cheap tract houses or mobile homes which will inundate both the Sheely and Schwartz historic areas .

The Sheely barn (General Patrick's headquarters) in 1987.

The Aaron Sheely farm in 1987, showing the barn on the left and the ruins of the house on the right. White Run is to the right, out of sight. "Red Hill" or "Slaty Ridge" is to the left.

PART V
Hospitals of the Gettysburg Campaign Located in Other Nearby Towns

Immediately during and for days and weeks following the battle, many other towns, in addition to Gettysburg, felt an immediate surge of the overflow of Union and Confederate wounded generated by the greatest battle in American history. Some of the Pennsylvania and Maryland locations, in addition to the larger cities where permanent military hospitals had already been established, were: Carlisle, Chambersburg, Hanover, Harrisburg, Littlestown, Shippensburg, and York. Also affected were Funkstown, Hagerstown, and Westminster, Maryland, plus Martinsburg and Winchester, Virginia.

In this section, a few of these towns and their field hospitals will be summarized.

HANOVER, PENNSYLVANIA

Located about fifteen miles east of Gettysburg, this prosperous village opened several small field hospitals on June 30, just prior to the battle at Gettysburg. The hospital operations began after a skirmish between Federal cavalry commanded by General H. Judson Kilpatrick and some Confederate horsemen under General James E.B. Stuart.

C.T.S. Pierce, a member of the 5th New York Cavalry, which suffered nine killed and thirty-one wounded, said that townspeople kindly provided for these wounded. They threw, "open the doors of the Dutch Reformed Church, where the wounded of both friend and foe received equal care. . . . None who were wounded, sick and sore, can ever forget the kindness of the women of this quiet, little town."[5]

Another source, a local newspaper called *The Spectator,* reported that wounded soldiers were taken care of by the citizens at their private residences, one of which was the Karl Forney house. The paper also noted that the government "has taken Eckert's Concert Hall, on Market Square, Marion Hall, on Foundry Alley, Albright's Hall, on Broadway, and Pleasant Hill Hotel, on Baltimore Street, for Hospitals, to accommodate the large number of wounded soldiers."

The other town newspaper, *The Citizen,* noted that at an early hour on Wednesday, July 1,

> Surgeon Gardner, in charge of all the wounded cavalry, reported as the surgeon of the hospital at this point, bringing with him an official corps of stewards and nurses, and soon brought order out of confusion. Soon the wounded (at Marion Hall) were mounted upon snug bunks furnished by the carpenters of this place. . . . The majority of the wounds received in this action were of a most serious character, requiring many capital operations. . . .

A citizen of Hanover, Pastor William Zieber, did much to aid the fallen men, both Northern and Southern. He said that several local physicians assisted these wounded, among them, Drs. William Bange, Smith, Culbertson, Eckert and Hinkle. Zieber also mentioned Marion Hall as being the *principle* hospital, while another one was located in the Flickinger foundry on York Street.

LITTLESTOWN, PENNSYLVANIA

The Baltimore Pike, which ran from the interior of the Union battle lines near Gettysburg, became a natural conduit directly southeast into villages like Littlestown, Pennsylvania and Westminster, Maryland. When a soldier was wounded, and if he could walk or find transportation, he usually travelled as far away

Lieutenant Colonel William W. Dudley. (MOLLUS-MASS)

from the battlefield as possible. Littlestown was about ten miles away, and being unaffected by the battle it made an ideal destination for the wounded. One soldier who made his way to this town was Captain John Adams of the 19th Massachusetts Infantry. He and a comrade paid $5 each to a farmer to take them from the Second Corps hospital to Littlestown. He wrote:

> There was no organization of the hospital. Two of the town doctors were doing all they could, being assisted by the women. . . . I cannot speak in too high praise of the women of Littlestown.[6]

Mr. J.W. Monfort, a military relief agent from Indiana, made a report of his visit to Gettysburg. Here is an extract:

> At Littlestown, (July 7) hundreds of wounded were in church and school house, in barns and shops. Here we found Dr. Garver, Assistant Surgeon of the Nineteenth Indiana Volunteers, sick, but giving his attention to the wounded, and having been detailed to wait upon Lieutenant Colonel Dudley, (19th Indiana) who was dangerously wounded, and who has since lost a leg by amputation.

Dudley, who spent some time at the First Corps hospital in White Church where one amputation was performed, ended up at Ephraim Myers' house *in* Littlestown. This house was on the south side of Baltimore Street, just past the railroad depot. Monfort also mentioned that he was on his way to see General Solomon Meredith, who was at a farmhouse four miles toward Gettysburg.

In a diary entry dated July 8, 1863, E.H. Rhodes, 2nd Rhode Island Infantry, remarked:
"At a place called Littlestown we saw large numbers of our wounded men, and all kinds of carriages were being used to take them to the hospitals."

WESTMINSTER, MARYLAND

During and after the fighting at Gettysburg, which was almost thirty miles to the north, Westminster became a collecting point for troops, supplies, wounded men, and prisoners going and coming from the great battlefield. In 1863, Westminster was a terminus of the Western Maryland Railroad coming out of Baltimore.

In her recollections written after the war, Mary B. Shellman, a young girl during the war, remembered:

> On July 2nd, the first prisoners, numbering 500, passed through town, and on the morning of July 3rd, temporary hospitals were established, one at the old 'Union Meeting House' and the other in the large shady yard adjoining the Roman Catholic Church. As the wounded were brought in, the citizens hastened to their relief, . . . The City Hotel with its cool shady rooms also served as a temporary hospital, and sheltered for several days men who had served with distinction in the three days conflict.[7]

A Christian Commission report issued soon after the battle said:

> At Westminster, meeting hundreds of the wounded from the battle-field, without a surgeon to care for them, a part (of the group of Commission delegates) halted and assisted in the establishment of hospitals in that place. . . . Among those to whom they ministered were Major-General Hancock and his aid, General (sic) Miller.

General John Gibbon, wounded on July 3, was with Hancock for a while in a hospital on Rock Creek, then,

> . . . I left (this) hospital in an ambulance for Westminster, thirty miles distant, reaching there just at daylight to learn that no train would leave for Baltimore till late in the day. . . . I was tenderly cared for at the house of my wife's aunt, Mrs. Neal, who poor lady, was torn with anxiety for one of her sons serving in the Rebel army. . . .
> Late in afternoon (July 4) I was placed in a box car on a train with many other wounded which ran out only a mile or two to a side track where we remained all night in a pouring rain, arriving the next day. . . .[8]

On July 9, Surgeon Henry Janes, who was in charge of all of the hospitals at Gettysburg, reported to the Medical Director of the Army of the Potomac:

"I have sent away from this place 3,500 slightly wounded. The railroad authorities say that 4,000 have gone from Littlestown and Westminster. The number of wounded (near Gettysburg) have probably exceeded 20,000."[9]

One officer who was known to have died in a Westminster field hospital was Colonel Paul J. Revere, 20th Massachusetts Infantry. On July 5, this grandson of Boston's famed Paul Revere succumbed of wounds received at Gettysburg.

CARLISLE, PENNSYLVANIA

This, the county seat of Cumberland County, was about twenty-seven miles north of Gettysburg. A relief agent for the Sanitary Commission, Isaac Harris, kept a diary during the Gettysburg Campaign and was one of the few chroniclers of the hospitals established in Carlisle and Chambersburg.

On July 6, Harris wrote:

Rec'd message from Gov. Curtin to call on him and did so at once. Requested me to take supplies for 1,000 patients to Carlisle. . . .

(July 7) The (Christian Commission) were in high spirits when they ascertained the San. Com. had no stores at Carlisle and hoped by their numbers to supply the Hospital there before I could. The train came to a stand about one mile N. of the town on account of a broken bridge . . . I left the train and walked into town through a drenching rain to the Hospital which was located in Dickinson College. Had a talk with Dr. Tomlinson the Surgeon in charge, and with the lady nurses . . . Loaded the wagons and drove to the Hospital and was unloading when the CC's again appeared and offered assistance which was refused by Dr. Palmer, saying, the San. Com. had supplied every want of his patients.[10]

An eyewitness in Carlisle found two Confederate surgeons at the hospital there; Dr. H.V. Budd and a "Dr. Coleman." Both were said to be "bitter secesh."

One Union physician was noted also, Dr. Stephen Kieffer, who was also at the college.

Interestingly enough, in the report filed by the Christian Commission, mention is made of another hospital several miles southwest of Carlisle. It reads:

Part of the delegates returned from Carlisle with the sick and wounded sent to Harrisburg. John Patterson, however, went on with the troops. At Pine Grove, a wheelwright's shop was obtained near Watt's iron

furnace, and about forty disabled men gathered into it. They had lain twenty four hours without food or care. Mr. Patterson distributed to them all his remaining stores, and greatly relieved them.

Pine Grove is today a state park where you can visit Watt's buildings and furnace area.

CHAMBERSBURG, PENNSYLVANIA

Isaac Harris, who contributed some of the information above, mentioned this about hospitals around Chambersburg:

July 6th—Numbers of wounded and sick principally Rebels are reported to be at Shippensburg and Chambersburg and sadly deficient in Hospital material.

July 9th—Up early. . . . Started for Shippensburg at 10 AM . . . arriving at 1 . . . Returned to Carlisle on train . . . Left (Carlisle) at 5.30 and reached Shippensburg 22 miles at 9 PM. Pleasant ride. Turned in at Black Boar Tavern and slept on the floor . . . Up at 5 o'clock (July 10) after a hard night . . . reached Chambersburg at 10 AM . . . I stopped for the day to rest the horse and visit the Hospitals. Found 70 Reb. patients under charge of Dr. Hamilton M. Gamble—20th Va. Inf. (Reb) and nephew of Gov. Gamble of Mo. Hospital in horrible condition and without supplies of any kind, the patients lying on the bare floors, without covering of any kind, and even without dressing for their wounds, and the entire place infested with vermin. The sight was sickening, in fact, the most horrible I have yet met with. Telegraphed to . . . send complete outfit for the Hospital . . . Informed Dr. Gamble who returned profuse thanks in behalf of his patients.

July 11—Saw Dr. G. at breakfast. He informed me that he had never regularly studied medicine, but after acting as Hospital Steward one year, he had been appointed Surgeon. When the Rebs evacuated Chambersburg he voluntarily remained with his patients.[11]

David Z. Shook, a resident of Greencastle, recalled these scenes:

At day-break on Sunday morning, July 5th, I was called from my bed and requested to proceed immediately to the King Street hospital to assist in removing from wagons a number of wounded Confederates. The teamsters . . . had lost their way during the night and had come into Chambersburg. Arriving at the hospital I found in the street four or five wagons . . . all loaded with wounded men . . . O what a terrible sight these men presented! Filthy, bloody, with wounds undressed and swarming with vermin, and almost famished for food and water. . . . After they were all taken into the hospital, arrangements were at once made to have their wounds dressed and food supplied.

Mr. Shook also remembered a wagon train of one hundred wagons and one thousand wounded Confederates that was captured on July 4—the wounded men were, "taken from the wagons and placed in the Theological Seminary buildings and other improvised hospitals" (in Chambersburg).[12]

Another source listed three hospitals in use during the Antietam campaign of 1862. They were the "School House Hospital," Franklin Hall, and the "Academy Hospital," all in or near town. The School House hospital was on King Street (adjoining the old jail) and is probably the "King Street Hospital" mentioned earlier. It was also in operation from "early July to August 21, 1863" and was said to be a large brick building.

The Academy General Hospital, near Chambersburg, was opened in July and closed on September 3, 1863, when the patients were transferred to the "Town Hall Hospital" which is listed in the National Archives as the same hospital as the Odd Fellows Hall. The Odd Fellows Hall held several wounded for a while until they were removed to a "stone house on the corner of Main and Catherine Streets" until September of 1863.

PART VI
Camp Letterman, The United States General Hospital on the George Wolf Farm

158

Within just two weeks or so after the Battle of Gettysburg, it became obvious to the Medical Department that something had to be done to consolidate the thousands of wounded left behind by the two armies. Henry Janes, a U.S. volunteer surgeon born in Vermont, who had served in the 3rd Vermont Infantry, reported that in early July he was placed in command of "all field hospitals" around Gettysburg and had "under my charge some 60 different hospitals with over 20,000 Union and Rebel wounded needing prompt attention."[13] Of these numbers, he stated that 5,456 were Confederates in twenty-four of those hospital camps.

When the medical director of the Army of the Potomac, Jonathan Letterman, left with the army on July 6, he ordered 106 surgeons to remain behind with these wounded. Shortly afterwards, the army dispatched a few more doctors to assist those left at Gettysburg. Very slowly, these injured men were either sent away to permanent military hospitals in cities along the east coast, or moved to Camp Letterman which was established on July 20. By July 25, 16,125 wounded had been sent away from Gettysburg, and approximately 4,217 remained because they were unfit to travel.

There were good reasons to position a "general hospital" near the battlefield. The most important reason was that there were the thousands of severely injured men who could not go anywhere else, and had to remain behind for a while to recuperate. As it turned out, the hospital did not actually close until November 20, one day after Lincoln's visit. Also, it was a very difficult task to supply so many outlying field hospitals, where conditions were becoming even more unhealthy as time passed.

The site chosen by U.S. Medical Inspectors E.P.

Medical Director Jonathan Letterman.

Vollum and G.K. Johnston and Surgeon Janes, was about one mile east of town, along the York Pike. This location was a good one for other reasons. At that time, it was on high, mostly well-drained ground, in a large grove, which provided both shade and free movement of fresh air. Initially, the camp area was drained and the tents were pitched under the direction of Surgeon Cyrus N. Chamberlain. The railroad was only thirty rods away, which permitted litters to be walked to the cars. A good spring on the property, along with several wells that were later dug, provided a neverending supply of clean, fresh water.

A scene at Camp Letterman in 1863. (G.N.M.P.)

Possibly the cookhouse at Camp Letterman in the late fall of 1863. (MOLLUS-MASS)

The land, itself, was part of George Wolf's large farm, and was locally called "Wolf's Woods," a place used by many county residents as a picnic spot. Mr. Wolf's house, barn, and outbuildings stood about one thousand yards southwest of the grove. In fact, his farm may have been a temporary aid station on July 2, as six identified Confederate burials were found on the property after the battle.

A Christian Commission delegate was one of the only persons to recall those burials. He said:

The General Hospital (tents) . . . (were) located . . . within a few feet (of the) graves of several men who were killed in the battle. The site was upon a large farm . . . high and healthy."

Oddly enough, in 1861–62, there had been several wooden military barracks constructed on this farm to shelter a regiment of New York cavalry stationed in the Gettysburg area. Whether or not these barracks remained standing in 1863, has never been determined.

After a while, the general hospital, became the very model of a clean, efficient, and well-run medical facility, one of the first of its kind actually on a battlefield anywhere. It was commanded by Dr. Cyrus Chamberlain, a U.S. volunteer medical officer, formerly a member of the 10th Massachusetts Infantry. At its peak, the hospital had more than four hundred hospital tents, set up in six double rows, about ten feet apart. Each tent held up to ten patients, and was heated (in the fall) with a Sibley stove. Every medical officer had charge of from forty to seventy patients, which totalled 1,600 on August 30, but dropped to about three hundred in late October, and ran as low as one hundred on November 10.

Many eyewitness accounts remain today of this large and interesting establishment. Several of these are worth renumerating here.

A man who was among the first to help open the new general hospital was Chaplain Lyman D. Ames of the 29th Ohio Infantry. In his diary, he wrote how he worked with the wounded there from July 23 to August 3. During the first week, Ames wrote several times that, "many are sinking and must go down—a number died today," etc. On July 29, he gave the number of wounded taken from the morning report: "307 Rebel and 308 Union, total 615." This is a good indication of how large the general hospital was before all of the field hospitals were emptied and transferred there.[14]

A 62nd Pennsylvania Infantry soldier, Jacob Shenkel, was assigned to nurse the wounded at Camp Letterman on Friday, July 31, when the wounded from the Fifth Corps hospital were moved in from the field to the general hospital. His diary mentioned several colorful incidents. For instance, on August 2, he noted that he had the cleanest tent in the ward, (Tent 5 of Ward 8), and that during the evening a choir from Gettysburg visited the camp and serenaded the patients. On August 5, Shenkel said that he had six amputees in Tent 5. August 9, a fist fight occurred between a Federal and a Confederate—"the Latter got used up pretty Bad." On August 10, Shenkel had his photograph taken, saying, "I took three smiles." On August 11, a fire broke out in the dispensary—causing the destruction of $100 worth of sheets, etc. He was very busy on Wednesday, August 26—"dressed five Stumps, one shoulder (and) one spine." September 8 was cloudy with a chance of rain, but a picnic in camp went on as scheduled and that night he attended a stag dance. However, on September 9, Nurse Shenkel reported that he "felt Pretty Boozy after Last Night's Performance." On November 17, he recalled—"the Ohio Boys Left to Day. . . ."[15]

A letter written by Chaplain William C. Way, 24th Michigan Infantry, on August 7, gave a fine, concise

168

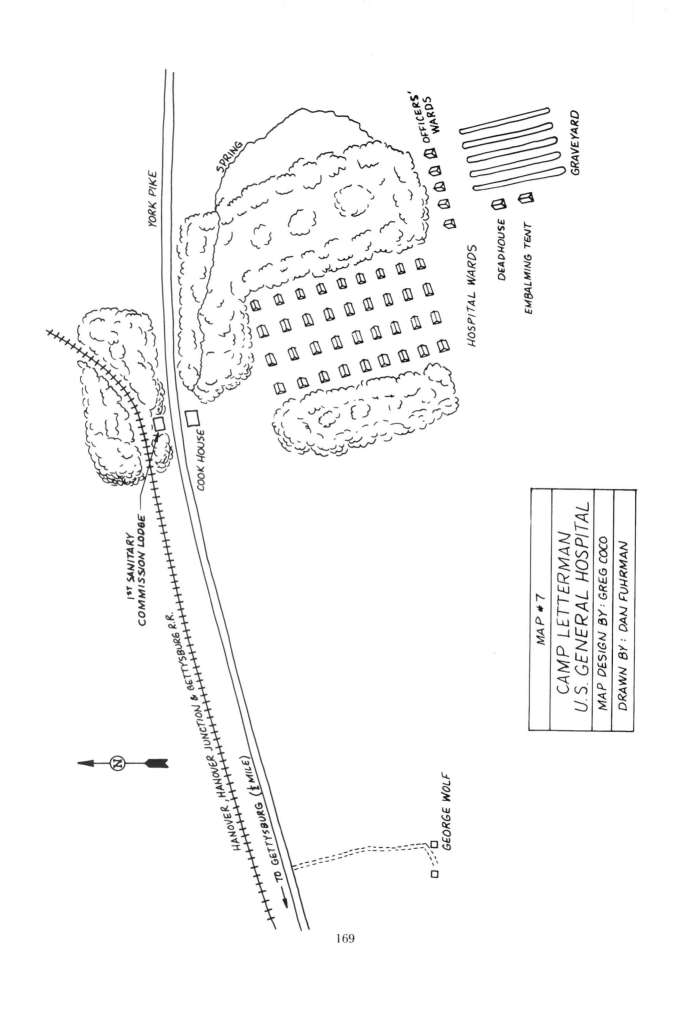

MAP #7

CAMP LETTERMAN
U.S. GENERAL HOSPITAL

MAP DESIGN BY: GREG COCO

DRAWN BY: DAN FUHRMAN

description of the camp:

> To-day we visited the General Hospital, and found it . . . neat, clean, and systematic. The hospital is located on a rise of ground, skirted on two sides by an oak grove. . . . The tents are pitched in an open field, which descends gently toward the west and north. A fine spring, sufficient for a bountiful supply of good water is located near the cook-house. There are about 126 tents already up, each of which is occupied by 12 persons. The prospect is that the area of the hospital will be materially enlarged, as tents are being put up daily.[16]

Just two weeks later, a member of the Christian Commission visited Camp Letterman and remarked:

> When visited, the General Hospital was in charge of thirty surgeons, one of whom, Dr. Janes, was the Superintendent, or Medical Director. There was an Assistant Superintendent, seven Division and twenty six Ward surgeons. Dr. Chamberlain was the Assistant Superintendent. . . . At (this) hospital there were 1,600 patients, about half Confederates.

Another soldier who recalled the picnic previously mentioned by Nurse Shenkel was J.M. Silliman, 17th Connecticut Infantry, who had been wounded on July 1. He wrote home to his mother on August 11:

> We had a famous picnic here a few days since, the benefactors set a table about large enough to accomodate 1/3 of our wounded who collected around them while they were singing. When the invitation was given for the wounded to partake of the good things, many of the rebel nurses wedged their way to the table and crowded our wounded out. About two thirds of the number present were rebels wounded and otherwise.

In a second letter on September 9, he repeated: ". . . the reb nurses with their characteristic chivalry made a rush for the table . . . and gorged themselves with dainties."

On September 15, just a few days prior to this banquet, the local newspaper reported that there were still 1,300 wounded at "hospitals," a large portion of these had compound fractures. And on October 6, the

An amputation scene at Camp Letterman in 1863. (G.N.M.P.)

Another amputation scene at Camp Letterman in 1863. (MOLLUS-MASS)

Confederate wounded prisoners and medical personnel at Camp Letterman in 1863. (MOLLUS-MASS)

General Hospital listed 1,183 patients still left, with over ten thousand men in several hospitals around the state of Pennsylvania.

The *Star and Sentinel*, a Gettysburg newspaper, remarked on September 29 of a large banquet that was given on September 23 for the wounded at Camp Letterman by the Christian Commission and the ladies of the town. This article said that four hundred to five hundred chickens, twenty to thirty hams, and fifty tongues were donated, along with oysters, pies, and ice cream. At dark, amusements were held, such as foot races, minstrel performers, greased pole climbing, "gander" pulling, and a band from York played. The day was a beautiful one, and all went well.

Frank Stoke, a Pennsylvania militia guard at Camp Letterman, wrote this news home on October 26, 1863:

This hospital is composed of large tents which cover eighty acres of ground; it is laid off in streets or avenues which give it the appearance of a city. When we first came here there were five thousand sick and wounded . . . as high as seventeen die per day. . . . Those who die . . . are buried in the field south of the hospital; there is a large grave-yard there already. The dead . . . are nearly all Confederates. . . . The amputated limbs are put into barrels and buried and left in the ground until they are decomposed, then lifted and sent to the Medical College at Washington. A great number of bodies are embalmed here and sent to their friends. Close to the grave-yard is a large tent called the dead-house, another where they embalm.[17]

Sophronia E. Bucklin, one of the first female nurses to arrive at this hospital, (the number of women soon increased to forty), wrote in 1869 about her experiences at Camp Letterman where she had spent many weeks in 1863:

"The hospital tents were set in rows—five hundred

of them. . . . Walks were thrown up between these rows, in order that they might dry quickly after the summer rains. The ground . . . was the only floor in the wards or in our quarters."

Miss Bucklin gave a good description of the Confederate wounded, saying,

It was universally shown . . . that (they) bore their suffering with far less fortitude than our brave soldiers who had been taught, in sober quiet homes in the North. . . . Many more of the rebels died than of our own men. . . .

Of twenty-two rebels who were brought into my ward at one time, thirteen died, after receiving the same care that was given to our men.

Bucklin recalled, too, that of the 1,200 graves in the camp cemetery, over two-thirds were Confederates.

She continued by commenting that among the Southerners, "a hydrophobic fear of water seemed to prevail." Her duties in the ward consisted of passing out beef tea three times a day, "stimulants three times, and extra diet three times—making nine visits which each woman nurse made a day, to each of the two hundred men under her charge. This was done, besides washing the faces and combing the hair . . . preparing the extra drinks ordered by the surgeons, and seeing that the bedding and clothing of every man was kept clean. . . ." All this while being required to wear "close shakers," a type of woman's headgear required by the surgeons.[18]

Another equally good description of Camp Letterman was left by nurse Cornelia Hancock who narrated on August 8:

Our hospital is on rising ground, divided off into six avenues, and eighteen tents holding twelve men each on each avenue. We call four tents a ward and name them by a letter; mine is Ward E. . . . Our cook-house alone is a sight; they have meals cooked for thirteen hundred men, so you may know that they have to have the pots middling size.[19]

The preceding description closely matches one left by Surgeon William F. Norris, who served in the Third Division, First Corps. He moved his patients to the General Hospital from the Catholic Church on July 23.

> I succeeded in having everything moved out by 7 P.M. . . . Our patients bore the journey better than I had anticipated. . . . (Dr. Goodman) has put me in charge of the row of tents appropriated to the 1st Corps, 16 tents holding 192 beds. These are subdivided into wards, 48 beds to the ward, each under charge of an assistant surgeon.[20]

The official closing of the hospital took place in late November. A medical officer in Washington, D.C. reported: "All patients remaining in that hospital were transferred during the week ending November 21, 1863. All medical officers were relieved on November 20, 1863."[21]

This unique and important hospital was a concentration of thousands of interesting people and the even more thousands of incidents which affected them all. Camp Letterman was a world of its own, with every known human emotion brought together in its long four months of operation. The last tents were finally struck about the time President Abraham Lincoln visited Gettysburg. Nurse Bucklin said of the disbanding which took place in late fall:

> The hospital tents were removed—each bare and dust-trampled space marking where corpses had lain after the death-agony was passed, and where the wounded had groaned in pain. Tears filled my eyes when I looked on that great field, so checkered with the ditches that had drained it dry. So many of them I had seen depart to the silent land; so many I had learned to respect. . . .[22]

So now the story of the field hospitals and their wounded was over. The sites that Ms. Bucklin wept over would soon pass into history, to be commented over briefly in the generations to follow, as did John B. Bachelder, an historian, who visited "Hospital Hill" (as it was called then) in 1878:

> Not withstanding the mournful memories of this hill, it is still a very charming spot. Its commanding location, its leafy shades of hickory and oak, its spring of delicious and pure water, indeed, all its surroundings, invite the traveller to pause and rest and ponder.[23]

Or as a Christian Commission delegate had predicted in 1863:

> . . . the record was closed, and the meadow, like the great field around it, (is) left to the hallowing influences of time, never to be forgotten, but ever to be brightening in the grateful affections of a free people, for whom the great sacrifice had been made.

U.S. medical personnel at Camp Letterman in 1863. Left to right: Mr. Holstein, Steward King, Mrs. Backman (?), Mrs. Anna Holstein, Dr. May, Mrs. May, Rev. Dr. Winslow. (MOLLUS-MASS) Rev. Gordon Winslow was superintendant of the U.S. Sanitary Commission at Camp Letterman.

Georgiana Woolsey Bacon, a civilian nurse, who served at Gettysburg. (MOLLUS-MASS)

Well, a "grateful and free people" have certainly and clearly made their choices.

In 1988, the Camp Letterman "Hospital Woods" site, is a national and historical disgrace. Most of the original one-hundred-acre hospital grounds is now a shabby trailer court with an all-too common discount store shopping center nearby. And as I write this, plans are being completed for the erection of a fast-food burger joint on what is left of the site. The spring with its cool waters which had refreshed the parched throats of suffering and dying men, is now dead and mud-clogged and filled with debris. The once proud and ancient oak and hickory-filled woods have been replaced by an acre or two of trash-covered and scrawny second growth scrub trees.

All of Camp Letterman that is left to us who care of such things is about ten or so acres, all clearly marked "for sale," and, of course, advertised as "prime development potential."

How far must suffering and misery go before we see that even in the day of vast cities and powerful machines, the good earth is our mother and that if we destroy her, we destroy ourselves?

Paul Bigelow Sears

Tents at Camp Letterman General Hospital in 1863, looking west, toward Gettysburg. The Trinity German Reformed Church can be seen in the distance. (G.N.M.P.)

Looking west toward Gettysburg along the York Pike. Camp Letterman was where the trees can be seen in this 1986 photograph.

A portion of Camp Letterman (looking east) prior to the construction of the shopping center and fast-food complex in 1986–88.

A portion of Camp Letterman in 1986. The cookhouse site is to the right, out of the photograph.

A portion of Camp Letterman in 1986 (looking north) prior to the construction of the shopping center. The graveyard was just south of here.

A portion of Camp Letterman (looking east) prior to the shopping center being built in 1986.

The old spring at Camp Letterman in 1986.

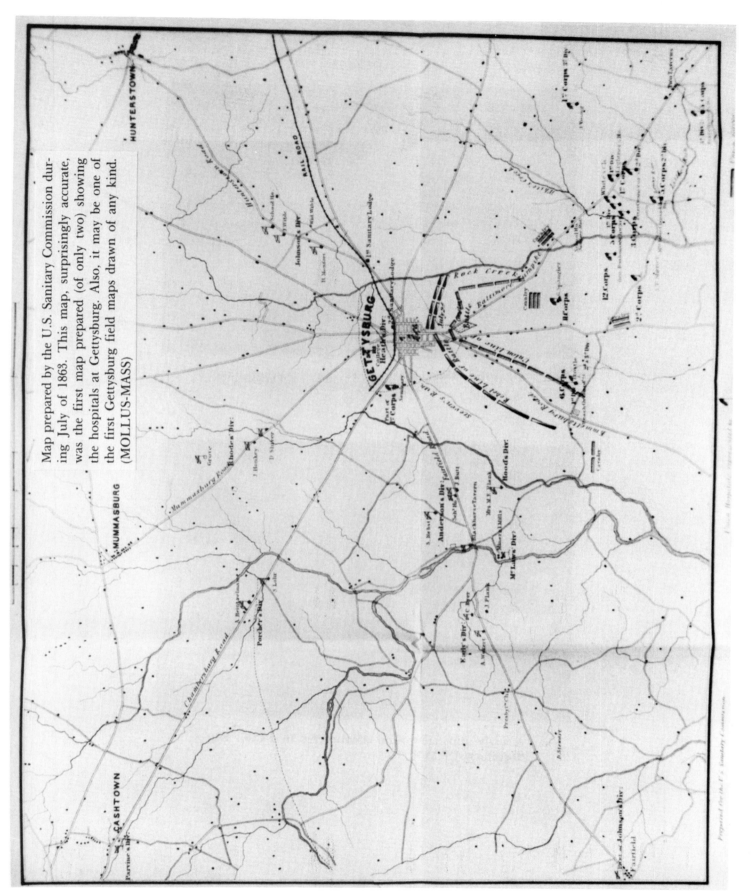

Map prepared by the U.S. Sanitary Commission during July of 1863. This map, surprisingly accurate, was the first map prepared (of only two) showing the hospitals at Gettysburg. Also, it may be one of the first Gettysburg field maps drawn of any kind. (MOLLUS-MASS)

175

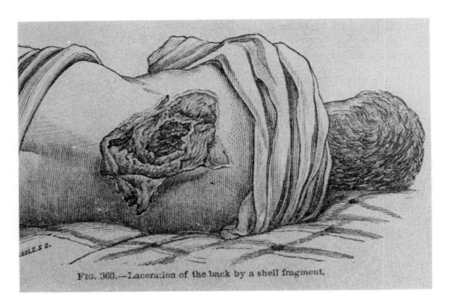

FIG. 360.—Laceration of the back by a shell fragment.

A typical wound encountered in a Civil War hospital.
(A.F.M.M.)

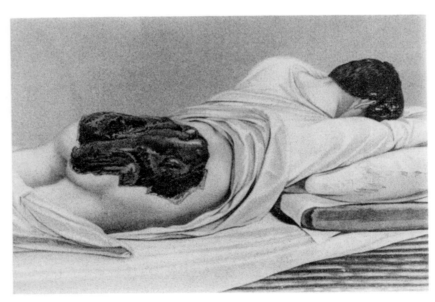

A fairly unusual wound encountered in a Civil War
hospital. (A.F.M.M.)

APPENDIX I
Surgeons and Physicians at Gettysburg

"Possibly the surgeons, who bound up these wounds, alone can some day tell the world how savagely men fought upon the bloody field of Gettysburg. Certainly no one else can."

From a *"History of Adams County"*

"It requires a man with a steel nerve and a case-hardened heart to be a army sergeon...."

James Houghton
4th Maine Infantry

This partial list of United States and Confederate States surgeons and other volunteer or contract physicians, is an attempt to assemble a roster of those men who appeared in sources relating to medical work actually done during and after the Battle of Gettysburg. It is obviously incomplete, (especially the Confederate section) and I apologize for that, however, the focus of this book is *not* a complete story of the medical history of the battle. This compilation is only a beginning, and may give interested readers a key, or a starting place from which to begin his or her own research.

UNION SURGEONS

Surgeon	Organization	Hospital
Adams, Z.B., Surgeon	32nd Mass. Inf.	regt. aid station near Wheatfield
Akin, Jno.	71st Pa. Inf.	2nd Div., 2nd Corps
Alexander, Charles, Surgeon	16th Me. Inf.	Christ Lutheran Church
Allen, Samuel J., Surgeon	4th Vt. Inf.	2nd Div., 6th Corps
Altman, William	28th Pa. Inf.	Abraham Spangler Farm
Arewald, A.W.		
Armstrong, James A., Med. Officer in charge of Corps Hospital	75th Pa. Inf.	11th Corps, G. Spangler Farm
Asch, M.J.	U.S. Volunteers	Med. Dir., Artillery Reserve
Bache, Richard M., Surgeon, Reynolds' Staff		Chas. Krauth House
Bache, Thomas H.	U.S. Volunteers	
Bacon, Cyrus, Jr.	Mich. Inf. and U.S. Regulars (?)	Jacob Weikert Farm
Ball, J. Alfred	50th Ohio Inf.	2nd Div., 12th Corps
Barnett	64th N.Y. Inf.	
Beck		Presbyterian Church

Beech, John H.	24th Mich. Inf.	Express Office
Bennett, W.C.	5th Ct. Inf.	1st. Div., 12th Corps
Benton, J.D. Assistant Surgeon	111th N.Y. Inf.	3rd Div., 2nd Corps
Billings, John S. Surgeon	U.S. Volunteers	Jacob Weikert Farm
Bissell, Evelyn Lyman Surgeon, Records, Food, Shelter Officer	5th Ct. Inf.	12th Corps
Boughman, George W. Acting Asst. Surgeon		Camp Letterman
Breakey, William F. Assistant Surgeon	16th Mich. Inf.	Camp Letterman
Breneman, Edward DeW.	U.S. Regulars	Jacob Weikert Farm
Brinton, Daniel G. Surgeon	U.S. Volunteers	2nd Div., 11th Corps
Brinton, Jeremiah B. Assistant Surgeon	Medical Purveyor	Gettysburg
Brinton, John H.	U.S. Volunteers	Special duty for Surgeon General
Brown		
Brubaker, David M. Assistant Surgeon	109th Pa. Inf.	Camp Letterman
Buck, H.B.	U.S. Volunteers	Granite Schoolhouse
Buckman, John H. Surgeon	5th N.H. Inf.	
Bunton, Sylvanus Surgeon	2nd N.H. Inf.	
Burchfield, James P.	83rd Pa. Inf.	Cared for Col. S. Vincent at L.A. Bushman Farm
Burke, George W. Surgeon, Records, Food, Shelter Officer	46th Pa. Inf.	12th Corps
Burmeister, Frederick F. Surgeon	69th Pa. Inf.	2nd Corps
Burn, William J. Surgeon	42nd Mass. Inf.	2nd Corps
Burr, W.J. Surgeon	47th N.Y. Inf.	2nd Div., 2nd Corps
Bush, W.P. Assistant Surgeon	61st N.Y. Inf.	1st Div., 2nd Corps
Butcher, Benjamin F. Acting Asst. Surgeon		Camp Letterman
Butcher		Presbyterian Church
Calhoun, J.T. Assistant Surgeon	3rd Corps Med. Dir. (temporary)	2nd Div., 3rd Corps, amputated Sickles' leg
Campbell, Cornelius M.	150th N.Y. Inf.	Abraham Spangler Farm
Cantwell, Jacob Y.	82nd Ohio Inf.	11th Corps
Capehart, Henry Surgeon	1st W.Va. Cavalry	3rd Div., Cavalry Corps
Carbee, Samuel P. Assistant Surgeon	12th N.H. Inf.	
Carpenter, James B. Acting Asst. Surgeon	U.S. Volunteers	Camp Letterman
Chamberlain, Cyrus N. Surgeon	U.S. Volunteers	Med. Officer in Charge of 6th Corps Hosp., and Camp Letterman
Chambers, William B.		Surgeon in Charge, 2nd Div., 1st Corps

Chapel, Artemus Surgeon	U.S. Volunteers	Chief Med. Officer of 1st Div., 12th Corps
Cheney, William F.	U.S. Sanitary Commission	In charge of U.S.S.C. camp
Child, William, Surgeon	5th N.H. Inf.	
Clark, Augustus M. Surgeon	U.S. Volunteers	Med. Officer in Charge of 5th Corps
Cobb, Albion Assistant Surgeon	4th Me. Inf.	
Collar, Alexander Assistant Surgeon	24th Mich. Inf.	Express Office Hospital
Cooper, W.S. Surgeon	125th N.Y. Inf.	
Cornish, Theodore O. Assistant Surgeon	15th Mass. Inf.	2nd Corps
Cotton		5th Corps (?)
Cress, James	Gettysburg Civilian	Miscellaneous houses, churches, etc.
Cuyler, John M. Med. Inspector, U.S.A.		Gettysburg, July 10-25
Davenport, Civilian Physician	Michigan	
Davis, U.Q. Surgeon	148th Pa. Inf.	1st Div., 2nd Corps
Day, Ebenezer Surgeon	39th N.Y. Inf.	Surgeon in Charge of 3rd Div., 2nd Corps
Dean, Henry C.	140th N.Y. Inf.	L.A. Bushman Farm
Dickson, John Civilian Surgeon w/Christian Commission	155th Pa. Inf.	
Dickson, Joseph Civilian Vol. Surgeon w/Christian Commission		
Dimon, Theodore Physician and Civilian Surgeon w/state of New York	3rd N.Y. Inf.	Washington House or Eagle Hotel
Dwinell, Justin Surgeon	108th Pa. Inf.	Med. Officer in Charge of Corps Hosp., 2nd Corps
Dougherty, Alexander N. Surgeon	U.S. Volunteers	Med. Director of 2nd Corps
Dunn, James L.	109th Pa. Inf.	2nd Div., 12th Corps
Dyer, J. Franklin Surgeon	19th Mass. Inf.	2nd Div., 2nd Corps
Ebersole, Jacob Surgeon	19th Ind. Inf.	Railroad Depot and Express Office
Edson, P. O'Meara Assistant Surgeon	1st Vt. Cavalry	
Emanuel, Louis M. Surgeon	82nd Pa. Inf.	Camp Letterman
Everett, Robert A. Assistant Surgeon	16th Mich. Inf.	
Farley, Henry L.	14th Brooklyn	Washington House Hotel
Fifield, Amos K.	7th Ohio Inf.	2nd Div., 12th Corps
Flood, Patrick H.	107th N.Y. Inf.	
Fowler, Hadley B. Surgeon	12th N.H. Inf.	3rd Corps
Free, Jared	83rd Pa. Inf.	

Freeman, J.A. Records, Food, Shelter Officer	13th N.J. Inf.	12th Corps left with wounded
Fulton, James Surgeon	143rd Pa. Inf.	3rd Div., 1st Corps, St. Francis Roman Catholic Church
Gallaher, Thomas J. Civilian Vol. Surgeon w/Christian Commission		
Gardner, Perin Surgeon		Hanover, Pa.
Garver, Henry F. Assistant Surgeon	19th Ind. Inf.	Cared for Lt. Col. Dudley in Littlestown
Gates		Presbyterian & Roman Catholic Churches
Gauntt, Charles S. Acting Asst. Surgeon	U.S. Volunteers	Camp Letterman
Gibbs, A.F. Acting Asst. Surgeon	U.S. Volunteers	Camp Letterman
Good, Daniel R. Acting Asst. Surgeon	U.S. Volunteers	Camp Letterman
Goodman, H. Earnest Surgeon	28th Pa. Inf.	Med. Officer in Charge of Corps Hosp., 12th Corps
Gorton Civilian Physician from Michigan		
Gunn Civilian Physician from Michigan		
Guth, E.F. Acting Asst. Surgeon	U.S. Volunteers	Camp Letterman
Hadden, James	95th N.Y. Inf.	
Hall, John C.	6th Wisc. Inf.	Express Office
Hamilton, Alfred T.	148th Pa. Inf.	J. Hummelbaugh Farm, Cared for Gen. Barksdale
Hamilton, Charles A.	76th N.Y. Inf.	Camp Letterman
Hard, Abner Surgeon	8th Ill. Cavalry	1st Div., Cavalry Corps, Presbyterian Church, Railroad Depot
Hays, William L. Acting Asst. Surgeon	U.S. Volunteers	Camp Letterman 1st Div., 3rd Corps
Hayward, Nathan Surgeon	20th Mass. Inf.	2nd Corps
Heard, Theodore J. Assistant Surgeon Gen. Reynolds' Staff	U.S. Volunteers	Med. Dir., 1st Corps
Herbst, John E. Surgeon	U.S. Volunteers	2nd Div., 12th Corps
Hildreth, Thaddeus Surgeon	3rd Me. Inf.	Med. Officer in Charge of Corps Hosp., 3rd Corps
Hodge, Lennox		In Charge of Pa. College Hospital
Holman, Silas A. Surgeon	7th Mass. Inf.	3rd Div., 6th Corps
Hooper Civilian Vol. Surgeon Boston, Mass.	U.S. Sanitary Commission	Relief Lodge
Horner, Charles Gettysburg Civilian Physician		Christ Lutheran Church

Horner, Robert Gettysburg Civilian Physician		Houses, churches, etc.
Howard, Benjamin	U.S. Volunteers	5th Corps, J. Weikert Farm
Hubbard, Robert	17th Ct. Inf.	Med. Insp. 11th Corps, Dr. O'Neal's home
Humphrey, Charles E.	142nd Pa. Inf.	
Humphrey, William F. Surgeon	149th Pa. Inf.	3rd Div., 1st Corps
Hunt, Charles W. Assistant Surgeon	12th N.H. Inf.	
Hursam, Nahum A. Surgeon	17th Me. Inf.	
James, Bushrod W. Civilian Physician from Philadelphia		2nd Corps
Janes, Henry Surgeon	U.S. Volunteers	Surgeon in Charge of all hosp. in Gettysburg area, Camp Letterman
Johnston, G.K. Surgeon	1st Mich. Cavalry	Medical Inspector
Jones, A. Stokes Assistant Surgeon	72nd Pa. Inf.	2nd Corps
Jones, William B. Ward Surgeon	U.S. Volunteers (13th Pa. Reserves)	Camp Letterman
Kelsey, Charles T. Surgeon		Surgeon in Charge, 1st Div., 2nd Corps
Kibby		11th Corps
King Civilian Physician from New York		
Koerper, Egon A. Acting Asst. Surgeon	75th Pa. Inf.	Camp Letterman
Kohler, John P.	153rd Pa. Inf.	
Kollock, John Assistant Surgeon	118th Pa. Inf.	
Kreffer, Stephen		Hospital in Carlisle
Ladd Civilian Physician		
Lanning, J.T. Acting Asst. Surgeon		Camp Letterman
Leaman, Henry Acting Asst. Surgeon		Lutheran Theo. Seminary, Camp Letterman
Levensaller, Henry C. Assistant Surgeon	19th Me. Inf.	2nd Corps
Leisenring, P.S. Acting Asst. Surgeon		Camp Letterman
Letterman, Jonathan Surgeon	U.S. Volunteers	Med. Dir. of the Army of the Potomac
Lord, C.H. Records, Food, Shelter Officer	107th N.Y. Inf.	12th Corps
Lord, Mathias L. Assistant Surgeon	140th N.Y. Inf.	L.A. Bushman Farm
Loughran, Robert Surgeon	80th N.Y. Inf.	Roman Catholic Church, Lutheran Theo. Seminary, Officer in Charge of 1st Corps (7 weeks)

Love, John H.	13th N.J. Inf.	1st Div., 12th Corps, at G. Bushman Farm 1st Div., 3rd Corps
Lyman, Jonas W. Surgeon	57th Pa. Inf.	1st Div., 3rd Corps
May, Henry A. Assistant Surgeon	145th N.Y. Inf.	12th Corps and Camp Letterman
McAbee, H.M. Reynolds' Staff	4th Ohio Inf.	2nd Corps Hosp., near Round Top, Catherine Guinn Farm
McCabe, H.M.	4th Ohio Inf.	3rd Div., 2nd Corps
McCook, George L. Civilian Vol. Surgeon w/Christian Commission		
McClarren(?)	38th Pa. (Reserves)	At Div. "Barn Hosp."
McCullough, J.W. Assistant Surgeon	1st Del. Inf.	3rd Div., 2nd Corps
McGregor, Murdock Assistant Surgeon	33rd Mass. Inf.	George George House
McNulty, John	U.S. Volunteers	Med. Dir. of 12th Corps
McWilliams, Alex Acting Asst. Surgeon		Camp Letterman
Meyer, Louis C.	25th Ohio Inf.	1st Div., 11th Corps
Milhau, John J. Surgeon	U.S. Regulars	Med. Dir. of 5th Corps
Mitchell, S. Weir		
Montfort, Robert V.K. Surgeon	124th N.Y. Inf.	
Moore, W.S. Surgeon	61st Ohio Inf.	11th Corps (was wounded and died July 6)
Neff, Henry K. Surgeon	8th Pa. (Reserves)	Poorhouse-taken prisoner
Neill, (John?)	U.S. Volunteers (?)	Pine Grove Furnace Hosp.
New, George W. Surgeon	7th Ind. Inf.	Surgeon in Chief, 1st Div., 1st Corps, Lutheran Theo. Seminary, White Church
Newcombe, James Acting Asst. Surgeon		Camp Letterman
Nordquist, Charles J. Surgeon	83rd N.Y. Inf.	2nd Div., 1st Corps
Norris, William F. Surgeon		3rd Div., 1st Corps, Roman Catholic Church, and Camp Letterman
Oakley, Lewis W. Surgeon	2nd N.J. Inf.	Camp Letterman
O'Leary, Charles Surgeon	U.S. Volunteers	Med. Dir. of 6th Corps
O'Neal, J.W.C. Gettysburg Civilian Physician		Miscellaneous houses, churches, etc., D. Stem, Almshouse, D. Shriver
Osborne, Joseph D. Surgeon	4th N.J. Inf.	Reserve Artillery and Camp Letterman
Osborne, William F. Assistant Surgeon	11th Pa. Inf.	2nd Div., 1st Corps, Lutheran Theo. Seminary
Paine, Robert T., Jr. Records, Food, Shelter Officer, Asst. Surgeon	28th N.Y. Inf.	12th Corps
Palmer		Hosp. in Carlisle
Pancoast, George L. Surgeon	U.S. Volunteers	Med. Dir. of Cavalry Corps

Parker, Edgar Assistant Surgeon (wounded)	13th Mass. Inf.	Christ Lutheran Church
Peltier, Pierre D. Surgeon	126th N.Y. Inf.	J. Schwartz Farm, 2nd Corps
Phillips, William W.L. Surgeon	1st N.J. Cavalry	2nd Div., Cavalry Corps
Place, Simon G. Assistant Surgeon	147th N.Y. Inf.	
Plunkett, Philip M.	2nd Del. Inf.	
Potter, George L. Assistant Surgeon	5th U.S. Cavalry	
Potter, William W. Surgeon	57th N.Y. Inf.	Surgeon in Charge, 1st Div., 2nd Corps, Taneytown Road and with Gen. Zook at death
Porter Surgeon		Surgeon in Charge of 5th Corps
Preston, A.W.	6th Wisc. Inf.	
Quackenbush, Surgeon General (?)	N.Y. Inf. (?)	
Quinan, Philip A.	150th Pa. Inf.	Roman Catholic Church Officer in Charge, 3rd Div., 1st Corps
Ramsey, George W. Surgeon	95th N.Y. Inf.	Surgeon in Charge, 1st Div., 1st Corps
Read, Louis W. Surgeon	U.S. Volunteers	3rd Div., 5th Corps
Reed, J.A.E. Surgeon	155th Pa. Inf.	
Rizer, Martin Surgeon	72nd Pa. Inf.	2nd Corps
Rogers, William C. Surgeon	46th Pa. Inf.	Chief Operating Surgeon, 1st Div., 12th Corps
Roher, Benjamin Surgeon	10th Pa. Reserves	
Ross, Lucretius Assistant Surgeon	14th Vt. Inf.	3rd Div., 1st Corps
Rowand, J.R. Acting Asst. Surgeon	U.S. Volunteers	Camp Letterman
Rulison, William H.	9th N.Y. Inf.	Med. Officer in Charge of Corps Hospital, Presbyterian Church
Runkles		Presbyterian Church
Russell, Ira Surgeon	U.S. Volunteers	5th Corps, J. Weikert Farm, stayed w/General Weed
Sanborn, John H. Assistant Surgeon	12th N.H. Inf.	
Sanger, Eugene F.	U.S. Volunteers	Presbyterian Church
Scott, Isaac Surgeon	7th W.Va. Inf.	3rd Div., 2nd Corps
Senseny, A.H.		Chambersburg Hospitals
Senegar (?)	7th Ind. Inf.	
Sharp, W.W. Assistant Surgeon	140th Pa. Inf.	1st Div., 2nd Corps
Shaw, Thomas W. Civilian Vol. Surgeon w/Christian Commission		

Shekell, A.B. Acting Asst. Surgeon	U.S. Volunteers	Camp Letterman
Shippen, Edward Surgeon	U.S. Volunteers	1st Div., 5th Corps
Shivers, James K. Acting Asst. Surgeon	U.S. Volunteers	College Hospital, Camp Letterman
Sim, Thomas Surgeon	U.S. Volunteers	3rd Corps Med. Dir. of Corps, Left battlefield w/Gen. Sickles
Smiley, Thomas L. Acting Asst. Surgeon	U.S. Volunteers	Camp Letterman
Smith E.		
Smith, F.H. Acting Asst. Surgeon	U.S. Volunteers	Camp Letterman
Stearns, Isaac H. Surgeon	22nd Mass. Inf.	1st Div., 5th Corps- A. Spangler barn
Stem, William Civilian Physician at Cashtown		Cashtown
Stevens, George T. Surgeon	77th N.Y. Inf.	with regiment
Stiles, Richard C. Surgeon	U.S. Volunteers	1st Div., 2nd Corps
Stonedale		
Stonelake, A.B. Acting Asst. Surgeon	U.S. Volunteers	Camp Letterman
Stout, Abraham Assistant Surgeon	153rd Pa. Inf.	11th Corps, M.L. Stoever House
Sturdevant, Samuel B. Assistant Surgeon	139th Pa. Inf.	Camp Letterman
Suckley, George Surgeon	U.S. Volunteers	Med. Dir. of 11th Corps, 11th Corps
Sutton, H.H. Acting Asst. Surgeon	U.S. Volunteers	Camp Letterman
Swart, Charles Assistant Surgeon	63rd N.Y. Inf.	1st Div., 2nd Corps
Tate, Theodore H.	3rd Pa. Cavalry	with C.S. wounded in Schoolhouse Hospital
Taylor, Edward F. Surgeon	1st N.J. Inf.	1st Div., 6th Corps
Taylor, William Civilian Physician in Gettysburg		Miscellaneous homes, public buildings, etc.
Taylor		Med. Inspector of the Army of the Potomac
Thomas, Joseph	118th Pa. Inf.	J. Weikert Farm Camp Letterman
Thome, W.H. Surgeon	U.S. Volunteers	3rd Div., 11th Corps
Thompson, John H. Surgeon	124th N.Y. Infantry	
Tibbals, William T. Records, Food, Shelter Officer	5th Ohio Inf.	12th Corps
Tomlinson		Hospital in Carlisle
Towar, George W. Assistant Surgeon	24th Mich. Inf.	with regiment
Townsend, E.P. Acting Asst. Surgeon	U.S. Volunteers	Camp Letterman
Twiford, W.H.	27th Ind. Inf.	1st Div., 12th Corps

Van Benst, B.	U.S. Volunteers	1st Div., 11th Corps
Vollum, Edward P.	U.S. Regulars	Medical Inspector
Vosburg, Hiram D. Assistant Surgeon	8th N.Y. Cavalry	Presbyterian Church, Camp Letterman
Wafer, Francis M. Assistant Surgeon	108th N.Y. Inf.	Peter Frey Farm-2nd Corps
Wagner, Clinton Assistant Surgeon	U.S. Regulars	Surgeon in Charge, 2nd Div., 5th Corps, J. Weikert Farm
Walker, Mary Civilian Volunteer		
Walker, T.H. Acting Asst. Surgeon		Camp Letterman
Wallace, Ellerslie		
Walsh, R.S.L. Acting Asst. Surgeon	U.S. Volunteers	Camp Letterman
Ward, Andrew J. Surgeon	2nd Wisc. Inf.	Officer in Charge of Corps Hospital, 1st Corps
Ward, George W. Acting Asst. Surgeon	U.S. Volunteers	Camp Letterman
Watson, James D. Assistant Surgeon	3rd Me. Inf.	Camp Letterman
Watson, William Surgeon	105th Pa. Inf.	Div. Hospital— 3rd Corps "Barn"
Weidman, William W.	2nd Pa. Cavalry	"Treated Rebs"
Wescott, William Assistant Surgeon	17th Me. Inf.	
Whittier, Samuel C. Assistant Surgeon	11th Mass. Inf.	
Whittingham, Edward T.	U.S. Regulars	5th Corps, J. Weikert Farm
Wilson, W. Stockton Assistant Surgeon	155th Pa. Inf.	
Wishart, J. Wilson Surgeon	140th Pa. Inf.	
Wolf, Fred Surgeon	39th N.Y. Inf.	3rd Div., 2nd Corps
Wood, Charles Squire		treated General Zook— at Corps Aid Station
Woodward, A.T. Surgeon		Surgeon in Charge, 3rd Div., 1st Corps

CONFEDERATE SURGEONS

Baker, Daniel	12th Va. Inf.	Camp Letterman
Baruch, Simon Assistant Surgeon	3rd S.C. Inf.	Black Horse Tavern
Black		
Bodly, John R. (?)	Georgia	J.E. Plank Farm
Briggs Surgeon	30th N.C. Inf.	
Brown, C.H. Acting Asst. Surgeon	18th Miss. Inf.	
Brown, J.R.	3rd Ark. Inf.	with regiment
Budd, H.V. Surgeon		Hospital in Carlisle
Butler, Matt	37th Va. Inf.	
Clifton, James B.	Semmes' Brigade	George Rose Barn

Name	Unit	Location/Notes
Cullen, J.S. Dorsey Surgeon		Med. Dir. Longstreet's Corps, Black Horse Tavern
Edwards	8th Va. Inf.	
Eldridge	McLaws' Div.	J. Cunningham Farm
Eliason, Talcot	Stuart's Cav.	Barn east of Gettysburg
Frazer (?)	Heth's (?)	From Texas
Frazier		Surgeon in Charge of Pa. College
Gamble, H.M.	20th Va. Inf.	Chambersburg Hospitals
Gott		Surgeon in Charge of Early's Div.
Gray, H.V. Assistant Surgeon	Alexander's Artillery Battalion	Black Horse Tavern
Green	55th N.C. Inf.	Heth's Div. Hospital
Guild, Lafayette		Med. Dir. of Army of Northern Virginia
Hayes	Rodes' Div. Ala. Bde. Surgeon	Mummasburg Road area
Hays		mentioned by Gen. Trimble
Hays, J.M.		Camp Letterman
Hobgood, S.P. Surgeon	Semmes' Brigade	
Holt, Joseph Assistant Surgeon	11th Miss. Inf.	
Hubbard	Davis' Brigade	Samuel Lohr Farm
Kead, J.B. (?)		
Kleinschmidth, H.C.	3rd Ark. Inf.	with regiment
Knox, R.L. Acting Asst. Surgeon	17th Miss. Inf.	
Madden Assistant Surgeon	Florida	
McAdams	Pickett's Div.	Surgeon in Charge
McCorkey	Pickett's Div.	
McGuire, Hunter H.	Ewell's Corps	H.A. Picking Farm
Means, F.A.	11th Ga. Inf.	J.E. Plank Farm and Camp Letterman
Minor, H.A.	8th Ala. Inf. Anderson's Div.	Surgeon in Charge, Butt's Schoolhouse on Fairfield Road. Camp Letterman
Monteiro, Aristides	Alexander's Battalion	Black Horse Tavern
Montgomery Assistant Surgeon	Archer's Brigade	Cashtown area
Morton Surgeon	Kemper's Brigade	
Myers, Robert P. Surgeon	16th Ga. Inf.	with regiment
Nance, W.F.	2nd Fla. Inf.	Camp Letterman
Nott, H.J. Assistant Surgeon	2nd S.C. Inf.	Black Horse Tavern for 6 weeks
Parker, D.H.		Camp Letterman
Parramore, H.J. Assistant Surgeon	58th Ga. Inf.	
Patterson		Presbyterian Church
Patterson, F.W. Surgeon	McLaws' Div.	Surgeon in Charge, Bream's Mill

186

Pearce, J.F.	18th S.C. Inf.	Black Horse Tavern for 6 weeks
Potts	Early's Div.	Fairfield Road
Ramsaur, D.H. Acting Asst. Surgeon	18th Ga. Inf.	
Ransom	McLaws' Div.	J. Cunningham Farm
Reeves	Pickett's Div.	Surgeon in Charge at Bream's Tavern & Farm
Richardson, W.F.	9th Ala. Inf.	Camp Letterman
Salmond, T.W.	Kershaw's Brigade	Brigade Surgeon
Sayers	Johnson's Div.	Surgeon in Charge
Scott	7th Va. Inf.	2nd Corps
Sethall, R.B.		Camp Letterman
Sewell, F.H. Acting Asst. Surgeon	Artillery Battalion	
Shields	Davis' Brigade	
Shivers		Surgeon in Charge, Pa. College Hospital
Smiley	Heth's Div.	Pa. College
Southhall	Ala. Brigade	
Spence, W.A.	Archer's Brigade	Chief Surgeon, Cashtown
Stewart	Johnson's Div (?)	Fairfield Road
Taylor, William H. Assistant Surgeon	19th Va. Inf.	(was wounded)
Vance, F.J.		Camp Letterman
Ward, B.F.	11th Miss. Inf. (?) Heth's Div.	Surgeon in Charge, (3 weeks) at Fairfield & on Chambersburg Road
Warren (?)	11th or 26th N.C. Inf. (?)	Chambersburg Road
Warren, L.P. Brigade Surgeon	52nd N.C. Inf.	Pettigrew's Brigade
Watson, Major	Alabama	Dr. M.L. Stoever house
Welch, Spencer G. Surgeon	13th S.C. Inf.	Pender's Div. Hosp.
Whitehead, William R.	Johnson's Div.	"In charge of C.S. wounded at Gettysburg" "Old Barn"
Whitfield, George Surgeon	12th Ala. Inf.	
Wilson		Fairfield Hospitals
Wilson	McLaws' Div.	at Cashtown
Wilson Assistant Surgeon	1st Va. Cavalry	Cavalry wounded
Wilson, Legrand J.	42nd Miss. Inf.	Willoughby's Run, Samuel Lohr Farm
Woods, J.R.	2nd Ga. Battalion	
Yates, Joseph	1st S.C. Cavalry	Hosp. on East Cavalry Field

Appendix II
Finding a Field Hospital in 1863

It was not always easy for a wounded soldier to locate a field hospital. After visiting the regimental aid station just in rear of the battle line, the injured man would usually be directed to the brigade, or more likely the division hospital, further to the rear. If the individual was slightly wounded he may have actually walked back, while seriously injured men would naturally be carried by litter to an ambulance collecting point, and from there transported to the field hospital. If they were fortunate, the walking wounded, as well as ambulance drivers followed markers which designated the route to the hospital. An eyewitness recorded one way in which his route was so marked: "We noticed as we were going through the woods a red flag flying alongside of a board on which we read: '1700 wounded down this way.'"

Even though a general order issued by the Headquarters of the Army of the Potomac on March 24, 1862, stated that, "Hospitals will be distinguished by a yellow flag," red flags seemed to be predominantly used during and after the Battle of Gettysburg. In fact, out of the thirty or so references in my files to hospital flags, thirteen mention scarlet or red for the color noted while only four list yellow as the color in question. One source even indicated that at night he observed "red lights" in use while hunting for the wounded.

Badly hurt soldiers who were unable to move, often placed a white cloth on a ramrod jammed into the ground next to their persons to let the medical attendants know where to find them.

In January of 1864, a new hospital flag was designated for the U.S. medical service. It was yellow with a large green "H" in the center. Like its northern counterpart, the Confederate army seemed to use whatever color was available. At the large Confederate States hospital at Bream's Tavern, a yellow flag was flown on the lightning rod of the barn, while at many other sites a red flag served as the indicator. In fact, for a short time on July 2 at the John Cunningham farm, the Confederates used a pair of Mrs. Cunningham's white undergarments as a flag on the lightning rod of the family's barn.

Appendix III
Movement of the Wounded to Field Hospitals

When a wounded soldier was unable to walk or otherwise make his own way to a hospital, he generally waited for the stretcher bearers to carry him to an ambulance collecting point where he was then usually transported to a division hospital. If the task of moving thousands of injured men became too great for the regular ambulance corps, civilian wagons and carriages were often utilized. Many wounded at Gettysburg even paid local farmers to take them to hospitals or to the railroad depot. When litters became unavailable, boards, window shutters, or doors were used as substitutes.

Overall, during and after the Battle of Gettysburg, the ambulance corps probably did a better-than-average job of removing the wounded from the field and carrying them to hospitals. Several of my sources seem to indicate this to be the case.

One of the best descriptions of a division ambulance corps at Gettysburg was left to us by Thomas Livermore who was then chief of ambulances for the Union Second Corps. He wrote:

> The ambulance corps consisted of three trains, one for each division of the army corps. Each train consisted of forty, two horse ambulances (in the proportion of three ambulances to each regiment, I think), with a few for the artillery, several wagons with four horses to carry forage and rations in, and a forge wagon for repairs and horseshoeing, with several old-style four-horse ambulances. The men were selected proportionately from the regiments, and consisted of a driver for each ambulance and wagon, two stretcher-carriers for each wagon, and several blacksmiths and supernumeraries. . . .
>
> The total force of the ambulance corps was, in round numbers, 13 officers, 350 to 400 men, and 300 or more horses, with a little over 100 ambulances and 10 or 12 forage and forge wagons; and these were my command. Each two-horse ambulance was a stout spring wagon very much like an ordinary express or grocer's wagon, with sides a little higher than theirs along each side. Inside this wagon were two seats the whole length, like those

of an omnibus, stuffed and covered with leather. Hinged to the inner edges of each of these seats was another leather-covered seat, which could be let down perpendicularly so as to allow the wounded to sit on the first seats facing each other, or could be raised and supported horizontally on a level with the first seats, and, as they filled all the space between the first seats, thus made a couch on which three men could lie lengthwise of the ambulance.

In the rear end of the ambulance under each seat was a water keg with the end out and containing a faucet, which contained fresh water for the wounded. In front, under the driver's seat, was a supply of beef stock, and I believe bandages and other hospital stores. On each side of the ambulance there was hung a canvas-covered stretcher to carry the wounded on, and the whole ambulance was neatly covered with white canvas on bows.

Taking the information just given, the Union army, then at Gettysburg, must have had about eight hundred ambulances on the field, and at least 1,600 litter bearers. It is plain to see why, when Surgeon Letterman left only about thirty ambulances and a few wagons behind when the army left the area, the remaining medical personnel were quite upset and seriously handicapped. This meant that 21,000 wounded would have had to make do with only these few conveyances.

Appendix IV
Medical Observations at Gettysburg

During the research period for this book, I came across several medical practices, some of which, to the casual reader, may seem somewhat unusual. Briefly, here are a few of those interesting items.

—Special shirts were issued to seriously wounded men. They were made in sections for ease of donning, and were held on with tape.

—A lieutenant colonel of the 8th Virginia Infantry noted that it took twenty-one inches of flesh and muscle to stop a Minié ball at 150 yards.

—Another officer in the 53rd Virginia recalled that in his army, whiskey was called "Confederate chloroform."

—A visitor to the battlefield on July 5 remembered that the soldiers were speaking in very loud voices due to being nearly deaf from battle noise.

—One soldier said that in his field hospital chloroform was administered with the aid of a cow's horn.

—A surgeon had the distinct impression after visiting many hospitals around Gettysburg that the wounded in town sites were not doing as well as the wounded on the country farms.

—Chloride of lime was used to kill the terrible smell of rotting flesh.

—Tea was used to loosen and remove blood-caked or blood-soaked bandages.

—Several spectators on the field remembered medical students and others boiling down the limbs and bodies of soldiers so that the bones could be taken away as medical specimens.

—One nurse was seen using camphor and potatoes on wounds to aid in their healing.

—One surgeon cleaned the maggots out of wounds by spitting a mouthful of turpentine onto the creatures. Kerosene was used also.

—Many people who visited the battlefield the week after the fighting were taken ill, some very seriously by the horrible odor of rotting human and animal corpses.

—Although it was a common practice during the Civil War to keep wounds wet, some new medical literature of the day stated that wounds kept dry and clean had better results.

—One report issued said that out of eight thousand cases treated with chloroform, thirty-seven patients died, and out of eight thousand cases treated with ether, four were fatal. Many died from lack of resuscitation after being under chloroform or ether.

—Eight inch square *Pads* filled with bran or sawdust were in great demand and were in short supply. They were probably used to support wounded limbs, or heads of patients. One nurse made his own pads, stuffed with sawdust which had filled brandy crates. Lint was also scarce, and dried "rusk" was often mentioned as being needed.

—At Gettysburg, several serious wounds of the chest were "hermetically" sealed, a fairly new method of treatment. All died within a short time afterwards.

—Straw was extremely scarce, but was one item that was almost indispensible. Many wounded did not even have a thin layer of hay to lie on—even for days at a time.

—One surgeon noted: "I saw few that were *slightly* hurt." This sentence tells it all.

—Flies were one of the most terrible scourges of Gettysburg, especially the large "green bottle" kind. A soldier in one of the field hospitals noted that every fence post near him was "black with flies." This is why so many wounds contained maggots.

—When available, cornstarch was administered to wounded men every hour.

—One wounded soldier said that water became so scarce on July 4 that he had to walk six miles to find a well not dry.

—It is readily known that one or two Federal units used "explosive bullets" in the Battle of Gettysburg. A surgeon noted that the Confederates were also using these fearful projectiles. He said: "When these balls burst in the body the destruction of the parts is terrible. They must greatly add to the mortality of the wounded."

—The same surgeon observed that soldiers who purchased or were issued field tourniquets often left them on too long, causing serious damage to the circulatory system. He recommended that they not be used: "It is very rare indeed that death occurs from Primary Hemorrhage in consequence of gun-shot wounds. More lives are lost than saved by (their) use. . . ."

—Another doctor, this one a Confederate in one of Longstreet's division hospitals, remarked that, ". . .many surgeons in their haste were resorting to primitive methods, cutting and sawing through skin, muscle, and bone, then cauterizing the stump with a searing hot iron, not ligating or tying the arteries. . . ."

Notes

Any reference in the text to "Duncan" can be traced to the book written by Louis C. Duncan, *The Medical Department of the United States Army in the Civil War* Washington, D.C. (?) 1915 (?), pp. 211–267.

Likewise, the Federal or State claims were not footnoted. They may be found in the damage claim applications file, 1871–79 from the Pennsylvania Historical and Museum Commission, Harrisburg, Pennsylvania 17108, or in the Quartermaster General's claims files, record group 92, National Archives, Washington, D.C., 20408.

When the U.S. Sanitary Commission is referred to, the reader will probably find the information in *Report on the Operations of the Sanitary Commission During and After the Battles at Gettysburg* (New York, 1863), and *The Sanitary Commission of The United States Army, A Succinct Narrative of Its Works and Purposes* (New York, 1864). Information on the U.S. Christian Commission was taken from the *United States Christian Commission for the Army and Navy, Work and Incidents, First Annual Report* (Philadelphia, 1863), and *The Battle of Gettysburg and the Christian Commission* by Andrew B. Cross (Baltimore, 1865).

If gravesites or burial rosters are noted, these are all courtesy of their compiler, Kathleen Georg Harrison, Gettysburg National Military Park historian.

Due to the brevity of the footnotes, if anyone would like additional information concerning any particular source, please feel free to write the author, in care of Thomas Publications, P.O. Box 3031, Gettysburg, Pennsylvania 17325.

Part I
Borough of Gettysburg Area Field Hospital Sites

1. U.S. Christian Commission Report, 1863. Hereafter cited as U.S.C.C. Report, 1863.
2. Hard, Abner, *History of the Eighth Cavalry Regiment Illinois Volunteers, During the Great Rebellion* (Aurora, Ill., 1868).
3. Ebersole, Jacob, *Incidents of Field Hospital Life with the Army of the Potomac*, Military Order of the Loyal Legion of the United States (MOLLUS) Ohio papers, Vol. 4.
4. Blanchard, Eli A., copy of unpublished personal letters in author's files.
5. Jones, Francis B., copy of unpublished memoir in files of the Gettysburg National Military Park library (G.N.M.P. library).
6. Vautier, John D., "At Gettysburg," Philadelphia *Weekly Press*, 1886.
7. Gardner, Leonard M., *Sunset Memories* (Gettysburg Times Publishing Co., 1929).
8. Ziegler, Hugh M., copy of unpublished memoirs in author's files.
9. New, George W., letter to John B. Bachelder, September 1865, in the G.N.M.P. library.
10. Powell, Robert M., memoir, Philadelphia *Weekly Times*, 1884.
11. Trimble, Isaac R., diary, *Maryland Historical Magazine* (March 1922).
12. Schantz, F.J.F., recollections (Lebanon County Historical Society, 1963), Vol. 2.
13. Broadhead, Sarah M., copy of diary, G.N.M.P. library.
14. Douglas, Henry K., *I Rode With Stonewall* (University of North Carolina Press, Chapel Hill, 1986).
15. McClean, Elizabeth M., article, Gettysburg *Compiler*, June 8, 1908.
    Elher, C.A., *Hospital Scenes After The Battle of Gettysburg*, The Patriot Daughters of Lancaster (Philadelphia, 1864).
16. Buehler, Fannie J., *Recollections of the Rebel Invasion and One Woman's Experience During the Battle of Gettysburg* (Gettysburg, 1896).
17. Moore, Frank, "Miss Carrie Sheads of Gettysburg," *Grand Army Scout and Soldiers Mail*, Vol. 2, #13.
18. Foster, Catherine M.W., obituary, Gettysburg *Compiler*, January 20, 1917. (Also article, Gettysburg *Compiler*, September 1, 1896.)
19. McCreary, Albertus, memoir, *McClure's* Magazine (July, 1909).
20. Kiefer, William R., *History of the 153rd Regiment Pennsylvania Volunteers Infantry . . .*, Newton H. Mack (Press of the Chemical Publishing Company, Easton, 1909).
21. Ibid.
22. Silliman, Justus M., *A New Canaan Private in the Civil War*, New Canaan Historical Society (Connecticut), ed. by Edward Marcus (1984).
23. Huidekoper, Henry S., *Historic Church and Hospital on the Battlefield of Gettysburg*, illustrated pamphlet, G.N.M.P. library.
24. Myers, Elizabeth Salome, memoir, Philadelphia *North American* (July 4, 1909).

Linn, John B. Diary in the collection of the Gettysburg National Military Park library.
25. Norris, William F., "A Hospital at Gettysburg," *General Magazine and Historical Chronicle* (1942-45), Vol. 45. Linn, John B., op. cit.
26. McCreary, Albertus, opere citato (op. cit.).
27. Camp Letterman Papers, gift from Lewis Leigh, Jr., in G.N.M.P. library.
28. McCurdy, Charles M., *Gettysburg, A Memoir* (Pittsburgh, 1929).
29. Walker, Melvin H., "A Captive of Lee's Army at Gettysburg," *National Tribune* (Washington, D.C., October 1925).
30. Croll, Jennie C., memoir of Mary A. Horner, Philadelphia *Weekly Press*, November 16, 1887.
31. Elher, C.A., op. cit.
32. McAllister, Mary, a memoir published in four articles, Philadelphia *Inquirer,* June 26-29, 1938.
33. Vail, Enos B., *Reminiscences of a Boy in the Civil War* (Brooklyn, New York, 1915), courtesy of Seward R. Osborne.
34. Fahnestock, Gates D., memoir, Adams County Historical Society, Gettysburg. Hereafter cited as A.C.H.S.
35. U.S. Sanitary Commission Report, 1863. Hereafter cited as U.S.S.C., 1863 or 1864.
36. Buehler, Fannie J., op. cit.
37. McClean, Elizabeth M., op. cit.
38. Swallow, William H., "The Third Day at Gettysburg," *Southern Bivouac*, Vol. 4 (1886). Linn, John B., op. cit.
39. Smith, Donald L., *The Twenty-fourth Michigan of the Iron Brigade* (The Stackpole Co., Harrisburg, 1962).
40. Wills, John C., memoir, files of the A.C.H.S.
41. Camp Letterman Papers, op. cit.
42. New, George W., letter, op. cit.
43. Dimon, Theodore, unpublished diary, State University of Iowa, Iowa City, Iowa.
44. U.S.S.C. Report, 1863.
45. Pierce, Matilda J. (Mrs. M.J. "Tillie" Alleman), *At Gettysburg; What a Girl Saw and Heard of the Battle* (New York, 1889).
46. Broadhead, Sarah M., op. cit.
47. Warren, Leander H., *My Recollections of What I Saw Before, During and After The Battle of Gettysburg* (Gettysburg, 1926).
48. Aughinbaugh, Nellie E., *Personal Experiences of a Young Girl During The Battle of Gettysburg* (Washington, D.C., 1926?).
49. Harvey, William, letter, Detroit *Advertiser and Tribune,* July 9, 1863.
50. Camp Letterman Papers, op. cit.
51. Kiefer, William R., op. cit.
52. Way, William C., letter, Detroit *Free Press,* July 9, 1863.
53. Silliman, Justus M., op. cit.
54. U.S.C.C. Report, 1863.
55. Kendlehart, Margaretta, "A Story of Early's Raid," Gettysburg *Compiler,* June 30, 1923.
56. Shepherd, Henry E., "Wounded and Captured," article, *Blue and Gray* Magazine (Philadelphia, July 1893).
57. Hollinger, Liberty A., *Some Personal Recollections of the Battle of Gettysburg* (Mrs. L.A. Clutz) (privately printed, no date).
58. Silliman, Justus M., op. cit.
59. Kiefer, William R., op. cit.
60. Ibid.
61. Schantz, F.J.F., op. cit.
62. Colver, Michael, article, Pennsylvania College yearbook, *The Spectrum* (1902).
63. Unknown officer's diary, Vol. 2, *The Land We Love* (Charlotte, North Carolina, 1866-67). Linn, John B., op. cit.
64. Powell, Robert M., op. cit.
65. Barziza, Decimus et Ultimus, *The Adventures of a Prisoner of War*, ed. by R.H. Shuffler (University of Austin Press, Austin, Texas, 1964).
66. Article, Harrisburg *Telegraph,* July 18, 1863.
67. Kimball, George, memoir, *Rebellion Echoes*, Boston *Journal* (May 2, 1885).
68. Jones, Francis B., op. cit.
69. Rexford, William H., letter, Detroit *Advertiser and Tribune,* July 9, 1863.
70. Howard, Rowland B., diary, (American Peace Society, Boston, May and June, 1887). A copy of this article is at the A.C.H.S.
71. Howard, Oliver O., *Autobiography of Oliver O. Howard* (Baker and Taylor Company, New York, 1907-1908).
72. McCreary, Jennie, letter, Philadelphia *Evening Bulletin,* July 2, 1938.
73. Wert, J. Howard, taken from one of twelve articles published in the Harrisburg *Telegraph,* July 2-October 7, 1907. Hereafter cited as Wert, J. Howard.
Osborn, William F., published letter, "Newspaper Clippings File" p. 163, G.N.M.P. library.

74. Trimble, Isaac R., op. cit.
75. McCurdy, Charles M., op. cit.
76. Hanna, Thomas L., "A Day at Gettysburg," article, *National Tribune*, May 23, 1901.
77. McAllister, Mary, op. cit.
78. Reinecker (Rupp) Amanda E., article, Gettysburg *Compiler*, March 17, 1928.
79. Croll, Jennie C., op. cit.
80. McAllister, Mary, op. cit.
    Way, William C., letter, Detroit *Advertiser and Tribune*, July 24, 1863.
81. Schantz, F.J.F., op. cit.
82. Laracy, Richard, letter (published copy), files of the A.C.H.S.
83. Gilbert, Elizabeth, memoir, Gettysburg *Compiler*, September 6, 1905.
84. Broadhead, Sarah, op. cit.
85. "Reminiscences of the Battle of Gettysburg," article, Gettysburg *Star and Sentinel*, March 8, 1872.
    Trowbridge, John T., "The Field of Gettysburg," *Atlantic Monthly* (November 16, 1865).
86. Stoever, Sue Elizabeth, "A Woman's Story of the Battle," article, Gettysburg *Compiler*, June 24, 1903.
87. Ibid.
88. McClean, Elizabeth M., op. cit.
89. Buehler, Fannie J., op. cit.
90. Gilbert, Elizabeth, op. cit.
91. Marsh, Henry C., letter, Indianapolis *Daily Journal*, August 1, 1863.
92. Copy of a letter written to J.W.C. O'Neal in Scott, J.K.P., *The Story of the Battles at Gettysburg*, (The Telegraph Press, Harrisburg, 1927).
93. McCreary, Albertus, op. cit.
94. See "Newspaper Clippings File" #5, p. 88, G.N.M.P. library.
95. Souder, Emily Bliss Thacher, *Leaves from the Battle-field of Gettysburg . . .* (Philadelphia, 1864).
96. Pierce, Matilda J., op. cit.
97. Roberts, Charles W., *At Gettysburg in 1863 and 1888*, (MOLLUS-MASS papers), Vol. 1.
98. Souder, Emily B.T., op. cit.
99. Thorn, Elizabeth, article, Gettysburg *Compiler*, July 26, 1905.
100. Article about Rosa A. Snyder in the Wymore, (Nebraska) *Arbor State* May 30 (?), 1944.
101. Copy of a receipt given to Mr. George by Surgeon McGregor in the G.N.M.P. library. In the 1840s, Mr. George still spelled his name "Georg Georg."
102. Myers, Elizabeth Salome "Sallie," "How A Gettysburg Schoolteacher Spent Her Vacation in 1863," article, San Francisco *Sunday Call*, August 16, 1903.
103. Wert, J. Howard, op. cit.
104. Wert, J. Howard, op. cit.
105. Powers, Alice, memoir, Gettysburg *Compiler*, July 1, 1903.
106. Fulton, James, "Gettysburg Reminiscences," *National Tribune*, October 20, 1898.
107. Jacobs, Henry E., article, Philadelphia *North American*, June 29, 1913.
108. McCreary, Jennie, op. cit.
109. Article, Gettysburg *Compiler*, August 4, 1909.
110. Fuller, Charles A., *Personal Recollections of the War of 1861* (Sherborne, New York, 1905).
111. King, Sarah Barrett, "Battle Days in 1863." Gettysburg *Compiler*, July 4, 1906.
112. Montfort, Mary Elizabeth, *Mary Elizabeth and Mr. Lincoln*, by Margaret M. Seylar (Chicago, 1961, and copy of Montfort's diary at the A.C.H.S. The 1860 census does list Mary, age nine, living with Sarah E. Montfort, age thirty-three in Gettysburg.
     Linn, John B., op. cit.
113. King, Sarah B., op. cit.
114. Hollinger, Liberty A., op. cit.
115. Dawes, Rufus R., *Service with the Sixth Wisconsin Volunteers* (Marietta, Ohio, E.R. Alderman & Sons, 1890).

Part II
The Union Army-Controlled Area Field Hospital Sites

1. Article, Gettysburg *Compiler*, July 6, 1880.
   Article, *Yankee* Magazine (July 1977).
   Article, Philadelphia *Press*, July 4, 1888.
   Article, *North American Review* (February, 1891).
2. Clifton, James B., unpublished diary, North Carolina Department of Archives and History (Raleigh, North Carolina).
3. Skelly, Daniel A., *A Boy's Experience During the Battles of Gettysburg* (Gettysburg, 1932).
4. Peabody, Charles N., *ZAB* (Harvard University Press, Boston, 1984).

5. *History of Cumberland and Adams Counties, Pennsylvania* (Warner, Beers, & Co., Chicago, 1886). Hereafter cited as History of Adams County.
6. Meade, George G. Jr., *With Meade at Gettysburg* (John C. Winston Co., Philadelphia, 1930).
7. Belknap, Charles W., copy of diary in files at G.N.M.P. library.
8. Thompson, Benjamin W., *Personal Narrative of Experiences in the Civil War, 1861–1865* manuscript owned by John A. Thompson, Minneapolis, Minnesota.
   (*Civil War Times Illustrated*, August–November, 1973.)
9. Skelly, Daniel A., op. cit.
10. Hitchcock, Charles A., letter in files of G.N.M.P. library.
11. Wafer, Francis M., original diary, Douglas Library, Queen's University at Kingston, Kingston, Ontario, Canada.
12. Bigham, H.H., letter in files of G.N.M.P. library.
13. Muffly, Joseph W., *The Story of Our Regiment, a History of the 148th Pennsylvania Volunteers, . . .* (Kenyon Print and Manufacturing Co., Des Moines, Iowa, 1904).
14. Duncan, Louis C., op. cit. (see explanation under NOTES).
15. Houghton, James, diary, archives of the University of Michigan, Ann Arbor, Michigan.
16. Livermore, Thomas L., *Day and Events, 1860–1866* (H. Mifflin Company, Boston and New York, 1920).
17. Colver, Michael, op. cit.
18. Wagner, Clinton, letter to George Torney on August 7, 1911, in files of G.N.M.P. library.
    Dwinell, Justin. Manuscript report of the Second Corps hospital operations during the Battle of Gettysburg, National Library of Medicine, Bethesda, Maryland.
19. Carter, Robert G., *Four Brothers in Blue* (University of Texas Press, Austin and London, 1978).
20. Fuller, Charles A., op. cit.
21. Billings, John S., *The Medical and Surgical History of the War of the Rebellion . . .*, prepared under the direction of Surgeon General J.K. Barnes (Washington, Government Printing Office, 1870).
22. Pierce, Matilda J., op. cit.
23. Powell, Robert M., op. cit.
    Graham, Ziba B., *On To Gettysburg . . .* (Winn and Hammond, Detroit, 1893.)
24. *History of the Third Pennsylvania Cavalry, . . . 1861–1865* (Franklin Printing Co., Philadelphia, 1905).
25. Farley, Porter, *Reminiscences of the 140th Regiment New York Volunteer Infantry*, Rochester Historical Society-Publications #22 (DuBois Press, Rochester, New York, 1944).
26. Case, A. Pierson, "Notes on the Taking and Holding of Little Round Top at Gettysburg" (Vernon, New York, 1866).
27. Carter, Robert G., op. cit.
    Norton, Oliver W., letter dated September 28, 1888, in files of G.N.M.P. library.
    Norton, Oliver W., *The Attack and Defense of Little Round Top* (Neale Publishing Co., 1913).
28. Bachelder, John B., *Notes on the Services of Troops at the Battle of Gettysburg*, Huntington Library, San Marino, California 91108.
    Dwinell, Justin, op. cit.
29. Thorn, Elizabeth, op. cit.
30. Simpson, William T., article, Philadelphia *North American* (June 29, 1913).
31. Carter, Robert G., op. cit.
32. Benton, Charles E., *As Seen from the Ranks: A Boy in the Civil War* (G.P. Putnam's Sons, New York, 1902).
33. Muller, Charles, memoir, Minnesota Historical Society, St. Paul, Minnesota 55101.
34. Colvill, William, article, Minneapolis *Daily Tribune*, July 28, 1884.
35. Lightner, Nathaniel, article, Gettysburg *Compiler*, July 6, 1910.
36. Tawney, William, memoir, in files of G.N.M.P. library.
37. McClean, William, article, Gettysburg *Compiler*, July 1, 1908.
    Tallman, William, memoir of military service, courtesy of Charles Rhodes, Lexington, Kentucky.
    Dwinell, Justin, op. cit.
38. Favill, Josiah M., *The Diary of a Young Officer Serving with the Armies of the United States During the War of the Rebellion* (R.R. Donnelley & Sons, Chicago, 1909).
39. Wert, J. Howard, op. cit.
40. Gardner, Leonard M., op. cit.
    Linn, John B., op. cit.
41. Article, Gettysburg *Star and Sentinel*, April 19, 1905.
    Article, Gettysburg *Star and Sentinel*, August 23, 1882.
42. Wert, J. Howard, *A Complete Hand-book of the Monuments and Idications . . .* (B.M. Sturgeon & Company, Harrisburg, 1886).
43. Thorn, Elizabeth, op. cit.
    Thorn, George D., article, Gettysburg *Compiler*, July 9, 1932.
44. Article, "Newspaper Clippings File" #3 at G.N.M.P. library.
45. New, George W., op. cit.

46. Marsh, Henry C., letter, op. cit.
47. Chase, John F., memoir, *Deeds of Valor . . .* Vol 1, (The Perrien-Keydel Company, Detroit, 1900). Chase was wounded 48 times by the premature explosion of a case shot he was loading into a cannon tube on July 3.
48. Camp Letterman Papers, op. cit.
49. Wert, J. Howard, op. cit.
50. Thorn, Elizabeth, op. cit.
51. Durboraw, Isaac N., memoir, in files of A.C.H.S.
52. J.W. Monfort, letter, in files of G.N.M.P. library.
53. Cowles, Luther E., *History of the Fifth Massachusetts Battery* (Boston, 1902).
54. Article, New York *Herald,* July 24, 1863.
55. O'Neal, John W.C., *Physician's Handbook for 1863* in files of A.C.H.S. Hereafter cited as O'Neal, J.W.C.—Physician's Handbook.
56. Wert, J. Howard, op. cit.
57. Livermore, Thomas L., op. cit.
    Dwinell, Justin, op. cit.
58. Hancock, Cornelia, *South After Gettysburg, Letters of . . . from the Army of the Potomac 1863-1865,* ed. by Henrietta S. Jaquette, (University of Pennsylvania Press, Philadelphia, 1937).
    Nickerson, Azor H. *Personal Recollections of Two Visits to Gettysburg.* Scribner's Magazine. Volume 14. (Charles Scribner's Sons, New York, 1893.)
59. Dooley, John. *John Dooley, Confederate Soldier, His War Journal,* ed. by Joseph T. Durkin (Georgetown University Press, Washington, D.C., 1945).
60. James, Bushrod, W., *Echoes of Battle* (Henry T. Coates & Co., Philadelphia, 1895).
61. Adams, John G.B., *Reminiscences of the Nineteenth Massachusetts Regiment* (Wright & Potter Printing Co., Boston, 1899).
62. Peltz, H.S., "Two Brass Buttons," article, Gettysburg *Compiler,* March 15, 1887.
63. Thompson, Benjamin W., op. cit.
64. U.S.C.C. Report, 1863.
    Hancock, Cornelia, op. cit.
    Souder, Emily B.T., op. cit.
    Dwinell, Justin, op. cit.
65. Wert, J. Howard, op. cit.
    Report of the General Agent of the State of New York . . . (Comstock & Cassidy Printers, Albany, New York, 1864).
    U.S.C.C. Report, 1863.
    Clark, Augustus M., letter to D. McConaughy on August 16, 1869, in files of G.N.M.P. library.
66. Clark, William H., unpublished memoir in the files of G.N.M.P. library.
67. Shenkel, Jacob, 1863 diary in the possession of Mr. Timothy Brooks, East Liverpool, Ohio.
68. Bacon, Cyrus, from his "daily register" located in the archives of the University of Michigan, Ann Arbor.
69. Hunt, Mark, letter, *The Legacy I Leave, 1839-1899,* through the courtesy of William Frassanito and Harry C. Shriver.
70. Dimon, Theodore, op. cit.
71. Article, New York *Herald,* July 24, 1863.
72. Schaeffer, Lewis, unpublished diary in files of West Virginia University, Morgantown, West Virginia 26505.
73. Musgrove, Richard W., *Autobiography of Richard W. Musgrove,* privately published by Mary D. Musgrove, 1921.
74. Watson, William, *Letters of a Civil War Surgeon,* ed. by Paul Fatout, (Perdue University Press, West Lafayette, 1961).
75. Cross, Andrew, U.S.C.C. Report, 1865—op. cit.
76. Wescott, James B., letter dated February 1896, in the "J.L. Chamberlain Papers," Library of Congress, Washington, D.C.
77. Samuel Toombs, *New Jersey Troops in the Gettysburg Campaign,* Chapter 15, (The Evening Mail Publishing House, Orange, New Jersey, 1888).
78. Phillips, Richard C., *Richard and Rhoda: Letters from the Civil War,* ed. by M.G. Phillips and V.P. Parsegian.
79. Ames, Lyman D., unpublished diary in the possession of Mr. Edwin L. Ames, San Francisco, California.
80. Barziza, Decimus et Ultimus, op. cit.
81. Bushman, Sadie, memoir, in files of A.C.H.S.
82. Report of the General Agent . . . New York, op. cit.
    U.S.C.C. Report, 1863.
    Mesnard, Luther, "The Rise and Survival of Private Mesnard, Part II," article, *Civil War Times Illustrated* (February 1986).
83. Silliman, Justus M., op. cit.
84. Kiefer, William R., op. cit.
85. Schurz, Carl, "The Battle of Gettysburg," *McClure's* Magazine, Vol. 29 (July 1907).
86. Schantz, F.J.F. op. cit.
87. Brinton, Daniel G., "From Chancellorsville to Gettysburg, A Doctor's Diary," *The Pennsylvania Magazine of History*

and Biography, Vol. 89, (1965).

88. Hubbard, Robert. Copies of unpublished letters in author's files.
89. Wert, J. Howard, op. cit.
90. Eliason, Talcot, letter to H.B. McClellan, July 23, 1885, in files of the G.N.M.P. library. Dr. Eliason was one of Stuart's Cavalry corps surgeons.
91. King, Sarah B., op. cit.
92. Baird, William, unpublished memoirs in archives of the University of Michigan, Ann Arbor.
93. Hebert, T.W., "In Occupied Pennsylvania," *The Georgia Review,* Vol. IV (The University of Georgia, Athens, 1950).

Part III
The Confederate Army-Controlled Area Field Hospital Sites

1. Johnson, Clifton, *Battleground Adventures* (Houghton Mifflin Co., Boston and New York, 1915).
2. Wert, J. Howard, *Physician's Handbook, 1863,* in files of A.C.H.S.
3. Article in "Newspaper Clippings File" #5, at G.N.M.P. library.
4. Silliman, Justus M., op. cit.
5. Douglas, Henry K., op. cit.
6. *History of Adams County, 1886,* op. cit.
7. Barlow, Francis C., letter, Massachusetts Historical Society, Boston, Massachusetts 02215.
8. Smith, Jane, diary account, Gettysburg *Star and Sentinel,* July 2, 1913.
9. Young, Anna Mary, *The Soldier of Indiana in the War for the Union, Vol. 2,* by Catherine Merrill, (Indianapolis, 1866).
10. "Company Officer," *Reminiscences of the Gettysburg Battle,* Lippincott's Magazine, Vol. 6 (J.B. Lippincott & Co., Philadelphia, 1883.)
11. Dodge, Theodore A., "Left Wounded on the Field," Putnam's *Monthly Magazine,* Vol. 4 (September 1869).
12. Barlow, Francis C., letters, op. cit.
13. McIlhenny, Mrs. Hugh, Sr., memoir, in files of G.N.M.P. library.
14. Bayly, William H., memoir, in files of G.N.M.P. library and A.C.H.S.
15. O'Neal, John W.C., memoir, the *Gettysburg Compiler,* July 5, 1905. Hereafter cited as memoir.
16. Keppel, Ruth Hamilton, letter to Melchoir Sheads, March 4, 1935, in files of A.C.H.S.
17. Article, *Gettysburg Times,* August 9, 1937.
18. Blacknall, Oscar W., memoir, North Carolina Department of Archives and History, Raleigh, North Carolina 27611.
19. O'Neal, John W.C., memoir.
20. McClean, Elizabeth M., "The Rebels Are Coming!", Gettysburg *Compiler,* June 8, 1908.
21. Blacknall, Oscar W., op. cit.
22. Johnson, Clifton, op. cit.
23. Wilson, LeGrand J., *The Confederate Soldier,* ed. by James W. Silver (Memphis State University Press, Memphis, 1973).
24. Reinecker, Amanda E., op. cit.
25. Johnson, Clifton, op. cit.
26. Witherspoon, T.D., letter to Lieutenant J.W. Phillips, January 5, 1864. The original is in the possession of Robert S. Phillips, Tunica, Mississippi.
    Witherspoon, T.D., article, "Prison Life at Fort McHenry," *The Southern Historical Society Papers,* Vol. 8 (Richmond, Virginia, 1880).
27. Wilson, Le Grand J., op. cit.
28. Leinbach, Julias A., "Scenes at the Battle of Gettysburg," *The Salem Band,* by B.J. Pfohl (privately printed, Winston-Salem, 1953).
29. Welch, Spencer Glasgow, *A Confederate Surgeon's Letters To His Wife* (Neale Publishing Company, New York and Washington, D.C., 1911).
30. Dickert, D. Augustus, *History of Kershaw's Brigade* (Elbert H. Hull Co., Newberry, South Carolina, 1899).
31. *History of Adams County,* op. cit.
32. O'Neal, John W.C., memoir, op. cit.
33. Myers, Robert P., unpublished diary, Museum of the Confederacy, Richmond, Virginia.
34. Ward, W.C., "Incidents and Personal Experiences on the Battlefield at Gettysburg," *Confederate Veteran* Magazine, Vol. 8 (1900).
35. Beard, Elizabeth Plank, unpublished memoir, in files of G.N.M.P. library, collected by Ann Reaver.
36. Miller, O.H., memoir
    U.S.C.C. Report of 1865, by Andrew Cross, op. cit.
37. Haskell, John C., *The Haskell Memoirs,* ed. by G.E. Govan and J.W. Livingood (G.P. Putnam's Sons, New York, 1960).

Colston, F.M., memoir, "Gettysburg As I Saw It," *Confederate Veteran* Magazine, Vol. 5, p. 551.

Fremantle, James A.L., *Three Months in the Southern States: April–June, 1863* (William Blackwood & Sons, Edinburgh and London, 1863).

38. O'Neal, John W.C., *Physician's Handbook*, op. cit.

Baruch, Simon, article, New York *Times*, December 8, 1912, and *Confederate Veteran* Magazine, Vol. 22 (1914).

39. Monteiro, Aristides, *Confederate Surgeon*, ed. by S.G.L. Dannett and R.H. Burkart (Dodd, Mead & Company, New York, 1969).

40. It might interest the reader to know that Monteiro later joined John S. Mosby's partisan command and served with it until the end of the war.

41. Ross, Fitzgerald, *A Visit to the Cities and Camps of the Confederate States* (William Blackwood & Sons, Edinburgh and London, 1865).

42. Johnston, David W., *Four Years a Soldier* (Princeton, West Virginia, 1887.)

43. Warren, Leander H., op. cit.

44. Information concerning Fraser, courtesy of Kathy G. Harrison.

45. Way, William C., letter written August 7, 1863, Detroit *Advertiser and Tribune*.

46. Bigham, Mrs. J. Paxton, memoir, *Gettysburg Times*, April 22, 1941.

47. Paxton, John R., *Sword and Gown* . . . (Knickerbocker Press, New York, 1926).

Tolson, Thomas H., diary published in the *Baltimore Telegram*, 1879.

48. Stevens, George T., *Three Years in the Sixth Corps* (D. Van Nostrand Publisher, New York, 1870).

49. Neese, George M., *Three Years in the Confederate Horse Artillery* (Neale Publishing Co., New York, 1911).

50. Fremantle, James A.L., op. cit.

Parts IV, V, & VI

IV Other Important Sites Associated With the Treatment of Wounded During the Battle of Gettysburg

V Hospitals of the Gettysburg Campaign Located in Nearby Towns

VI Camp Letterman, The U.S. General Hospital on the George Wolf Farm

1. U.S.S.C. Report, 1863, op. cit.

2. U.S.S.C. Report, 1863, op. cit.

3. Patrick, Marsena R., *Inside Lincoln's Army; The Diary of General Marsena R. Patrick, Provost Marshall General, Army of the Potomac*, ed. by D.S. Sparks (Thomas Yoseloff, New York and London, 1964).

4. Sheely, Aaron, memoir, in files of A.C.H.S.

5. Pierce, C.T.S., article in what is commonly called *New York at Gettysburg*, ed. by William F. Fox (J.B. Lyon Co. Printers, Albany, 1900).

6. Adams, John G.B., op. cit.

7. Shellman, Mary B., *Recollections of Stuart's Raid*, manuscript, Carroll County Historical Society, Maryland.

8. Gibbon, John, *Personal Recollections of the Civil War* (G.P. Putnam's Sons, New York, 1928).

9. *Official Records of the War of the Rebellion*, Series I, Vol. 27, Part 3, p. 620, (Government Printing Office, Washington, D.C., 1889).

10. Harris, Isaac, unpublished diary, Harrisburg Public Library, Harrisburg, Pennsylvania.

11. Ibid.

12. Hoke, Jacob, memoir of D.Z. Shook, op. cit.

13. Camp Letterman Papers, op. cit.

14. Ames, Lyman D., op. cit.

15. Shenkel, Jacob, op. cit.

16. Way, William C., letter, August 7, 1863, op. cit.

17. Silliman, Justus M., op. cit.

Stoke, Frank M., letter, Gettysburg College Library (Gettysburg, Pennsylvania).

18. Bucklin, Sophronia E., *In Hospital and Camp* (John E. Potter and Co., Philadelphia, 1869).

19. Hancock, Cornelia, op. cit.

20. Norris, William F., op. cit.

21. Camp Letterman Papers, op. cit.

22. Bucklin, Sophronia E., op. cit.

23. Bachelder, John B., *Business Enterprise* . . . , booklet accompanying his "steel engraving" of the Battle of Gettysburg (Boston, 1878).

INDEX

Academy General Hospital, 166
Adair, James, 53
Adair, John, 48
Adams County: 20, 59; 1858/1872
    map of, 86, 128, 135, 138, 139,
    140; lack of patriotism by farm-
    ers, 94, 99; oldest brick house in,
    80; one of oldest farms in, 117,
    147; sheriff of, 84, 144
Adams County Almshouse and Farm,
    13, 29, 30, 105; barn, 30
Adams County Courthouse, 7, 22, 44,
    50, 53, 54
Adams County Historical Society, 8,
    121, 134, 142
Adams County, history book of, 61,
    139, 154
Adams County Prison, 27
Adams County Schools; Butt School,
    140; Picking School, 117; Pitzer
    School, 144; Union School, 27;
    White Run School, 159
Adams, C.P., 75
Adams Express Office, 4
Adams, John, 94; at Littlestown, 164
Adams Sentinel, 34, 78
Adams, Zabdiel B., 61
Aid station, duties of a surgeon at, 60,
    63, 133
Alabama Infantry Regiments: 4th,
    142; 8th, 141; 12th, 125; 15th, 74
"Alabama, Lieutenant Colonel,"
    probably Isaac B. Feagin, 15th
    Alabama Infantry, 74
Albright's Hall, 163
Alexander's Artillery Battalion, 146
Allewalt, John Q., 134
Allman, H.V., 7
Almshouse. See Adams County
    Almshouse and Farm.
Altman, William, 73
Ambulance train, Second Division,
    Second Corps, 74
Ames, Lyman D.: 103; states number
    of wounded at Camp Letterman,
    168
Anderson's Division hospital: at A.
    Butt's farm, 140, 141; number of
    wounded in, 141
Archer, James J.: 139; sword of, 37
Armed Forces Medical Museum, 82
Armistead, Lewis A., at G. Spangler
    farm, 105, 107
Armstrong, James A., 105
Army of Northern Virginia, 113, 144,
    151, 154
Army of the Potomac: 57, 61, 80,
    117, 165; artillery reserve of, 66,
    87; cavalry corps, 65, 86, 107;

headquarters of, 62, 63, 68, 83,
    161; provost marshal general, 65,
    83, 159, 161
Arnold, Caleb H., 1
Artillery Reserve, Confederate, at S.
    Johns house, 151
Artillery Reserve, Union: headquar-
    ters at M. Frey farm, 66, 87; hos-
    pital near Two Taverns, 88; hos-
    pital near White Church, 87;
    possible hospital near Granite
    Schoolhouse, 72
Ashworth, James, 51
Aughenbaugh, Nellie E., 26
"Aunt Katy." See Catharine H. Wert.
Avery, Isaac, 115
Avery's Brigade hospital, at E. Weible
    farm, 118

Bache, Richard M., 9
Bachelder, John B., 172
Bacon, Cyrus J., 99
Bacon, Georgiana W., 172
Bair, J., (James W. Barr), 89
Baird, William, 109
Baker, G.M., 98
Baker, Melissa, Baltimore nurse, 142
Baldwin, M.R., 43
Ballou, Thomas, 53
Balsey, Joseph R., 17
Baltimore and Ohio Railroad, 51
Bane, Lewis, 148
Bange, William, 163
Bank of Gettysburg, 53
Barksdale, William, 64, 65
Barksdale's Brigade hospital: at John
    Crawford farm, 150
Barlow, Francis C.: at G. Spangler
    farm, 107; at J. Crawford house,
    121; at J. Benner farm, 123, 124
Barlow's Knoll. See Blocher's Hill.
Barnard, Mrs., nurse, 151
Barnes Family, 141
Barr, Agnes S., 27
Barr, Elizabeth, 89
Barr, James W., 89
Baruch, Simon, 145, 146
Barziza, Decimus et. Ultimus, 32, 103
Bates, James L., 79
Battleflag, Second Mississippi In-
    fantry, 56
Baugher, Henry L., 20, 32
Bayly, Evaline, 128
Bayly, William H., 127
Beath, R.B., 5
Beck, Surgeon, 12
Beech, John H., 4
Beely, John, 56
Beitler, Andrew, 81
Beitler, Henry: 85, 86; farm, 85, 86;
    farm near L. Bushman house, 72;

farm on the Baltimore Pike, 86;
    headquarters of Alfred Pleason-
    ton, 86; store on property of, 86
Beitler, Matilda, 86
Belknap, C.W., 62
Bendersville, Pa., 33, 140
Benner, Christian: 115; farm of, 115
Benner, Christian Sr., 115
Benner, H.S., 115
Benner, Josiah: 80, 125; farm, 121,
    123, 127; Francis Barlow at farm,
    123; Richard S. Ewell at farm,
    121, 123
Benner, Susan (Snyder), 115
Benton, Charles E., 74
Bevans, Milton L., 48
Biesecker, Frank, 150
Bigelow, John, 66
Biggs, Basil, 150
Biggs, Mary, 150
Bigham, H.H., 63
Bigham, Mrs. J. Paxton, 151
Big Round Top: 71; First Division,
    Fifth Corps hospital nearby, 98
Billings, Charles W., 98
Billings, John S., 69
Bird, Peter, 26
Black Boar Tavern, 165
Black Horse Tavern. See F. Bream's
    Tavern.
Blacknall, Charles, 128, 130, 131
Blacknall, Oscar, 128
Blacksmith shops: 28; Hamilton's,
    127, 128; Whisler's, 28
Blair, Bruce, 51
Blanchard, Eli A., 4
Blocher's Hill, 29, 30, 119, 125
Boll, Father Joseph A., 18
Bough, Mrs., (Cashtown), 140
Brain, Mrs., nurse, 151
Bream, Francis: 148, "Black Horse
    Tavern" and farm, 142, 144-147,
    152; McLaws' Division hospital
    at, 144; number of Pickett's Di-
    vision wounded at, 145; Pickett's
    Division hospital at, 145
Bream, Elizabeth (Slaybaugh), 144
Bream, Henry, 144
Bream, Robert, 144
Bream's Mill: 145, 147-150; Pickett's
    Division hospital at, 145
Bricker, Leonard, 68
Brinkerhoff, J., farm, 108
Brinton, Daniel G., 107
Broadhead, Joseph, 42
Broadhead, Sarah M., 1, 7, 25, 42
Brooks, Lieutenant, 109
Broom, Charles H.H., 78
Brown, Mrs., Philadelphia nurse, 43
Bucher, Samuel, 120
Buck, H.B., 73

Gregory Ashton Coco, born in 1946, grew up in Mansura, Avoyelles Parish, Louisiana. He graduated from the University of Southwestern Louisiana in 1972 with a B.A. degree in history. From 1967 to 1969, Coco served in the U.S. Army, including a tour in Vietnam, where as an infantryman, he was wounded twice. Since his return to civilian life, Coco has worked as a Louisiana state trooper, and as a battlefield guide, park ranger, historian, and maintenance worker at the Gettysburg National Military Park.

Kathleen Georg Harrison was born in Johnstown, Pa., and attended public schools there. She received degrees in education (B.A.) and history (M.A.) from the University of Pittsburgh. Employed at the Gettysburg National Military Park since 1974, she has served as research historian since 1976 and as chief historian since 1984. Kathy spends her office hours trying to preserve the cultural resources of the Gettysburg battlefield, and her leisure hours trying to preserve an eighteenth century stone home south of Hanover. Her hobbies include reading, oil painting, folk art and cross stitching.

Daniel E. Fuhrman was born in 1961, in Hanover, Pa., where he now lives with his wife of five years, Cynthia S. Roller. He graduated from Southwestern High School in 1979, and then studied drafting and design for three years at the Electronics Institute of Harrisburg. Dan is currently employed as a draftsman at the P.H. Glatfelter Company of Spring Grove. Besides his love of art, he is an avid outdoor enthusiast as he enjoys sports such as running, biking and racewalking.